PACIFIC

OCEAN

PHILIPPINES

Manila

Sulu
Sea

ndakan

wau

Celebes
Sea

SULAWESI
(Celebes)

•Makassar

N   E   S   I   A

Equator

BIAK

WEST
IRIAN

250   500

Approximate   Miles

Malaysia
Indonesia
Philippines

TIMOR

Dorothy deFontaine

D1217471

THE FORMATION OF
MALAYSIA
NEW FACTOR IN WORLD POLITICS

THE FORMATION OF

MALAYSIA

NEW FACTOR IN WORLD POLITICS

An analytical history and assessment of the prospects of the newest state in Southeast Asia, based on a series of Reports written for the American Universities Field Staff.

By WILLARD A. HANNA

P. H. WELSHIMER MEMORIAL LIBRARY
MILLIGAN COLLEGE, TENN. 37682

AMERICAN UNIVERSITIES FIELD STAFF, INC.

366 MADISON AVENUE   NEW YORK, N.Y. 10017

DS
597.2
H3

© 1962, 1963, 1964 BY

AMERICAN UNIVERSITIES FIELD STAFF, INC.

ALL RIGHTS RESERVED

Library of Congress catalog card number: 64-19390

Design by John Woodlock
Composition by M. Martinez
Map by Dorothy deFontaine

PRINTED IN THE UNITED STATES OF AMERICA

CONTENTS

6.50

Amer. Univ. Field Staff

5-1469

50316

Acknowledgment

In writing Chapter XVII, "Tengku Abdul Rahman, *Bapa* Malaysia," I drew extensively on two published biographies:

Miller, Harry. *Prince and Premier*. London: George G. Harrap and Co., Ltd., 1959.

Abdul Aziz bin Ishak, Wan King Cheong, and Tan Kah Jee. *The Architect of Merdeka, Tengku Abdul Rahman*. Singapore: Tan Kan Jee, 1957.

W. A. H.

PREFACE

In his long periods of residence in Indonesia, Malaya, and Singapore and frequent regional travels, Willard A. Hanna has kept the affairs of Southeast Asia under sustained observation for almost twenty years. The volume of his written work and the quality of his judgments have earned him a place in the front rank of Southeast Asian specialists. Since joining the American Universities Field Staff in 1954, he has written more than 130 AUFS Reports, most of them commenting on the policies and leaders of Indonesia and the neighboring countries.

Mr. Hanna was among the first to recognize the implications of the proposal to federate several former British colonies. He saw it as a major development in international affairs, long before it could be called a plan — when it was no more than a tentative idea. The first of his twenty-four AUFS Reports on *Malaysia, a Federation in Prospect* was written in February 1962. Nineteen months later, when the prospect was reality and Malaysia had become the focus of regional and global conflicts of interest, other writers inevitably looked to Hanna as they started studying the pressures generated by the formation of this new political entity.

Mr. Hanna's sparkling analysis of the contending forces in Southeast Asia's domestic and international politics gains luster from his use of paradox, near-pun, and triple modifier. His writing style, which is always fresh and often striking, is also highly functional; it helps compress into a chapter enough facts, impressions, and interpretations to keep most writers busy for a full booklength.

The Formation of Malaysia is as authoritative and timely as his earlier book, *Bung Karno's Indonesia*. Pessimistic about Indonesia's future, Mr. Hanna has more hope for Malaysia. Yet, whatever hope he expresses for Malaysia's ability to withstand the confrontation of an intransigent Indonesia comes of careful analysis, not wishful thinking. His deep personal desire for a community of economically and politically viable Southeast Asian countries does not get in the way of his perception of the people, events, and trends on which he bases his judgments. Whether or not Malaysia survives the stresses it will suffer under the leverage of confrontation, this book will stand as a valued contribution to the literature on Southeast Asia and as a basic reference for researchers on the history and problems of the Federation of Malaysia.

Teg C. Grondahl
Executive Director
American Universities Field Staff

New York
April 15, 1964

INTRODUCTION

CONFRONTATION IN SOUTHEAST ASIA

With the birth of the Federation of Malaysia on September 16, 1963, there took definite shape on the Southeast Asian scene not only a new nation of bright promise but also a new crisis of dark omen. In order to form the new Malaysia, three flourishing ex-colonies of Great Britain—Singapore, Sarawak, and Sabah (North Borneo)—voluntarily federated with Malaya, which, since it achieved its independence from Great Britain in 1957, has proved to be a very model of orderly development. Even so, the new Federation of Malaysia, although it promised to become a stabilizing factor in a shaky area, has itself become yet another center of regional conflict. The Philippines vigorously and Indonesia violently objected to its formation, and recurrent efforts to resolve the dispute have resulted in fact in its exacerbation.

The new Malaysia, with a population of 10 million people, a nation which is militarily weak but is strongly supported by Great Britain, now finds itself forced to divert both attention and revenues from national development to national defense. The Philippines, a nation of 30 million people closely tied to the United States, has become involved in agitating a dispute which it is seeking simultaneously to mediate. Indonesia, with a population of 100 million hungry, impoverished people whose leaders have mortgaged themselves to the Soviet Union for US$1 billion worth of armaments has undertaken to "smash" Malaysia, to oust the British, and to gain for itself the decisive role in Southeast Asia. With Great Britain, the United States, and the Soviet Union directly involved and Communist China by no means idle on the sidelines, Indonesia's "confrontation" of Malaysia, with ambivalent Philippine support, is the unhappy sequel to the hopeful Malaya-Singapore-Sarawak-Sabah merger.

The formation of Malaysia is the subject of a series of 24 reports originally written for separate publication by the American Universities Field Staff between February 1962 and September 1963 and now brought together in this book. These reports deal with the component parts of the new nation, its citizens, both ordinary and prominent, and the problems and process of federation. Written at different times on a wide variety of topics while the final shape and substance, indeed the very emergence, of the new nation was still uncertain, the reports trace the evolution of Malaysia to a point just one day short of the climax, the actual proclamation of the Federation on September 16, 1963. There then developed the not altogether unanticipated anticlimax: the Philippines withheld and the Indonesian government refused recognition; Malaysia broke off diplomatic relations with both; Indonesia staged anti-Malaysia riots, embargoed its own Malaysia trade, and mounted a crescendo campaign of military provocation. Thus the fulfillment of the Malaysia plan signaled the detonation of the Malaysia crisis.

The 24 reports on the formation of Malaysia show how a tentative proposal of federation was systematically transformed into a definite agenda and timetable, also how people of widely divergent racial, religious, social, economic, and political backgrounds achieved mutual accommodation on the basis of give and take negotiations and free elections. The Malaysia story, thus, is one of peaceful self-determination (Brunei, which failed to join, being the exception), a remarkably sophisticated political performance on the part of diverse peoples, many of whom are commonly regarded as being politically quite immature. The new Malaysia, like any other nation, is faced with extremely difficult problems, such as racial integration and economic diversification, to mention only two of the most obvious. Even as it emerged, however, the new nation established a strong precedent for resolving its problems by rational adjustment of conflicting interests. Peace, progress, and prosperity would have been the logical forecast had Malaysia not by sheer chance stirred up opposition in the Philippines, which revived an almost forgotten historic claim to Sabah, and by merely being reasonable and successful stirred up outrage in Indonesia, where ultranationalistic irrationality has resulted in national deterioration.

The remarkable success story of Malaysia and the problems which could still induce failure constitute the continuing themes of the reports reproduced in this volume. The development of Philippine and Indonesian opposition to Malaysia constitutes an accompanying theme, one which needs to be clearly distinguished in order to report not only the Malaysia story but also the new Malaysia crisis. The story of Philippine and Indonesian opposition to Malaysia is both curious and tragic, that of the Philippines the more curious, that of Indo-

nesia the more tragic. Philippine objections to Malaysia seem now
to be waning as Indonesia's increase, but the triangular relationship
is subject to many changes which are likely to grow more not less
complicated, since for each of the principals national prestige is now
at issue.

The Philippine government, then, first became involved in the
Malaysia controversy because it contested the right of the British to
transfer Sabah, over which the Philippines itself claimed residual sovereignty. The original Philippine case was mainly legalistic. It was
based on a vague, in fact a vanished document, dated 1878 and signed
by the Sultan of Sulu, who either leased or ceded Borneo territory to
which his own claim of proprietorship was dubious. The British, no
doubt tactlessly, declined to discuss the Philippine claim that the document provided for lease, not cession, and that the Philippines succeeded to the Sulu rights. The Malayan government adopted the position that the dispute concerned only the Philippines and Great Britain.
The Philippine press, public, and politicians became incensed. Macapagal had himself raised the issue as a congressman in 1948; as President in 1962 he was in search of a foreign policy distinctively Filipino
and not American in inspiration. He seized upon North Borneo as his
personal cause.

The Philippine case thereafter went through successive modifications and elaborations which have stressed the following not altogether consistent arguments:

1) Malaysia is an artificial and unstable Federation, an invitation to Chinese Communist subversion which can readily spread from
Singapore through Borneo into the Philippines. In any event, Malaysia
is likely to be Chinese dominated and an affront, therefore, to all Southeast Asian nationalists.

2) Malaysia cannot protect North Borneo (from Communist China
or from Indonesia, for instance), but the Philippines can.

3) Indonesia is the coming power in Southeast Asia and, like it
or not, the Philippines must get along with Sukarno. By cautiously supporting Sukarno on the Malaysia issue, the Philippines can convert Indonesia into a responsible neighbor. Thus, the Philippines can assert
its own leadership in Southeast Asia and strengthen the anti-Communist cause.

4) The British have shamelessly manipulated Malaya and Malaysia. They exercised pressure upon Tengku Abdul Rahman to resist
Indonesian and Philippine moves of conciliation at the time of the Ma-

nila Conference and during the subsequent United Nations "assessment" of public opinion in Borneo. Malaysia is thus a creature of the British, the United Nations assessment is invalid, and the Tengku, just as Sukarno says, lends himself to British "neocolonial" designs by failing to support the basic new principle of Southeast Asian determination of Southeast Asian affairs.

5) "Maphilindo"—Macapagal's proposal for a "loose confederation" of the Philippines, Indonesia, and Malaysia, recently readjusted to allow for membership of all Southeast Asian states except North Vietnam is the answer to the Malaysia crisis.

The Philippines, however, has long been distressed by Indonesia's drift or drive toward communism, and it has experienced a very considerable degree of disenchantment in recent months regarding Sukarno and his aggressive "smash" Malaysia tactics. The Philippines, furthermore, has been a partner of Malaya's in the Association of Southeast Asia for economic and cultural co-operation; the small but notable achievements of ASA contrast sharply with the grandiose but elusive promise of Maphilindo. In the Philippines, therefore, realistic reconciliation to Malaysia is a definite, possibly even an imminent prospect —as in Indonesia it is not.

The Indonesian case against Malaysia is best summarized in President Sukarno's words—not his often reiterated charges that Malaysia is a "neocolonialist conspiracy" of "military encirclement" but his unguarded admission that "Malaysia is against our wishes and against our revolution." Malaysia was created without consulting Sukarno: that is one of his basic objections, for he has determined to make himself and Indonesia the decisive influence in Southeast Asia, and as his Foreign Minister declares for him, "Things will not go smoothly unless we are consulted." Malaysia, furthermore, was created as a result of non-violent evolution involving co-operation with the once colonial British. Sukarno has propounded an ultranationalistic, ultrarevolutionary ideology for Indonesia and, by extension, for the Afro-Asian world which he seeks to dominate. He advocates revolutionary violence in rejection of all once accepted codes and standards; for him the Marxist class conflict has been transformed into an inevitable and uncompromisable conflict between the "new emerging forces," of which Indonesia is the heroic leader, and the "old established order," of which Malaysia is the reactionary adherent. The presence of British military bases in Malaysia, the continuing prosperity there of British, Overseas Chinese, and other aliens, many of them large or small capitalists, the concession by Malays of political as well as economic privilege to non-Southeast Asians, the relative backwardness of the Malays in social and economic attainment—all signify to Sukarno failure on the part of Malaysia to adhere to the "sacred principles" of Afro-Asian nationalism.

Sukarno, of course, is quite right when he discerns in Malaysia a continuing tolerance for alien political, economic, social, and military interests. Malaysia's tolerance for exactly these interests is the basis, in fact, for its progress and prosperity, just as Indonesia's intolerance is the basis for its deterioration. The contrast between Malaysia and Indonesia constitutes, therefore, at once a provocative proof of Sukarno's thesis that Malaysia's policies correspond to what he calls "counterrevolutionary reaction" and an intolerable disproof of his corresponding thesis that Indonesia's revolutionary activism is the formula for progress.

The Republic of Indonesia, by practice of Sukarno's "Guided Democracy" and "Guided Economy," has worked itself into a political and economic state which amounts to neoanarchy. The government has deteriorated into an ineffectual dictatorship, while the military, the Communists, and the palace politicians stalemate each other in the contest to determine who will inherit Sukarno's authority. The economy has been wrecked beyond the ability of even a good government to put it together again in less than a decade. The currency is virtually worthless; consumption so far outdistances production that massive foreign aid serves mainly as a relief program; and manipulation rather than development has become a way of life. The swiftly growing population has been more or less distracted from its troubles by devices of domestic and international agitation—the Irian Barat campaign, for instance, to which the empty victory now dictates an even more diversionary sequel. The military establishment has been equipped with US$1 billion worth of Russian armaments and seeks to experiment in utilizing them. Sukarno is thus beset by domestic problems that are irresolvable because he has rejected the devices of rationality. Bemused by a sense of manifest destiny, he is driven to assert his own authority and Indonesia's throughout Southeast Asia. He is quite aware that relaxation of external crisis will lead to a violent recurrence of the domestic. Indonesian confrontation of Malaysia is the consequence.

Confrontation has led to Indonesian guerrilla action on the Sarawak and Sabah borders, piratical raids in the Strait of Malacca, and the constant threat of even more reckless military action. It has resulted also in the burning or seizure of British properties in Indonesia, an international propaganda campaign against Malaysia, and an embargo on US$100-US$200 million worth of trade between Indonesia and Singapore—trade which is important to Malaysia but absolutely vital to Indonesia. Within Malaysia, Indonesia's campaign has resulted in diversion of time, effort, and money to the build-up of defensive military forces and in certain incidental manifestations unhappily reminiscent of Indonesia itself, such as burnings in effigy and agitation of nationalistic sentiments.

Indonesia's campaign may eventually result, as Sukarno hopes, in the overthrow or subversion of the Malaysian government. It seems more likely to result, however, in explosive reintensification of Indonesia's domestic difficulties and a suicidal Sukarno outburst induced by sheer desperation. International recognition of the gravity of the problem has led to efforts at conciliation—a mission by United States Attorney General Robert F. Kennedy in late January 1964, a simultaneous mission by Prince Sihanouk of Cambodia, and other less publicized attempts. International interest may result at worst in appeasement of Sukarno, at best in some postponement of the collapse of his regime and of the chaos to follow—scarcely, however, unless some now unforeseen new factor emerges, in resolution of the real problem, which is not so much what to do about Malaysia as what to do about Indonesia.

Indonesia's confrontation of Malaysia constitutes, in fact, a confrontation in Southeast Asia between the forces of irrational, irresponsible untranationalism and those of rational, responsible co-operation between the Afro-Asian and the Western nations. The manner in which the Afro-Asian and the Western worlds react to the crisis will afford an important clue to the prospects for peaceful coexistence and for fruitful co-operation between the two. Indonesia stands for resentment toward and resistance to the Western presence in the non-Western world. Malaysia, as the following chapters will show, stands for mutually beneficial acceptance. Indonesia, however, is 100 million people; Malaysia is 10 million. Although Malaysia's rationality may spread to Indonesia, Indonesia's extremism seems more likely to infect Malaysia, unless Sukarno can be effectively restrained rather than, as in the case of the Irian Barat settlement in 1961, rewarded for his troublemaking.

CHAPTER
I

THE MALAYSIA PROPOSAL

February 23, 1962

Tengku Abdul Rahman, Prime Minister of the Federation of Malaya, appearing in Singapore before the Foreign Correspondents Association of Southeast Asia on May 27, 1961, slipped into his after-luncheon remarks an electrifying proposal:

> Sooner or later Malaya should have an understanding
> with Britain and the peoples of Singapore, North Bor-
> neo, Brunei, and Sarawak. It is premature for me to
> say now how this closer understanding can be brought
> about, but it is inevitable that we should look ahead to
> this objective and think of a plan whereby these terri-
> tories can be brought closer together in political and
> economic co-operation.

Was the Tengku, who had already many times rejected Singapore's importunities to join the Federation of Malaya, now himself suggesting a new kind of package deal by which Singapore might actually be admitted? Within a matter of a very few days it became clear: (A) that he was; and (B) that in Malaya, Singapore, Sarawak, Brunei, and North Borneo this was to be the political issue of the year—and of the next. It is one on which politicians of all degrees of vision and volume now have a very great deal to say, and the people are being called upon to express their wishes.

Prematurely or not, and there are many who agree with the Tengku's original suggestion that this is no occasion for haste, the proposal managed at once to acquire a name, an agenda, and a timetable. According to press and public, a "Greater Malaysia"—for some of the more zealous supporters and opponents, a "Mighty Malaysia"—was to be created by merging the four other states into an expanded and re-organized Federation of Malaya, and the whole complicated political process was to be well under way, if not actually consummated, in 1963.

Gradually, as a result of official clarifications, the name became the Federation of Malaysia, the process became one as much of partnership as of merger, and the target date became June 1963—with a hint, however, that an even earlier date might be possible.

Tengku Abdul Rahman had made a sudden 180° shift in policy course. Previously he had opposed Singapore's merger with the Federation on the grounds that it would result in a Malayan national population only 41% Malaysian but 44% Chinese. It would lead, therefore, in the opinion of the Tengku and many other Malay leaders, to acquisition by the Chinese of political power commensurate with their greater numbers if not with their overwhelmingly greater wealth. It would prejudice the Federation's prospects for political and economic stability by adding to its own problems those of policing Singapore's extreme left-wing political factions and of rationalizing its chancy economy. A series of developments had convinced the Tengku, however, that he must deal not by inaction but by action with the problem of his Singapore neighbor and that he could best do so by placing it in its larger—and still more troubled—context.

The most persuasive development of all was a number of political crises in Singapore, in which the People's Action Party (PAP), the moderately left-wing government party, had been seriously challenged by its own extremist faction. Unless the PAP government could now make good on its primary policy objective—that of achieving merger with the Federation—it seemed certain to collapse and Singapore seemed as certain to turn violent, Communist, or both at once. At the same time events in British Borneo (the most significant of them a Communist subversion scare in the Crown Colony of Sarawak) had raised the ogre of a series of miniature but highly infectious Indochina-cum-Congo crises arising out of incipient nationalist movements in North Borneo, Brunei, and Sarawak. Finally, the news from nearby Laos, Vietnam, Indonesia, and elsewhere indicated that the internal situation in most of the new nations of Southeast Asia was swiftly deteriorating and that regional security was increasingly threatened.

By introducing into the old dilemma regarding Federation-Singapore merger the new element of British Borneo participation, the Tengku opened the way for rethinking and perhaps resolving some of the more obvious difficulties not just in Federation-Singapore affairs but in British Borneo as well. Two of the major problems, those of Malay Chinese tension and Communist conspiracy, would be extended in scope but not necessarily worsened in degree by adding four multiracial and evolutionary states to the new Federation. A system of automatic counterbalances might conceivably come into effect, Malay right-wing fanaticism, for instance, offsetting rather than triggering Chinese left-wing extremism—a delicate and dangerous sort of political equilibrium, no doubt, but less hazardous than official inertia.

The advantages and the appeal of the Malaysia merger are so immediately apparent that local politicians are asking themselves why they failed to anticipate the Tengku's proposal. The conversion of five closely related but detached small national entities, each extremely vulnerable by itself and dependent upon the others, into one centrally organized larger nation, potentially far stronger in its whole than in its parts, is a political inspiration which seems, in retrospect, completely obvious. Although historical reconstructionists can find precedent for the idea and can trace in private, off-the-record conversations between the Tengku and Singapore's Prime Minister Lee Kuan Yew the origins of the present plan, it was actually not until the Tengku went on the record with his May 27 remarks that the real Malaysia idea began not only to take shape, but, what was far more important, to assume feasibility.

The difficulties inherent in the Federation of Malaysia proposal are at least as great as the prospective advantages. The proposal at once rallies and unites the forces of a wildly heterogeneous collection of politicians who find formidable anti-Malaysia arguments on the basis of the political, economic, racial, religious, linguistic, and purely private differences of a highly diversified Malaysian, Chinese, Indian, tribal, and European population. The present Federation of Malaya already harbors a 37% Chinese minority that fears Malaysian encroachment upon its traditional privilege; its 49.5% Malaysian population, meanwhile, fears Chinese exploitation and subversion. Either group—both include doctrinaire Marxists dedicated to class and race conflict—might be provoked or panicked into a pogrom. In Singapore, 1.7 million people—75% of them Chinese—are packed tightly into a 225-square-mile island where extremes of wealth and of poverty induce also extremes of political reaction and excitability. In British Borneo, three closely related and newly prosperous states—each with a Malay Chinese racial problem overlaid by tribal complications—are being swiftly propelled by 20th-century history toward the self-government for which they are quite unprepared. In the Federation, Singapore, and the states of Borneo, amorphous and potentially inimical political groups are impinging experimentally upon each other while the shadows and agents of Communist China—with expansionist drives—and of troubled Indonesia—with potential claims to British Borneo—darken not just the background but the immediate foreground as well. Given this regional montage of a thriving but threatened Federation, a confused but aspirant Singapore, a divided but promising Borneo, and an expansionist-minded China and Indonesia, plus a Philippine irredentist claim to North Borneo and the persistence of British colonial interests and influence throughout the area, Tengku Abdul Rahman came to a statesmanlike conclusion: better to spread and share than to dissemble the risks.

The Malaysia proposal has caught on both widely and rapidly. It would be extremely rash, however, to assume that the creation of Malaysia is now a foregone conclusion. The opposition is already powerful in each of the individual states and is just beginning to become effectively organized on a regional basis. The road to "Malaysia by 1963" is being simultaneously surveyed, mined, and bulldozed.

Among the more noteworthy judgments upon which the architects and observers of the new Federation of Malaysia find themselves in general agreement are the following:

1) The area is discontinuous, exposed, and unevenly developed. With a total land area of 130,000 squares miles, the proposed new state is still rather small in comparison with Thailand or Burma. The inclusion of one third of the island of Borneo, moreover, creates major problems of development and of defense in an area where potential danger threatens from many quarters and jungles are less readily penetrated by bulldozers than by bombs or bombast.

Land Areas
(in square miles)

Malaya	50,600
Singapore	240
North Borneo	29,360
Brunei	2,225
Sarawak	47,075
TOTAL	129,500

2) The population is complexly stratified on the basis of race, religion, social status, economic privilege, and political development.

Populations

	Malaya	Singapore	North Borneo	Brunei	Sarawak	Total
	6,916,000	1,497,500	454,800	83,960	743,300	9,695,560
Malaysian[1]	49.5%	13.5%	18%	49%	18%	41.5%
Other Indigenous[2]	0.5%	--	50%	27.5%	50%	10.5%
Chinese	37%	76%	23.5%	19%	31%	38%
Others[3]	13%	10.5%	8.5%	4.5%	1%	10%

[1] Malaysian includes people of Malay, Indonesian, and other closely related racial groups. Figures for Malaya include about 50,000 aborigines.

[2] Other Indigenous includes mainly tribal peoples — the Dayaks of Sarawak; the Kadayans of Brunei; the Kadayans, Muruts, and Bajaus of North Borneo, etc.

[3] Others includes mainly Indians, Pakistanis, and Ceylonese, plus about 22,500 Europeans in Singapore, 16,000 in Malaya, and 4,500 in Borneo.

The range is from primitive tribesmen to Malay sultans and Chinese
millionaires. Between these extremes are a great many persons and
groups indisposed to cherish aborigines, feudalists, capitalists, or each
other.

3) The economic systems are now prosperous yet highly vulnerable. Except for Brunei, which luxuriates in oil, prosperity is dependent upon high world market prices for rubber, tin, timber, copra,
and a few other raw materials. Cycles of boom and bust have been
characteristic of the past and might prove characteristic of the future.

Major Export Products
(Value Factor Indicated by Percentages)

	Rubber	Tin	Iron ore	Palm Products	Pepper and Spices	Timber	Petroleum
Malaya	60%	15%	6%	4%-5%	--	2%	--
Singapore	40%*	--	--	2%	--	--	15%*
North Borneo	20%	--	--	13%*	--	45%	--
Brunei	1%	--	--	--	--	--	99%
Sarawak	25%	--	--	--	7.5%	10%	55%*

*Re-exports.

4) The political systems are developing at different speeds and
in different directions. Malaya is quietly practicing a system of constitutional, democratic monarchy freakish in Southeast Asia. Singapore threatens momentarily to move into a "peoples' democracy"
phase. Brunei has a rudimentary form of constitutional monarchy with
an extreme left-wing opposition. Sarawak is embarking on a highly
tentative democratic experiment. North Borneo is still in predemo-
cratic state nursery school.

5) The indigenous military forces—basically Malaya's 12,000-
man army and its minute navy and air force—are inadequate to maintain security in the face of any serious internal or external challenge.
The retention of British land, sea, and air bases constitutes an invitation to the political agitator. The forces of international Communist
subversion and aggression are already formidable and are likely to
grow more so, in the area and in the near future.

GOVERNMENTAL SYSTEMS, MILITARY SERVICES, AND MALAYSIA PLAN, AS OF EARLY 1963

Federation of Malaya

Constitutional, parliamentary monarchy. Federation of nine Sultanates or Rajahdoms and two former British Straits Settlements. Paramount Ruler (Yang di-Pertuan Agong) elected for five-year term from and by the traditional rulers. Bicameral Parliament: 22 members of Senate elected from and by members of the 11 State Legislative Assemblies, an additional 16 appointed by the Paramount Ruler; all 104 members of House of Representatives popularly elected. Alliance Party (coalition of United Malay National Organization, Malayan Chinese Association, and Malayan Indian Congress) holds 73 seats. Prime Minister and Cabinet responsible to Parliament. Next elections scheduled for 1964. Military services: Army of 12,000 men; Air Force of about 15 planes; Navy of a few small patrol craft. British military base installations at Malacca, Penang, Johore, and Ipoh.

Singapore

Semiautonomous state within British Commonwealth. Chief of State (Yang di-Pertuan Negara) appointed by British Crown. Prime Minister and Cabinet responsible to fully elected 51-member Legislative Assembly. Current government party—left-wing People's Action Party—now in minority in Legislative Assembly; PAP's original 43 seats (1959) now reduced to 24 by death of one PAP incumbent whose seat's still unfilled and by defection of 18 PAP Assemblymen who formed Barisan Sosialis and United People's Party, both recklessly extremist. Next elections scheduled for 1964. Indigenous defense force: one battalion (1,000 men), a second being formed. Singapore is still a major British military base with land, sea, and air installations occupying 10% of land area and employing 9% of working population earning 5% of the national income.

North Borneo

British Crown Colony. Governor appointed by the Crown. Executive and Legislative Councils made up of ex-officio members and leading local citizens appointed by the Governor. Town Board members chosen in first general elections, November 1962, pro-Malaysia candidates scoring overwhelming victory. No local military services. Small British land-sea-air base on Labuan Island.

Brunei

British Protectorate. Sovereign ruler: Sultan of Brunei. Under 1959 Constitution, first general elections held August 1962; 54 out of 55 District Council seats (32 uncontested) won by anti-Malaysia Party Ra'ayat; 16 members new Legislative Assembly elected from and by District Council members; remaining 17 filled by ex-officio and appointed members. Upon outbreak of December 1962 armed insurrection, Party Ra'ayat banned, Legislative Assembly dissolved, Constitution suspended; new Executive Council appointed by Sultan and new elections now being tentatively planned. Armed forces: approximately 400 men, most of them in training in Malaya.

Sarawak

British Crown Colony. Governor appointed by the Crown. Supreme (executive) and State (legislative) Councils made up of ex-officio, appointed, and indirectly elected members. General elections for District Council members scheduled for May 1963; three-stage electoral system whereby voters choose District Councils, District Councils elect Divisional Councils, Divisional Councils elect majority of members of State Council, to which other members are appointed by government. Armed forces: 1,500 men, including constabulary, paramilitary recruits, and formerly separate Sarawak Rangers.

Federation of Malaysia

With formation of Federation of Malaysia, Sultan of Brunei to join Malaya's Conference of (traditional) Rulers. Malaya's House of Representatives to be expanded to include 15 members from Singapore, 16 from North Borneo, 24 from Sarawak, and an as-yet unstipulated number from Brunei. Singapore to accept less than proportional representation in return for high degree of local autonomy in finance, labor, and education. Borneo states to gain more than proportional representation, also special assurances about development funds (M$300 million* for Sarawak, M$200 million for North Borneo in first five years); local control over civil service and immigration; freedom of religion; continued use of English language in schools, courts, and offices; and other matters of special concern. New indigenous chiefs of state to be appointed for North Borneo and Sarawak; local civil servants gradually to replace the British. Many other details still to be worked out; some of the above possibly still subject to alteration.

*M$3.00=US$1.00.

The proposed state, if it is to prove truly viable, must go a long way toward meeting certain very difficult conditions:

In the first place, it must allow for the widely different aspirations and capacities of the component populations. Reconciliation of interest between Malays and Chinese is obviously so difficult and so essential that the majority of the population is prepared to make concessions. Reconciliation of interest among Malay groups themselves may prove almost as difficult and not nearly as well-recognized a political problem. Within the Federation, jealousy between the Malays of Kuala Lumpur and those of the conservative and retarded East Coast is a cause of constant bickering and occasional flare-up. An early experiment in regional technical and administrative co-operation, one between the governments of the Federation and of Brunei, has led to Brunei suspicion of Malaya's "colonial designs" and Federation indignation over Brunei's "ingratitude" and "obstructionism." Within the whole area of Malaysia, psychological and political sensitivities run high, as shown recently by resentment of Malaya's tactics of "bulldozing" Borneo into merger. Matters of civil service staffing, states' rights, official perquisites, politicians' prestige, and local pride are certain to prove highly tendentious.

Malaysia, furthermore, must achieve a rapidly increasing degree of economic diversification, integration, and industrialization in order to satisfy demands not merely for prosperity but for national self-sufficiency. The Federation, for instance, at present imposes high tariffs on imports, the Borneo states impose very low tariffs, and Singapore remains essentially a free port. All aspire to industrialization, but industrialization, if it is to be really impressive and co-operative rather than small and competitive, depends upon creation of a common market. Desultory consultations on such a move have as yet resulted in no agreement. All aspire to a major share in the development potentialities of the rich Borneo hinterland, but the states of Borneo exhibit marked reluctance freely to admit capital, skills, or labor, or to share their resources. In North Borneo, for instance, despite an official policy of welcoming foreign investment, Singapore Chinese capitalists have met with a very cool reception. In oil-rich Brunei, even native sons seeking to return after a few years' residence in Malaya are made to feel like inheritance hunters. In theory, then, Malaysia offers an exceedingly attractive prospect for swift, integrated economic development; in practice, it offers most perplexing conflicts of interest.

Malaysia must achieve also a high degree of mobility among

racial, social, occupational, and geographic groups. At present, the
privileged classes are too exclusively Malay aristocrats or Chinese
plutocrats. The middle classes are too exclusively nonindigenous.
The lower classes, both Malay and Chinese, are groups apart, little
known even to other classes of their own race. The achievement of a
truly healthy society will entail not only a very great deal of crossing
of social and racial barriers but also a relaxation of certain citizenship and residence regulations which some of the leading proponents
of the Malaysia merger scheme wish to maintain. Most specifically,
the densely overpopulated and in many respects overdeveloped island
of Singapore must be given the opportunity to export population, not
only laborers but also excess professional, business, and administrative personnel.

Finally, Malaysia must address itself to the extremely difficult
problem of adjusting its relations with its Asian neighbors and with
the Western world. The Federation itself has chosen to remain within
the British Commonwealth; to maintain a high degree of political, economic, and military co-operation with Great Britain; and to align itself
with Thailand and the Philippines in a newly coalescing anti-Communist
regional organization (Association of Southeast Asia—ASA) for economic
and cultural co-operation. Many Singapore politicians would prefer
greatly to weaken these Federation policies; many Borneo politicians
would prefer greatly to strengthen them. Politicians from all five
states are aware that Malaysia, if it emerges at all, will emerge into
an area throughout which political, economic, and military co-operation with Western nations and for anti-Communist causes is increasingly unpopular and nations which persist in such co-operation are increasingly suspect. On this score, Malaysia will itself be triply vulnerable. Already the Federation of Malaya is commonly regarded
throughout most of Southeast Asia as too soft on colonialism. Singapore is regarded as a reactionary center of British and Overseas Chinese capitalism. British Borneo is regarded as a deplorable anachronism to which Indonesian irredentist claims—at present officially
denied, as in the past Indonesian military intentions against Irian Barat
(Dutch New Guinea) were denied—are to be anticipated. The government of Malaysia will be confronted with an extremely difficult choice:
whether to maintain close and cordial relations with the West at the
risk of stirring up domestic and regional animosities, or whether to
prejudice prosperity and progress by yielding to nationalistic pressures.

CHAPTER
II

THE EARLY NEGOTIATIONS

February 26, 1962

In the nine months which have passed since Tengku Abdul Rahman, Prime Minister of the Federation of Malaya, first put forward his
proposal for creation of a new Federation of Malaysia by the merger
of Malaya, Singapore, North Borneo, Brunei, and Sarawak, official and
semiofficial representatives of the five states and of Great Britain have
reached a most impressive number of preliminary agreements. These
remain, as yet, agreements in principle only. They are only now in
process of being translated into a detailed official formula of merger.
The formula itself, once it is worked out, must be formally accepted
by the governments of Great Britain, the Federation of Malaya, Singapore, and Brunei. Even prior to such acceptance, it will in all probability constitute the major issue in general elections to be held in 1962
or 1963 in Singapore and in the Borneo states. The really serious road-
blocks are more likely to develop in the later rather than in the earlier
stages of the merger process. The very record of achieving one preliminary agreement after another, however, serves to throw an increasingly heavy weight of precedent in favor of ultimate success.

Whether by accident or by design, and it was probably a combination of both, the supporters of the Malaysia proposal hit upon a very
shrewd political strategy. First they made the proposal so vague that
the automatic opposition had an extremely difficult time defining its objections. The general idea of merger was so logical and so popular that
practically everyone had to profess himself in favor of merger, "in
principle." The opponents expressed grave misgivings, however, about
merger in practice and demanded full and immediate details. Gradually
the sponsors announced some of the provisional details, enough so that
the opposition could reject them as unsatisfactory and make its own demands. The merger plan, according to its critics, failed to safeguard
the special interests of the various states and the various racial groups
within the states. Then, on February 6, the Malaysia sponsors released

a lengthy "Memorandum for Malaysia." In it they made many concessions in response to the objections which had been raised against the previous and provisional terms. The opposition, thus, is now placed in the position of having to attack a merger proposal which corresponds in its specific details rather closely to its own demands. It is maneuvered, accordingly, into the logical but not necessarily politically precarious position of attacking not so much the details of merger as the very concept of merger, which it has all along professed to uphold.

The Malaysia negotiations have moved forward with such remarkable speed that month-to-month progress is readily apparent. On May 27, 1961, came the original and highly tentative proposal. In early June came official commitment from Singapore's People's Action Party government to the course of achieving merger in company with the Borneo states. In early July representatives of Malaya, Singapore, North Borneo, Brunei, and Sarawak attended a regional conference in Singapore of the Commonwealth Parliamentary Association. There they discussed the Malaysia proposal and came to general—but far from unanimous agreement—to push forward with it.

Major organizational and negotiating advances came in August and September. On August 21 a Malaysia Solidarity Consultative Committee, organized as an offshoot of the Commonwealth Parliamentary Association, met in Jesselton and began to plan a regional program of action. In later meetings the Committee expanded the scope of its membership and its operations so that it constitutes at present the major negotiating and propagandizing agency for the Malaysia scheme. On August 23 the Prime Ministers of the Federation of Malaya and of Singapore held their first formal conference on Malaysia. They announced an agreement whereby Singapore would concede to the new Federation responsibility for external affairs, defense, and security, and would in turn be conceded autonomy in matters of education and labor. In mid-September the two Prime Ministers conferred again, and on September 14 they announced further agreements in principle, also the delegation to working parties of the continuing negotiations and the intent actually to achieve merger "before June 1963."

On October 18 Prime Minister Abdul Rahman requested and achieved the approval of the Federation's Legislature of a motion for creation of a Federation of Malaysia in which the Borneo states would join as "members" but Singapore would join as a "partner . . . on a footing something like that which exists between the United Kingdom and Northern Ireland." The distinction between Borneo "membership" and Singapore "partnership" was that the Borneo states would be treated as

equal members but Singapore as a special member with both special
privilege and special handicap.   Neither in Singapore nor in Borneo
was the distinction very popular.   The Singapore "privilege" was the
concession of a high degree of local autonomy; the "handicap" the denial of equal citizenship rights.   The Borneo "equal membership" formula, on the other hand, involved the risk that as the least developed
and least experienced members, the Borneo states would in fact suffer
severe handicap in relation to the others.

In November Tengku Abdul Rahman carried the Malaysia proposal to London. From the British Foreign Office he gained acceptance
of the Malaysia concept as a "desirable aim." He gained acceptance
also of a special formula regarding British retention after merger of
its Singapore military base. The Singapore base, it was agreed, largely
as a result of Singapore's insistence, would be used only for British and
Commonwealth, not for SEATO purposes.

In December the Malaysia proposal, despite the increasing stir
of favorable interest in it, ran into some serious difficulties. On December 6 the Singapore Legislative Assembly voted approval in principle to the same motion which the Federation's Legislative Assembly
had passed in October, but it did so only after a heated 13-day debate
which ended with the walkout of Barisan Sosialis and other opposition
Assemblymen in protest against extension of the final session into the
evening hours. Later (January 30, 1962), as a result of opposition protest that the vote had been invalid, the motion was reintroduced. This
time it passed with somewhat equivocal amendment which satisfied the
Marshall-Ong factions but the Barisan Sosialis cast negative votes.
On December 19, after a conference in Kuching, Sarawak, the Malaysia Solidarity Consultative Committee issued a long communiqué in
which it itemized a whole series of reservations on behalf of Borneo,
which amounted in effect to an appeal for safeguards against Federation and Singapore domination.

In January and early February of this year the Malaysia program gathered great momentum. From January 6 through January 8
the Malaysia Solidarity Consultative Committee met in Kuala Lumpur,
and from February 1 through February 3 in Singapore. In both sessions
it made rapid progress toward resolving the negotiating problems, and
in each city it staged big public meetings to gain and to demonstrate
support for the proposal. Then, on February 6, simultaneously in the
five capital cities (Kuala Lumpur, Singapore, Kuching, Brunei Town,
and Jesselton) the Committee released its lengthy "Memorandum for
Malaysia," setting forth the consensus of the delegates from the five
states. This Memorandum constitutes the basis on which a joint Brit-

ish-Malaysian Commission will in late February begin an on-the-spot investigation to determine whether the heretofore inarticulate peoples of Borneo wish to accept merger for themselves and thus to make it possible for Singapore as well. It constitutes also the basis of an area-wide political debate which seems likely to increase in intensity during the next few months.

Some of the major points of the "Memorandum for Malaysia" are as follows:

1) External affairs, defense, and security will be the responsibility of the central government. Varying degrees of autonomy will be allowed the new member states in other matters.

2) Islam will be the state religion, but freedom of religion is guaranteed.

3) Malay will be the official language, but English and other languages will continue in use as languages of education and general affairs.

4) The Borneo governments will be gradually transformed on the model of state governments in the present Federation of Malaya where traditional rulers remain sovereign rulers, traditional states' rights remain largely intact, and provision is made for integration of former crown colonies.

5) The Borneo states will be enabled quickly to achieve educational, economic, and political advancement to bring them up to the level of the other members of the Federation.

6) The Borneo states will retain control over immigration, land development, and civil service positions, in order to safeguard themselves against domination or exploitation by their more developed associates; they will receive more than proportional numbers of representatives in the Federal Legislature and greater than proportional shares of development funds from Federal sources.

7) All Federation and Singapore citizens will automatically acquire Federation of Malaysia "nationality" and will enjoy equal rights and responsibilities.

8) The indigenous peoples of Borneo will enjoy the same special rights that Malay citizens now enjoy in Malaya, i.e., "reservation of such proportion as may be deemed reasonable of positions in the public service, scholarships and other similar educational or training programmes and special facilities relating to trade or business in order that they may be able to take their rightful places along with the other communities."

The Memorandum, as its critics immediately point out, is still far from being a "blueprint," but that is intentional—in part at least—on the part of the drafters. As its sponsors insist, it is a highly significant "consensus," one which was worked out by laboriously reconciling many conflicts, leaving many yet to be resolved, and leaving the door open for modification of compromises already agreed upon. It is a significant indication, furthermore, of the manner in which the focus of the problem is shifting. To begin with, the conflict of interests between Singapore and the Federation attracted the greatest concern and consumed the most attention. Now it is the conflict of interests between the Borneo states and the Singapore-Federation partners.

Almost everyone is now agreed, although for different reasons and with different reservations and often despite vigorous declaration to the contrary, that Singapore and the Borneo states constitute each a special case and require each a special status. Total assimilation as twelfth, thirteenth, fourteenth, and fifteenth states of the present eleven-state Federation, as proposed sometimes by the architects, sometimes by the critics of the Malaysia proposal, is no longer contemplated; nor, despite the wording of Malaysia documents, is "equal membership" or "equal partnership." Singapore's status is in fact to be a partnership of mutual concession; the Borneo states' status is in fact to be memberships of special privilege.

The major problems regarding Malaya-Singapore "partnership" in the new Federation have been those relating to the concessions which Malaya and Singapore must make to each other on such critical matters as the following: (1) the degree of autonomy, if any, to be conceded the Overseas Chinese city-state of Singapore in matters of foreign affairs, defense, security, finance, labor, and education; (2) the acquisition by Singapore citizens of Federation citizenship; (3) the number of seats to be assigned to Singapore in the new Federation Parliament; (4) the creation of a customs union and a common market; and (5) the status of British military bases on Singapore Island.

Preliminary compromise has been reached as follows, with clear signals, however, that in Singapore a political cyclone may be gathering. (1) Singapore, as noted above, will concede central government control of foreign affairs, defense, and security, and in turn will be conceded a high degree of autonomy in finance, labor, and education. With regard to finance, for instance, Singapore will retain 75% of its own revenue for its own purposes. (2) Singapore citizens will automatically acquire Federation "nationality." This compromise leaves unresolved, however, the highly controversial question whether they also will acquire full citizenship rights, including right of suffrage. According to a compromise arrangement contemplated a few months ago, Singapore was to accept imposition of Federation citizenship requirements which would, in effect, disenfranchise a high percentage of its present citizens. (3) Singapore is to be allocated 15 seats in the new 127-member Federal Legislature instead of the considerably greater number to which it would be entitled on the basis of proportional representation. (4) Both the Federation and the Singapore governments acknowledge the desirability of creating a customs union and a common market. They have made little progress, however, toward reaching the necessary agreements. (5) The British Singapore base, as noted, may be used for British and Commonwealth but not for SEATO purposes—a distinction extremely difficult to interpret but one intended, by all parties possibly, as much for the record as for the observance.

Although all of the special difficulties regarding Singapore's status were apparent from the moment the Malaysia proposal was made, relatively few of the special difficulties regarding the Borneo states were actually anticipated. To be sure, it was widely assumed that Brunei, like Singapore, but with more reason, would be concerned about its money; that Sarawak, which has been agitated for years about language and curriculum of education would be concerned about its schools; and that North Borneo, which has small British military bases, might want to control them, dismantle them, or even ask Britain greatly to expand them. Assurances were promptly forthcoming, therefore, that Brunei, which each year earns US$40 million and spends only US$18 million, might reserve for itself its reservoirs of oil and of black ink. Reassurances on education have also been forthcoming, but none regarding Borneo bases which nobody seems yet actually to have mentioned.

The real Borneo crisis, however, arose quite suddenly and quite unexpectedly. It arose as a result of suspicions on the part of the Borneo leaders that they were being pressured into a merger from which everyone else would profit far more than they would and largely at their expense. The really serious objection on the part of Brunei is not money or sharing its wealth but the sharing of its sovereignty. The really serious reservations in North Borneo and Sarawak have related to forfeit of control over the civil service, immigration, development of resources, taxation, and also to forfeit of prestige on the part of local politicians. Major concessions have accordingly been offered and constitute, in fact, the major emphasis of the new "Memorandum on Malaysia." Reassurance is repeatedly reiterated regarding sovereign states' rights. The Borneo civil service is to be subjected as swiftly as possible to a process of "Borneanization"; local immigration will be left under the control of the Borneo states themselves; development will be speeded up and will be carried out, insofar as possible, by and for the Borneo people but at no increase of expense to them; the Borneo financial system—and its extremely low tax system—will be subject only to gradual changes. Borneo, in other words, is to be reserved largely for the Borneans. Most important of all, perhaps, Borneo politicians have been conceded a major role in the Malaysia Solidarity Consultative Committee and have been promised, by implication, conspicuous positions in the new Federation of Malaysia.

Political handicappers in the area are predicting a rather better than 50-50 chance of bringing the Malaysia proposal to realization. Optimism at present runs highest in the Federation, high in Singapore, by no means so high in Borneo, but high enough to justify the bookmakers' odds. One major hazard is that the Malaysia proposal involves great and unwelcome concessions of sovereignty on the part of each of the member states and each of the racial communities at a time when nationalist and racial sentiment runs high throughout Southeast Asia. It runs highest of all in the newest, least populous states. In the case of Malaysia, this means the emergent states of Borneo where, except for Brunei, both politics and nationalism were almost quiescent until the Malaysia proposal itself stirred them up. The greatest hazard of all, however, is that the proposal is much too rational and responsible and too respectably official to arouse great emotional support among the politically illiterate. The demagogue can and does attack it as colonialistic, imperialistic, capitalistic, and Malay-feudalist inspired, and hence not in line with the "progressive" forces of the century. Still, in the Federation, Singapore, and British Borneo to date, the process of outgrowing colonialism has not as yet led to uncontrollable excesses of the anticolonialist and the pro-Marxist sort of nationalism which has defeated healthful national development in Indonesia, for instance. Having weathered the 1950's in a good state of political and economic health, the proposed member states of the new Malaysia have a head start in meeting the problems of the 1960's.

CHAPTER
III

SUPPORTING AND OPPOSING FACTIONS

February 27, 1962

Prime Minister Abdul Rahman's mid-1961 proposal for creation of a new nation of Malaysia, inclusive of Malaya, Singapore, North Borneo, Brunei, and Sarawak, has introduced a dynamic new element into the politics of the region. Progress toward realization of the proposal has been so unexpectedly swift, however, as to distract attention from the grave Singapore crisis which occasioned it and from the formidable opposition which is now being organized. It seems prudent, therefore, to trace the crisis and to define the forces of pro- and anti-Malaysia sentiment as a preface to the exciting political developments which may be anticipated in the next few months in the Malaysia area.

The Singapore Crisis

A serious threat is now posed to the Singapore left-wing People's Action Party government by Singapore extremist elements led by onetime members of the PAP hierarchy. Prime Minister Lee Kuan Yew, who represents the moderate wing of the PAP, has given Singapore good, honest government since he took office on June 3, 1959. He has been unable, however, to solve any of Singapore's long-term problems, most of which relate to decreasing opportunity for the growing population of his minute island city-state and the increasing strength of Communist elements. He has been harassed by a new wave of troubles with the labor unions which in 1955 and 1956 staged a paralyzing series of strikes and riots. He has seen his Legislative Assembly majority of 43 out of 51 seats whittled down to 26, by reason of the defection of onetime PAP Assemblymen and the return in spectacular and, to the PAP, almost disastrous by-elections of anti-PAP candidates.

Consequently, he is confronted with the continuous threat that Singapore state security will crumble and that Singapore's political leadership will pass from him to labor union leader Lim Chin Siong, whom he accuses, with compelling documentary evidence, of being a Communist.

Lim Chin Siong, whom most observers now regard as the architect of the new Singapore crisis, was originally an associate of Lee Kuan Yew's in organizing the PAP. He later usurped party leadership and implicated the party in a series of bloody labor and student riots which led, eventually, to troop action and to arrest and imprisonment of large numbers of "subversives." Lim went to jail along with the others, but on June 2, 1959, just after the PAP landslide election victory, on demand of Lee Kuan Yew and other PAP leaders, Lim and his chief associates were released. As reward for their long martyrdom and as a measure to keep them under close party surveillance, six of them were given specially created posts as "Parliamentary Secretaries." In these jobs they set about promptly to restore their personal power and to steer the party. They succeeded better in the first than in the second endeavor, and in the spring of 1961, after instigating a series of party intrigues and labor troubles they bolted the party and worked openly for its collapse.

Lim Chin Siong has a powerful but unreliable and not always friendly ally in Ong Eng Guan, from late 1957 until early 1959 the rabble-rousing, British-baiting Mayor of Singapore, famous for his chaotic administration and his vote-pulling demagoguery. For his services in helping to win the 1959 elections, Ong was named Minister for National Development. As Minister, he promoted such grandiose schemes as "volunteer" labor projects which focused the floodlights on himself. The other PAP leaders mistrusted him and showed that they did; he accused them of betraying their election promises and of turning soft toward capitalism and colonialism. The top PAP hierarchy thereupon sacked Ong as Minister and purged him from the party. Ong joined the opposition, as did several of his supporters in the Legislative Assembly. In December 1960 he accused the PAP leaders of nepotism, resigned his Legislative Assembly seat in protest against all PAP personalities and policies, and devoted himself to rebuilding his own political fences.

In 1961 Lim and Ong, singly and in co-operation, saw and took their big chance to destroy the PAP by parliamentary means. Two Legislative Assembly seats fell open by reason of the deaths of the incumbents and the government scheduled two sets of by-elections. Ong Eng

Guan entered the first, in his own home district, and on April 29, against
the most powerful opposition the PAP could mount, he won by a vote of
7,747 to 2,828 for his nearest rival, the PAP candidate. David Marshall,
Singapore's first Chief Minister, entered the second contest and on
July 15, thanks far less to his own efforts than to the extremely vigorous anti-PAP campaign staged by Lim, Ong, and their associates, defeated the PAP candidate by a vote of 3,598 to 3,052 for the PAP candidate. In the course of these election furors, the PAP government was
itself on the point of resigning—or of being forced to resign. Whole
blocks of PAP Assemblymen defected to the opposition. When Prime
Minister Lee had to face a vote of confidence after the second election
defeat, he won by just one more vote than was absolutely necessary,
27 out of 51.

The situation of the PAP government was most precarious. Lee
Kuan Yew might at any moment be forced to call for new elections, and
he had no confidence that he could win. In any event, he faces regularly
scheduled elections early in 1963. In order to retain its position and
regain its prestige, the PAP will have to point to some dramatic new
accomplishment. What was absolutely necessary, Lee Kuan Yew decided, while the crisis was still building up, was progress toward achievement of his major policy objective, the one which offered a solution or
at least amelioration of many of Singapore's problems and was, therefore, popular with the electorate. The objective was merger—merger
of small, shaky Singapore into the larger and stable Federation of Malaya. The alternative, said Lee Kuan Yew, was the certainty of PAP
defeat in any new elections and of Communist take-over.

Political certainties being what they are, in Singapore as elsewhere, failure to achieve merger, PAP defeat, and Communist take-
over may be neither identical nor consecutive contingencies nor the
present crisis the decisive one. Prime Minister Lee Kuan Yew, for
the time being at least, believes that his analysis is correct. So, too,
does the Federation's Prime Minister, Tengku Abdul Rahman. The
Tengku is not enthusiastic about Singapore as a Malaysia member, but
prefers that to Singapore as a Communist neighbor and therefore
came forward with his Malaysia proposal. A great many other highly
qualified participants and observers agree with Lee and the Tengku.
Prominent among them is Lim Chin Siong.

The Support and the Opposition

The major support for the Greater Malaysia proposal has come

from the leading officials of the governments concerned, from the responsible press, and from the well-informed segments of the public —
a trio of opinion-molders which, by joint acclaim, might all too readily
induce public repudiation of the scheme. The most powerful opposition,
naturally, comes from the political opposition to the established governments. Basically, this means both the extreme right and the extreme
left wings in Malaya; the extreme far-left wing in Singapore; some of
the emerging nationalists in Borneo; and some of the unreconstructible
colonialists among the British. Rightists, leftists, revolutionaries, and
colonialists, however, make common cause with each other, also at
times with men of ordinarily sounder judgment who perceive in the Malaysia proposal some very serious flaws. Conspicuous among the flaws
may be the denial to the West of the British military base in Singapore,
decline in the level of political and economic rationality in British Borneo, and the spread into areas now politically healthful of the Singapore
Communist contagion.

Official support in the Federation, to be specific, centers about
the Prime Minister and his close associates in the conservative, pro-
Western Alliance Party. Support in Singapore centers about Prime
Minister Lee and his top associates in the moderate wing of the leftist
People's Action Party. Support in Borneo centers about the Sultan and
his court in Brunei; in Sarawak and in North Borneo support centers
about the British colonial administrators and some of their indigenous
adherents. Opponents of the proposal, therefore, can and do all too
easily attack it as the cunning plot of Malay and Brunei feudalists and
colonial collaborators, of "stooges" of Singapore capitalists, and British imperialist die-hards, any or all of whom can be declared to benefit from the proposed merger.

The position of the British in supporting or opposing the proposal is particularly delicate. British opposition—as distinguished from
British misgiving—exists, in fact, more in the minds of the regional
proponents than in the minds of the British themselves. The majority
of the British, reluctant as they may be to give up colonial perquisites,
concede the necessity of doing so and prefer to make the renunciation
voluntarily under circumstances as favorable as possible to the other
party and hence to themselves. British officialdom, in particular, evidently acting on the sound political premise that a little British obstruction is the best possible disproof of British manipulation, has devoted
itself mainly to pointing out the necessary but tedious technicalities to
be overcome in the achievement of a worthy but imperfect objective.
They find themselves, in North Borneo and Sarawak, for instance, in
the extraordinary position of having to justify to the local people their

renunciation of colonialism—for most of the Chinese, at least, would
prefer that they remain. They feel impelled, furthermore, to describe
Malaysia only as a "desirable aim," in order to appease the local elements which most ardently support the plan but do not wish to have it appear to be a British scheme and hence, to them, indefensible. Rather
than to damn by strong support, the British today prefer to save by
faint praise.

The support for Malaysia has organized an area-wide Malaysia
Solidarity Consultative Committee, itself an outgrowth of a Borneo regional committee which was called together first in August 1961 to col-
lect and disseminate information about the proposal. The Malaysia
Solidarity Consultative Committee, despite its cumbersome name and
function, has now succeeded in holding successively bigger and better-
publicized meetings, first in Jesselton, later in Kuching, Kuala Lumpur,
and Singapore. Working mainly through government channels, it is
mounting a full-scale campaign to popularize the Malaysia plan and to
combat the opposition. On February 7 it released a "Memorandum for
Malaysia" which serves at present as the basis for further propaganda
and negotiations. The Committee has not as yet succeeded in popular-
izing the Malaysia proposal in areas where it was not originally very
popular—in Borneo, that is. It has achieved its greatest success in
actually working out many of the details of merger and in establishing
an area-wide political organization, one which may constitute not only
the support for the Malaysia plan but the basis of a stable and constructive Malaysia party or parties.

As noted above, opposition to the Malaysia proposal in the Federation and in Singapore comes mainly—but not entirely—from the political opposition to the established governments. In Brunei it is a far-
left-wing Brunei Malay element that professes to support the government. In North Borneo and Sarawak, paradoxically, it is the Chinese
—those who genuinely support the colonial regime.

The opposition was generally bumbling and inconclusive at first,
for, like the support, it was taken by surprise by the proposal. The
general public response was either so favorable, as in Singapore and
the Federation, or, in the case of Borneo, so enigmatic that the politicians had to play it safe by leaving all doors open. The original reaction of almost all politicians in Borneo was to reject in principle while
searching for popular grounds to support that stand or any other. Presently, objections began to be defined and members of the opposition began to assume fixed positions. At the beginning of 1962, while the support was itself becoming well organized on an area basis, the majority

of the more important opposition politicians came together and agreed upon a joint position which now seems likely to be the long-term basis for a powerful anti-Malaysia campaign.

The opposition's stand, as defined in a regional conference of "Socialist" parties in Kuala Lumpur in late January, includes the following more significant points:

1) The present Malaysia proposal is "hostile to the concept of Malaysia"; it is "directed against the progressive forces" in the area; most specifically, it is a "military threat to Indonesia."

2) The proper approach to Malaysia is the "slow association of Malaysian peoples" by exercise of the "right of self-determination" without "interference" by the British.

3) The stages toward achievement of Malaysia should be: "full merger" of Singapore as a totally assimilated "twelfth state" of the Federation, or, failing that, continuation of Singapore's own "constitutional advancement" through "democratic process"; achievement of "right of self-determination" by the Borneo states; voluntary formation of a Borneo regional federation; and only then, consideration of Borneo membership in the expanded Federation of Malaysia.

The organizers of the Socialist Conference in Kuala Lumpur were the leaders of the Federation's Socialist Front: Inche (Mr.) Ahmad Bustamam, Secretary-General of the Party Rakjat (Malay), and Dr. Lim Kean Siew, Secretary-General of the Labour Party (Chinese and Indian). The Federation's Party Rakjat maintains a branch in Singapore, is affiliated with the Party Ra'ayat of Brunei, and both the Singapore and the Brunei parties were also represented. The Socialist Front invited other Socialist parties to attend. Four Singapore parties accepted: Prime Minister Lee Kuan Yew's PAP, Lim Chin Siong's recently organized and increasingly powerful Barisan Sosialis, Ong Eng Guan's new United People's Party, and David Marshall's Workers' Party. Two Borneo parties also sent delegates: the aforementioned Party Ra'ayat of Brunei and the United People's Party of Sarawak. North Borneo, having no party which qualified as "Socialist" in the eyes of the conference sponsors, received no invitation and sent no representative.

The conference opened dramatically with a PAP bid for conference consideration of a working paper in defense of the Malaysia proposal. The conference rejected the working paper, the PAP delegates staged a walkout, and the conference expelled the PAP from the Socialist fraternity. There followed four days of vigorous and increasingly anti-Malaysia speechmaking, and the conference closed with unanimous

adoption of the resolutions noted above and with unanimous determination to work for the defeat of the Malaysia proposal.

Each of the newly associated or semiassociated Socialist parties contributed important elements to the new united front opposition,
as expressed in the resolutions and as elaborated upon in previous and
subsequent oratory. Although there were overlappings in definition
and timing of objections such as are difficult if not impossible now to
trace, the major contributions seem to have been approximately as follows:

Lim Chin Siong most clearly developed the thesis that merger
as proposed by the Tengku and the PAP was not "true merger" but
rather "phony merger" involving "second-class citizen status" for
Singapore, "betrayal" of the people by the colonialists, the capitalists,
and their PAP "stooges." David Marshall added florid oratory about
a PAP "sellout" by proposing a "sham" merger which would convert
Singapore into a "permanent slave and colony of the Federation,"
worse off than it was under the British, to whom, at least, it did not
pay taxes in return for its defense. Ong Eng Guan took part in the
anti-PAP diatribe and represented himself as the true apostle of "independence" and "anticolonialism"—an honor which David Marshall,
Lim Chin Siong, and all other Singapore politicians seek to share. The
Borneo delegates contributed the demand for successive stages of self-
determination and independence, tristate Borneo federation, and Malaysia after that, if at all.

The arguments regarding self-determination, independence, and
two preliminary merger schemes for Singapore and the Federation and
the Borneo states respectively, are not merely the tactics of appearing
to approve while in fact rallying forces to defeat the plan. Many of the
opponents of the Malaysia plan, particularly in Borneo, deeply and sin-
cerely believe their own arguments. They are genuinely concerned
about moving too fast, too soon, too ill-prepared into the great unknown
of national statehood. They fail to take into account, however, the fact
that the Malaysia proposal originated as a package deal whereby Singapore might join the Federation in company with the other three states
and only on that condition. To argue for phasing and delay of merger
is in fact to argue for increase of the very hazards which make immediate merger seem imperative and delayed merger impossible.

Antimerger arguments, furthermore, are being advanced more
and more commonly, not only by those who are genuinely worried about
reaching decision too soon but by those who are primarily intent upon

waging an anticolonial campaign. To them, only the unconditional demand for total and immediate independence for each small potential national entity is truly "revolutionary" and "progressive." Amicable negotiation for independence and a mutual concession prior to independence of a degree of national sovereignty to some larger national unit are somehow "reactionary" and "neocolonialistic." These are the semantic weapons which are potentially the most incendiary and hence the most dangerous. Many of those who adopt them look to Indonesia for inspiration and help.

The Party Rakjat and the Pan-Malayan Islamic Party (PMIP—an important Federation party of the extreme right wing) were the first to introduce Indonesia into the debate—but then, Indonesia was at the back of many people's minds and had for years loomed as a formidable factor in any plan for regional association. The Party Rakjat and the PMIP, accordingly, declared very early on that any really valid Malaysia concept must allow for inclusion of Indonesia and the Philippines, without any indication, however, whether Indonesia and the Philippines were to be consulted, or, if so, what might be their reactions. Presently, the Party Rakjat ventured even further afield and included also the four southern provinces of Thailand.

The Indonesian government has adopted the correct if cryptic attitude of wishing the Malayan government well, "if it can succeed with this plan." But the Indonesian Communist Party (PKI) in December issued a statement branding the Malaysia proposal as "neocolonialism." At just the same time, report spread in Singapore that the Barisan Sosialis (which Lee Kuan Yew brands as an "open Communist front") was not only making strenuous efforts to achieve understanding with the PKI but that Lim Chin Siong had himself expressed a preference for a merger of Singapore with Indonesia rather than with Malaya. Meanwhile, over in Borneo, the Party Ra'ayat of Brunei, a revolutionary party on the Indonesian model headed by a Brunei Malay educated in Indonesia, was combining anti-Malaysia pronouncements with a renewal of advances toward Indonesia; other Borneo factions were eying Indonesia across the border, most with apprehension, but some with favor. This intricate interrelationship with each other and with Indonesia of the right-wing PMIP, the left-wing Party Rakjat, the extremist Barisan Sosialis, and various other groups, including as yet indeterminate Sarawak and North Borneo politicians, has served to throw the Malaysia proposal into international politics of the area and to introduce, therefore, one further and greater element of hazard.

The Malaysia proposal, particularly as it ties in with international political controversy, induces a high pitch of political exchange regarding conspiracy, subversion, and Communist aggression.   Just as the Tengku's critics accuse him of being a puppet of the imperialists, so he accuses many of them—often with ample reason, but sometimes without—of being Communists. And just as Lee Kuan Yew's critics accuse him of being a "stooge" of the colonialists, so he accuses them—all too frequently with all too abundant reason—of being secret agents of world communism, men who take their orders from outside the country. Since Indonesia is at present the center of regional and growing Communist strength, the assumption, whether rightly or wrongly based, is that the Indonesian Communist Party is a prime mover in the program to sabotage the Malaysia plan, and that the Indonesian government, if it does nothing to abet, certainly does nothing to restrain the PKI. Among promerger groups in the Federation and in Singapore, suspicion and resentment of the PKI and of world Communist agents is now markedly on the increase. This fact makes for realism regarding the desirability of settling local differences and achieving stability in merger, but it makes even more difficult than usual the problem of maintaining friendly relations with Indonesia.

The opposition in the Federation is strong enough to cause serious trouble to the Alliance government in gaining acceptance of the Malaysia proposal, but does not seem strong enough to block it. The Singapore Barisan Sosialis opposition is strong enough that, in the opinion of most observers, it could defeat the PAP—and hence the proposal—if new elections were held today. Nevertheless, the Barisan Sosialis seems indisposed to force new elections in the immediate future. Presumably, it fears to assume responsibility for failure of merger negotiations, which the Federation would certainly cancel in case of a PAP defeat. The popularity with the electorate of the merger proposal is the basis on which the PAP has a good prospect of rebuilding its prestige and power before the regularly scheduled Singapore elections are held in 1963 with merger as the issue.

Although the relative strength and prospects of the pro- and anti-Malaysia forces in Malaya and Singapore are being made subject to such brief and categorical summary as the one above, the situation in British Borneo at the moment defies even the boldest analyst. Some of the suddenly overdeveloped political complexities of this long underdeveloped land have been indicated in the course of the preceding discussion. They will be treated in greater detail in subsequent chapters.

CHAPTER
IV

POLITICS IN BORNEO

February 28, 1962

The proposal for formation of a new Federation of Malaysia has stirred up intense controversy in each of the five prospective member states—Malaya, Singapore, Brunei, North Borneo, and Sarawak. Singapore's stagy politics, even more frenetic on the Malaysia issue than on most others, has relegated Borneo politics to the remote hinterground. Yet, unless the states of Borneo voluntarily throw in with Malaysia, the proposal seems futile, the merger of the Federation of Malaya and Singapore seems blocked, and the Singapore political crisis, which induced the proposal in the first place, seems intensified by failure of the one measure which seemed best calculated to resolve it. And it is by no means certain that the people of Borneo, acting on their own volition, will any or all of them elect to join Malaysia.

Public political volition, however, is a phenomenon which until quite recently has been difficult to associate with the British Borneo land-seascape. Only Brunei has had a political party of any long standing—the far-leftist Party Ra'ayat, organized a few years ago by Inche A.M. Azahari, a Brunei Malay of Indonesian revolutionary background. Sarawak has for the last three years had two parties: the Sarawak United People's Party, basically Chinese and left wing, and the Party Negara, basically Malay and right wing. Both were the result more of accident than of design. British colonial guidance toward organization of a single party misfired and two rival groups emerged in place of the one loyal government party which the British intended. North Borneo has had no political party at all. Several potential political leaders of different racial groups had been eying each other, awaiting the propitious moment for organizing, but heeding benevolent British colonial advisers advising circumspection. While modern political parties—or at any rate political activities—were getting slowly under way, a few potential leaders were emerging, but except in Brunei where the Party Ra'ayat claimed 19,000 members, no very great number of political followers.

Of the political leaders, the best known both inside Borneo and abroad was Brunei's Azahari who stood for some not very clearly defined but still revolutionary manner of nationalizing Brunei's wealth, modernizing its feudal sultanate, and restoring its former area-wide hegemony. The only other Borneo politician at all well known even in the immediate area was Sarawak's Mr. Ong Kee Hui, a wealthy Kuching banker and organizer of the United People's Party. One other Bornean, however, was being picked by more and more insiders as the coming Borneo politician. He was Mr. Donald Stephens, Jesselton newspaper editor, appointive member of the North Borneo Legislative and Executive Councils, a man who combined local British and Kadazan (Dusun) racial heritage and was related by marriage to leading Chinese families as well. Mr. Stephens seemed almost uniquely well qualified to represent the multiracial Borneo community.

The sudden announcement of the Malaysia proposal first threw Azahari, Ong, and Stephens together in formulating a common personal reaction. Then within a matter of days it separated them as each began to take political soundings in his home area and to respond to them. Very soon it brought Donald Stephens into a position of almost unrivaled prominence in the area, one which he still maintains. The repercussions of the announcement, meanwhile, flushed whole coveys of new political leaders and followers and parties. Each began to take a stand on the Malaysia proposal and on other local issues—now suddenly much more important—which related to it. British Borneo, long sheltered from the winds of Southeast Asian political change, began almost overnight to register squalls. Borneo political leaders, who had to admit that they did not yet know quite whom they were leading, or in what season the Borneo political monsoon might begin to blow and from what direction, suddenly found themselves trying at once to read and to set the signals.

A few facts, however, soon began to clarify. First, Azahari's Indonesia-oriented Brunei Malays would vigorously oppose the Malaysia proposal and seek instead to establish Brunei paramountcy in British Borneo and Brunei-Indonesia rapport within the area. Second, in North Borneo, the powerful Chinese community—one fourth of the population, but the propertied, moneyed, educated fourth, scornful on the whole of the other Asian elements of the community—would oppose the proposal, preferring to retain British colonialism, but willing in theory at least to settle for North Borneo independence and federation with its two neighbors. Third, in Sarawak the Chinese community would also oppose the proposal, far less unanimously than in North Borneo but powerfully all the same, and with about as much Chinese

Communist as Chinese racial bias. Fourth, the indigenous people were divided, if indeed informed at all on the subject, and while they might be inclined to support the Malaysia proposal, tended also to be factional and factious. The Brunei people, of course, constitute a special case, and their case — for Brunei hegemony — would have little appeal among the indigenous peoples of Sarawak or North Borneo where memories of Brunei rule are not nostalgic. Almost everyone who reacted at all, in short, did so on the basis of personal interest which he identified almost always with racial interest. Where there had previously been little political or racial friction, now suddenly there were two major but related problems — the Malaysia political issue and the racial issues which it caused suddenly to flare up.

The general pattern of Borneo reaction on state and racial lines was approximately as indicated above. The more detailed chronology and the ideology of the reaction warrant further consideration. They may indicate the emerging pattern of Borneo political leadership, organization, and affiliation which will greatly influence not only Malaysia's prospects but the whole political future of Borneo.

The principal leaders of the three states, Stephens, Azahari, and Ong, and some of their associates, conferred hurriedly in Jesselton in early July in order to decide, if possible, upon a united Bornean front. Tengku Abdul Rahman had just visited Brunei and in a public address there had formally invited Brunei to join the new Federation, and had advised North Borneo and Sarawak to do likewise. He had stopped over also in Sarawak where he made similar speeches. The Borneo leaders were united in indignation at what seemed to them the Tengku's peremptory tone and manner and at his apparent decision, without any consultation with the Borneo peoples themselves, regarding conditions of merger. There had already been criticism in Borneo of the Federation's "bulldozing" tactics, its "colonial" aspirations, its "patronizing" attitude, and the joint intent of Malaya and Singapore to "exploit" the backward Borneo territories.

Ong, Stephens, and Azahari came to an agreement, therefore, to declare that, "So far as the wishes of the people of the three territories are ascertainable [a significant qualification] any plan in accordance with the pronouncements made by Tengku Abdul Rahman in Brunei and Sarawak [another important qualification] would be totally unacceptable . . . ." They went on to state that they favored "constitutional advance," "constitutional links," and elections "where an undertaking has been given" [i.e., Brunei] for the three Borneo states, with suggestion but not specific mention of a three-state Borneo federation. The three thus left

P. H. WELSHIMER MEMORIAL LIBRARY
MILLIGAN COLLEGE, TENN. 37682

the door open for actually ascertaining the wishes of the Borneo people, which each in his own state next attempted to do; and for entertainment of other proposals than those explicitly announced in Brunei and Sarawak, proposals which were quickly forthcoming. But in raising the question of a three-state Borneo federation, they proposed a little merger as an alternative to—or perhaps a step toward—a bigger merger, and thus established an opposition arguing point which virtually every opponent of Malaysia has now adopted as his own.

The three-state Borneo federation idea, in point of fact, dates back to a proposal made a few years ago by the British Governor of North Borneo. The reaction among the people of North Borneo and Sarawak was apathetic. The reaction in Brunei was unfavorable, the Sultan himself announcing that he rejected the proposal. The British refrained from pushing federation and worked instead for increased economic co-operation among the three states and joint participation in various administrative matters. Then, after the Tengku made his Malaysia proposal, suddenly in Borneo—and in the Federation and Singapore as well—the three-state Borneo federation idea became the political fad and promotion of Bornean regionalism became a prime tactic of the opponents of Malaysia. The fact that the Sultan of Brunei had categorically rejected the proposal four years ago and rejects it still; and the further fact that the Sultan's own anti-Malaysia, antifeudal opposition in Brunei (Azahari's Party Ra'ayat) advocates, paradoxically, a three-state Borneo federation in which the Sultan will be the paramount ruler and tiny Brunei the focus of authority—none of this deters the advocates of Borneo federation in other states, even those who least like the Sultan, Azahari, or Brunei.

Stephens, Ong, and Azahari, then, in early July agreed to reject the original Malaysia proposal, to work for closer intra-Borneo relations, but also—mainly on Stephens' insistence—to leave the door open for the Tengku to appeal to them again. Then Stephens and Ong (but not Azahari) went to Singapore to attend the conference of the Commonwealth Parliamentary Association, there to hear a carefully restated version of the Malaysia plan. Stephens returned to North Borneo convinced that his early misgivings were unfounded and that the Malaysia proposal offered the Borneo states their brightest hope for achievement of independence together with security. Ong returned to Sarawak reconfirmed in his opposition and determined upon a platform of Sarawak independence first, three-state federation next, and merger with Malaysia much later, if at all. Azahari, who had declined to attend the Singapore conference, declined also to attend subsequent conferences in Borneo or elsewhere. At year's end he proceeded instead to Indone-

sia to seek support there. And from Indonesia, on December 30, came
an Indonesian Communist Party decision branding the Malaysia proposal as "neocolonialist."

The Malaysia proposal, read the PKI communiqué, is "an unacceptable colonial intrigue," one which "will strengthen the position of
the imperialists in Southeast Asia in implementing their SEATO activities which are also aimed against Indonesia, a country that does not
like SEATO and that wages a resolute struggle against imperialism and
colonialism." "The Indonesian people," the communiqué concluded,
"will certainly support the righteous, patriotic, and just resistance of
the people of Malaya, Singapore, Sarawak, Brunei, and North Borneo
against the efforts for the establishment of this Federation of Malaysia."

The PKI's stand on Malaysia does not correspond to the official
stand of the Indonesian government, which has been extremely correct
regarding the proposal, declaring merely that it has "no objections"
and that it wishes its neighbor well "if it can succeed with this plan."
The faint warmth of Indonesian official approval of Malaysia, as compared with the fierce heat of Indonesia's demand for creation of new
nations out of colonial territories elsewhere, is indicative to many Malaysian observers of strong Indonesian reservations about seeing a Federation of Malaysia spring up next door. Indonesia being at the moment
engaged in a frenzied campaign for "liberation" of Netherlands New
Guinea, the idea occurs to virtually all observers that after liberating
New Guinea, Indonesia may turn its attention to "liberating" British
Borneo, to which, on the basis of geography, history, culture, and many
other factors, it has a somewhat more plausible claim. In January of
1962 the Indonesian government established an Indonesian consulate in
Jesselton. The increasing numbers of migratory Indonesian laborers
in North Borneo have recently been assisted rather than obstructed by
the Indonesian government in their movements. These facts lead to a
distinct suspicion among North Borneo political observers that the Indonesian official attitude toward Malaysia is not, after all, so different
from that of the PKI, and that Indonesian aspirations to acquire British
Borneo supply one important reason.

The political leaders of the states of British Borneo, a segment
of the population which has grown rapidly since the Malaysia proposal
was announced, have been extremely busy in the last few months organizing and reorganizing political parties, seeking affiliation with other
parties in Borneo, the Federation, Singapore—and Indonesia—formulating and reformulating positions on Malaysia and other matters. As

of early February of this year, Sarawak's parties had grown from two
to four, Brunei's from one to four, North Borneo's from none to six,
and the political tide is still rising.

In Sarawak, the Malay-based Party Negara (PANAS), headed by
Datu Bandar, one of the important hereditary leaders of the Sarawak
Malay community, supports Malaysia on the basis that merger pro-
vides the only security against the Communist menace and that only as
a member of Malaysia can Sarawak's independence prove meaningful.
The Malay Iban-based Barisan Ra'ayat Jati Sarawak (BERJASA), headed
by Datu Tuanku Bujang bin Sayed Osman, declares itself strongly anti-
Communist but has not yet clarified its stand on Malaysia. The Sarawak National Party, recently organized and as yet little known, is anti-
Malaysia. So, too, as noted above, is the Sarawak United People's
Party (SUPP), both its moderate wing led by Ong Kee Hui and its radical wing led by a young Chinese lawyer, Mr. Stephen Yong, which has
constituted itself the primary anti-Malaysia force in the state. Because
it co-operates openly with the Barisan Sosialis in Singapore, SUPP is
suspected by the British and by the PAP of building affiliations also
with the Communists. It has recently distributed and displayed a whole
index of anti-Malaysia slogans which might well be PKI-scripted: "Condemn Reactionary Malaysia," "Wipe Out Colonialism," "Oppose to [sic]
Any Foreign Interference," "Smash All Intrigue," "Oppose to [sic] False
Accusations on the Anti-Colonial Movement," "Long Live the Unity of
the Peoples of Borneo," "Implement the Unity of the Peoples of the Afro-
Asian Countries," "Independence for Every Nation."

In Brunei, Azahari's Party Ra'ayat remains the paramount
party, although with nothing close to the 19,000 active members it claims;
and its anti-Malaysia, pro-Brunei hegemony, pro-Indonesia platform
exercises apparently potent appeal. Nevertheless, the Party Ra'ayat
has suffered recent defections, one splinter group having now organized
a Brunei United National Organization which denounces Azahari. Two
other new Brunei parties, the Brunei United Party and the Brunei National Organization, are now reported—and denied—to be in process
of merging with the Brunei United National Organization to constitute
a single and rather less confusingly named Alliance Party. These last
two parties, most of whose leaders are closely associated with the Brunei feudal court, have adopted an outspokenly pro-Malaysia platform.
The platform quite certainly reflects the personal views of the Sultan
who has declined as yet, however, to risk his prestige on open support
of Malaysia. He has chosen instead to appoint a "fact-finding commission"—of which Azahari is a member—which has already conducted a
survey of the wishes of the Brunei people and is compiling a report on

the basis of which he will make his decision.

The Malaysia issue may force what has long been impending in Brunei, namely, a show of strength between the Sultan and Azahari. Among Brunei's newly enriched and newly awakening Malay population, the relative appeals of feudal loyalty and modern revolution are extremely difficult to estimate. The evidence may come sometime in 1962 when the state's first general elections are held—elections which were originally scheduled for September 1961, but were then postponed. Now that the court group has created its own political parties and now, also, that the Malaysia plan and the Sultan's support for it may become the election issue, the elections may constitute in fact a referendum not only on Malaysia but on monarchy as well.

In North Borneo, Mr. Donald Stephens remains the most prominent leader, and his party, the United Kadazan National Organization, inaugurated in mid-1961 in Jesselton, remains not the only but still the major political group. The UKNO, which is mainly Kadazan in membership (although it also claims a few Chinese adherents), gives all-out support to Malaysia. In its pro-Malaysia stand it receives support from a second party, the United Sabah National Organization, headed by Datu Mustapha bin Datu Harun, a Malay chieftain (of Sulu descent) and timber-copra operator of the Kudat area. The two parties are more easily distinguished on the basis of leadership and geography than of membership or platform. Stephens and Datu Mustapha are political co-operators but personal rivals; the party membership in each case is made up mainly of indigenous peoples of the areas in which the party was organized. The USNO membership, however, is more distinctively Malay or Muslim indigenous, whereas the UKNO is more distinctively non-Muslim indigenous. Originally, the intention was that along with UKNO and USNO would be created also a UCNO, or United Chinese National Organization, and that the three together would form a tripartite alliance, on the model of the Alliance Party in the Federation of Malaya. But Chinese racial sentiments interfered with the plan, and the North Borneo Alliance Party now seems an unlikely prospect.

In North Borneo there is now one other indigenous party, the United National Pasok Momogun (Sons of the Soil) Organization, a West Coast rural party with strong tribal membership. The Pasok Momogun, of which a retired civil servant, Mr. G. S. Sundang, is chairman, seeks independence for North Borneo without any commitment regarding eventual merger.

The three other North Borneo parties are all basically, if not exclusively, Chinese in membership and are all strongly anti-Malaysia. The Democratic Party, based on Jesselton, and the Social Democratic Party, based on Sandakan, stand for independence first, merger later. The distinct implication is that merger might come very much later indeed and that independence is the immediate objective—not because independence is to be preferred to British colonialism, but because in the present state of world affairs it is more readily justified. The Liberal Party, also based on Sandakan and claiming indigenous as well as Chinese members, stands for a three-state Borneo federation of which the Sultan of Brunei would be the Yang di-Pertuan Agong, or paramount ruler. At the moment, the Social Democratic Party is the most important of the three, being headed by three very wealthy and influential Chinese members of the Legislative Assembly and attracting to it numerous younger men of ability and promise. Adherents to the Social Democratic Party on January 1, 1962, established a new English-language newspaper, The Borneo Times, published in Sandakan as rival to Mr. Stephens' North Borneo News and Sabah Times.

The opposition parties in Borneo, almost all of which support the independence first, three-state federation next, merger later sequence, point out also a whole series of drawbacks to the merger arrangement which the supporters of Malaysia themselves are worried about. The Borneo states, all of them declare, will suffer major disadvantages in a Federation of Malaysia, for they will be the most backward of the member states and will be subject to exploitation by their more advanced partners. Furthermore, they ask, even though the Federation of Malaysia should write into its Constitution special safeguards for the Borneo states, what is to prevent it from revising the Constitution after the Borneo states have already joined? What assurance is there that the next chief of state would be as generally acceptable to Borneo as is Tengku Abdul Rahman? Finally, was not the whole Malaysia scheme thought up in the first place as an expedient for achieving Singapore's merger with Malaya? Borneo must join to offset Singapore's big Chinese population and to provide hinterland for it. But Borneo itself, rather than profiting from the arrangement, would greatly worsen its own Chinese capitalist economic problem and its Chinese Communist political problem. Since Malaysia supporters themselves have posed these questions, it is difficult for them to argue altogether convincingly against the opposition, even in view of the fact that the new "Memorandum for Malaysia" provides that many safeguards will be established for the Borneo states.

Few people in Borneo are willing to risk anything other than a wishful prediction regarding chances for acceptance of the Malaysia proposal. A joint British-Malaysian Commission of Inquiry is about to go to work eliciting the views of the people of North Borneo and Sarawak and compiling recommendations to the British government. There, at the moment, it would seem that the Chinese minority would vote against, the indigenous majority would vote for, the proposal—but perhaps not enough of them to carry the decision. The Sultan of Brunei, as noted above, has already appointed a Commission of Inquiry and is awaiting its findings. Rumor reports that the findings so far have been discouraging to the Malaysia supporters. Still, in one manner or another, the Borneo people will have their say, probably this year in the course of Brunei's general and North Borneo's local elections (the first in North Borneo history), and perhaps in Sarawak elections as well.

As elections approach, Malaysia may look increasingly better in comparison with (1) sudden independence for each of the small, unprepared states, in what the British in their white papers describe as a "predatory world"; (2) three-state Borneo federation, which would require quite a lot of negotiation—if, indeed, it is negotiable at all; or (3) the resuscitation of colonialism, with huge Indonesia next door demanding its demise and presumably eager to inherit its properties. The decision of the Borneo people in any premerger election is likely to be just as wise as would be their decision in any postmerger election in the near future. It should be as good a test, therefore, whether under the special political circumstances which obtain in Borneo, the Malaysia plan is really workable.

CHAPTER
V

SABAH AND ITS CAPITAL

March 13, 1962

Malayan Prime Minister Abdul Rahman's proposal for a new
nation of Malaysia is now directing attention to an area which has long
been virtually overlooked even by many of the more serious students
of Southeast Asian affairs. It is the British Crown Colony of North
Borneo—racially the most complex, economically the most swiftly developing, politically the most retarded, strategically perhaps the most
important of all the prospective members of what could prove to be
Southeast Asia's most stable, prosperous, and progressive nation.

North Borneo has been in the past and remains today something of an international curiosity, an extreme and generally agreeable
combination of anomaly and anachronism. It was for many centuries
the domain of pirates, slavers, and head-hunters. It emerged late on
the stage of modern world history by way of three colonial experiments
which culminated rather remarkably, the first in victory for "the na-
tives"; the second in the investiture of a highly popular White Rajah;
and the third in the replacement of an American would-be rajah by the
most paternalistic and hence the least lucrative of the British chartered companies. North Borneo has been the scene most recently of
little-known heroism and tragedy during World War II, and in the postwar years of a colonialism so enlightened as to cast doubt on the wis-
dom of the dissolution of empire. But for better or for worse, the days
of colonialism are over, and the Crown Colony of North Borneo will
soon become independent, perhaps as a member state of Malaysia.
Since North Borneo's history has been generally accessible only to the
more persevering student and traveler,[1] the situation of the past and
the present warrants a brief summary as preface to the new era which
is about to set in.

The North Borneo Story

The early history of the present territory of North Borneo is also that of its immediate neighbors, the Sultanate of Brunei and the Crown Colony of Sarawak. The area now encompassed by the three states was subject for centuries to the paramount but disputed rule of the Sultan of Brunei, chief of a highly mobile lot of Malay pirates who in the 18th and 19th centuries terrorized the Bornean coastal waters and ranged far into the shipping lanes of the South China Sea. In the interior lived head-hunting tribesmen who frequently terrorized the pirates. With a society and an economy geared largely to piracy, the slave trade, and head-hunting, Borneo attracted the unfavorable attention of European intruders, who preferred peaceful seas for their voyages to China, peaceful seacoasts for their shipwrecks, and peaceful little islands as their way points.

The British East India Company, accordingly, in 1773 dispatched European settlers to establish a base on Balembangan Island, at the mouth of Marudu Bay. In 1775 the fierce Sulus and Illanuns wiped out the settlement. Pirates, aided by disease, conspired to defeat a second British attempt in 1803-04. It was 40 years before the British seriously tried again.

In 1839 the British adventurer James Brooke, sailing his private vessel, the "Royalist," happened to put in to Kuching and found the population engaged in insurrection against the tyrannical Viceroy of the Sultan of Brunei. He returned in 1841, and finding the insurrection still under way and the whole situation very much confused, he intervened to restore order. He was entreated by his Borneo friends to remain and did so, accepting the title of Rajah of Sarawak which the Sultan was induced to invest upon him. He accepted also a large segment of Borneo real estate which he expanded presently, by negotiation and by war, into the present territory of Sarawak.

Very early on in his effort to consolidate and to extend his own authority, Rajah Brooke solicited the attention of the Royal Navy to Borneo waters. In 1846 Captain Mundy of the British frigate "Iris" put in at Labuan and claimed the island for the British Crown. Operating out of Labuan and Singapore, the British gradually cleared the coasts of the most dangerous of the pirates. By thus destroying the

---

[1] For recent scholarly studies of North Borneo, see K. G. Tregonning's Under Chartered Company Rule: North Borneo, 1881-1946 (Singapore: University of Malaya, 1958) and North Borneo (London: Her Majesty's Stationery Office, 1960). For a popular account of life in prewar Sandakan, see Agnes Newton Keith's Land Below the Wind (Boston: Little, Brown, 1944).

base of Brunei's wealth and power, they secured Sarawak to Rajah Brooke and his successors. They opened up also to other men of vision the potentialities of the Sultan's domain.

The next man of vision to show up was an American, Claude Lee Moses by name, variously identified as a consular officer, a confidence man, a colonial dreamer, and a drunken sailor. Moses materialized rather mysteriously in Brunei in 1865 and persuaded the Sultan, for consideration of M$9,500 (M$3.00=US$1.00) per year in cash and promises, to grant him a ten-year concession to a tract of North Borneo presumably as extensive in area as it was vague in boundary.

Moses then hustled to Hong Kong where partnership rights passed to two other Americans as dubious as himself and to a succession of Hong Kong Chinese merchant-bankers who proved even more shifty. The partners set up the American Trading Company of Borneo and shipped off a colonizing expedition of 12 Americans and 60 Chinese under command of a member of the firm, one Joseph W. Torrey. Torrey meanwhile had prevailed upon the Sultan of Brunei who, possibly to annoy Rajah Sir Charles Brooke, conferred upon him the titles of Rajah of Ambong and Marudu and Sir Maharajah of North Borneo. Rajah and Sir Maharajah Torrey in early 1866 raised the American flag over a nonexistent town by name of Elenna on Kimanis Bay. Then, while the forlorn colony foundered, he returned to Hong Kong to raise more money and to be hounded by Moses whose own creditors were hounding him.

Sir Maharajah Torrey and his partners managed in 1875, just before the original lease expired, to off-load onto Baron Overbeck, Austrian Consul General in Hong Kong. Baron Overbeck bought the colony strictly on speculation. He prudently renewed the lease with the Sultan of Brunei and in 1878 secured overlapping concessions from the Sultan of Sulu who likewise claimed traditional rights in the area. The Baron had hawked his new property meanwhile among Austrian, German, British, American, and Chinese businessmen, as well as among the foreign offices of a dozen nations interested in empire. All of them displayed more suspicion of him and of each other than inclination to plunge in the Borneo jungle. Finally he succeeded in 1877 in stirring up both interest and capital from the Hong Kong British trading firm of the Dent brothers who in 1878-79 underwrote the founding of Sandakan.

Overbeck himself got out from under while he could. The Dent brothers ran into innumerable difficulties but by exercise of influence and of immense labor managed in 1881 to ensure themselves by acquiring in London a Royal Charter. Thus was born the British North Borneo (Chartered) Company, last and longest-lived of the 19th-century British companies which both developed and governed overseas possessions. Gladstone, who had opposed, then concurred, then opposed again, expressed absent-minded dismay at this new and shapeless accretion to empire, but decided presently, it appears, just to put it out of mind. In 1888 North Borneo, under the administration of the chartered company, was formally designated a British Protectorate.

The chartered company operated on the unbusinesslike presumption that its main function was not exploitation but administration. It bitterly disappointed the expectations of its stockholders, who for many years received no dividends at all, only invitations to put up additional capital. It did not itself participate directly in trade but created a situation in which trade could develop, then licensed business concerns and leased land. With a staff of about 70 European officers, it imposed and maintained law and order, and at the same time engaged in modest programs of developing communications, education, and public health. It managed, in the process, almost to eliminate the tribal practice of head-hunting—except, of course, during World War II when it encouraged from a distance the taking of Japanese heads. It managed also, at almost ruinous cost and with no expert advice, to run a 116-mile railroad down the West Coast, a line which until 1960 maintained an unblemished record of deficit operations but did lead to development of rubber and rice lands. The company's accomplishments were modest, but it bequeathed to the territory not a legacy of anticolonial outrage but a respect for honest government.

Chartered company rule collapsed when the Japanese staged their invasion in January 1942. North Borneo proved, however, to be an area in which Japanese occupation forces ran into unexpected troubles, as, for instance, when the West Coast Chinese in late 1943 staged the "Kwok Rebellion." The Japanese put down this insurrection violently and vindictively, executing a hundred of Jesselton's leading citizens and burning a large part of the town. The remaining sections of Jesselton and most other urban centers in North Borneo were practically wiped out in the course of the Japanese defeat and British reoccupation. British forces returned just too late, however, to prevent the forced march along a mountain jungle trail between Sandakan and Jesselton of some 1,500 Commonwealth prisoners of war; only 6 survived.

North Borneo at the end of the war was a bombed-out shambles. It was quietly transferred on July 15, 1946, from British military administration to control by the Colonial Office. Working on a strictly

limited budget and with strictly limited personnel, the government set
about the job of reconstruction.   As late as 1955 North Borneo still
seemed an area of wartime desolation. In 1962 it is one of the most
startlingly prosperous and progressive areas of Southeast Asia.

Jesselton

          Although the history of North Borneo since the war is not pre-
cisely that of its capital city, the story of Jesselton is close enough to
it to suffice. The citizens of Jesselton's twin and rival city, Sandakan,
would at once protest that Jesselton, as usual, gets far too much attention. Citizens of the rural hinterland—the Kadazans, Muruts, Bajaus,
and other indigenous people who constitute two thirds of North Borneo's
total population—would be justifiably annoyed at being relegated again
to the obscurity from which they have just emerged. But the story of
Jesselton, all must concede, is that of a little-known tropical outpost,
almost wiped out by war without the outside world paying any particular attention to it, before, during, or after; and of a city now almost
miraculously restored and immeasurably enhanced, just in time to
pose in the Southeast Asian political floodlights. This sequence of ob-
livion, neglect, and sudden prosperity and importance is essentially the
story of British Borneo.

          The new Jesselton is a town of over 22,000 inhabitants, of whom
15,000 are Chinese, 5,000 are indigenous peoples, 2,000 are other Asians,
and 750 are Europeans. It is a handsome, comfortable, thriving town
built along a sandy shore line against a backdrop of luxuriant trees and
tropical hills. Its most immediately conspicuous feature is its small
port area, where ocean-going ships tie up practically on the main street.
The most showy development is a new government complex, a confused
and miniature Pentagon in tropicalized modern style. Other civic features warrant itemization: a water-front promenade; a 250-bed hospital;
elementary and secondary schools, both public and mission-run; a well-
equipped radio station which broadcasts in English, Chinese, and local
languages; an international airport with a 6,000-foot runway; a race
course with regularly scheduled meets; a downtown playing green,
shared by a pair of sports clubs; a superlative public swimming beach,
farsightedly zoned to preserve its natural beauty; a yacht club; a golf
course; and a small resort hotel. The town also has adequate electric
power, a municipal water system, good paved streets, and plenty of
cheap, reliable public transportation. Fifty miles of paved road lead
northward, and the 116-mile railroad, soon to be replaced by a highway, follows the coast to the south.

Downtown Jesselton consists of about a dozen blocks of commercial buildings of two, three, and more stories, attractively designed and built of reinforced concrete. Many of them include air-conditioned office quarters. Suburban Jesselton features one section of luxury seaside villas built in California style. Nearby areas are given over to government quarters—pleasant, well-spaced homes raised on stilts and wide open to catch the breezes. Other real-estate developments offer US$3,000-US$15,000 homes on easy rental-purchase plan, all equipped with modern kitchen, bath, and carport facilities. The town also has rather more than the usual complement of movie theaters, restaurants, and downtown hotels. And almost everything is absolutely new.

Most of the old Jesselton disappeared during the war. The new town had its beginnings as a set of shabby frame buildings designed for temporary use which, as a result of frequent fires, proved even more temporary than was originally planned. Then in 1955 the town began to rebuild in earnest, the government advancing 60% of the cost for private construction and putting large sums into public construction. The result is the Jesselton of today. It is dominated by a handsome six-floor apartment building for senior government officers atop scenic Signal Hill above the harbor. It is distinguished by such business establishments as a supermarket stocked with processed and frozen gourmet foodstuffs from all over the world and displaying in its show windows dinner sets of spode china. It retains only a few surviving sections of the old Malay-style "water village." Here the rickety wood and thatch huts, built on stilts over the tidal flats, are being replaced by neat modern cottages built on concrete piles, provided with piped drinking water and electricity, but still virtually water-borne at high tide.

This glorified reincarnation of Jesselton—one that can be matched in varying scale in other towns of North Borneo—is the work of a highly competent British administration, of an enterprising Chinese minority, and an industrious indigenous population. It has been accomplished basically with local resources, although the British government, mainly through the Commonwealth Development Fund, has provided modest amounts of pump-priming money for budding enterprises and for a large number of public institutions, such as hospitals and schools.

The British colonial administration today is headed by a Governor, Sir William Goode (previously Governor of Singapore at the time of its achievement of semiautonomy), and a staff of a dozen British department heads. The civil service numbers a few hundred members, mainly British in the top echelons but with increasing numbers of Chinese working up into the higher brackets and an increasing number of indigenous people entering the lower. The Governor retains "reserved powers" of decision in all really critical matters, but he delegates to his Executive Council—largely ex-officio, partly appointive—the day-to-day conduct of administration, and to his appointive Legislative Council—now preponderantly nonofficial and non-British—matters of routine legislation. In all matters, he is guided by the advice of the Councils.

The government is now in process of rapid evolution from an outright British colonial to a representative system. The present stage, one of shared responsibility between colonial officials and leading local citizens, has been working very smoothly. Among the local people there has been more feeling that the British were pushing ahead too quickly toward democratic self-government than that they were seeking to preserve colonial privilege. The feeling is particularly strong among the Chinese, a great majority of whom would greatly prefer British to indigenous rule. Under the British they constitute by far the most important political and economic segment of the community, but under an indigenous regime they would have to take their chances as a minority people. The days of self-determination, however, are at hand, and the British are calmly urging others to reconcile themselves to this inescapable fact. The first stage in self-determination will be an election this year for local officials, an election in which the Malaysia issue will no doubt be the decisive one.

The political contrast between the old Jesselton and the new is illustrated by two of the town's leading figures. One is Sir William Goode, the traditional British colonial official, crisp and competent, resplendent on official occasions in gold braid and plumes. The other is Mr. Donald Stephens, the man of the people, a portly, middle-aged gentleman of mixed British and Kadazan ancestry, generally a bit wilted in appearance and casual in manner. He is a man of Junior Cambridge-level education, the self-made proprietor-editor of what was until recently North Borneo's one English-language newspaper.

Sir William Goode is the tenant of Government House, a sprawling frame bungalow set on a hilltop among tropical gardens, both house and garden reported to be haunted by the ghosts of his predecessors, virtually all of whom came to untoward ends. He plays host at the traditional British garden party where picture hats and flowered prints still appear. He presides at charity bazaars, school commencements, sports meets, and other public affairs, and manages at the same time to put in an overtime working day. His official perquisites include not only an annual stipend of £7,000 (£1=US$2.80) but allowances for family and personal staff, the usual official limousines, and rather an unusual little official yacht, so badly designed and so badly air conditioned as to be recommended only for calm, cool weather.

Mr. Stephens occupies a modest home of the US$10,000 price bracket in one of Jesselton's new suburban developments. He drives a modest car to his small downtown office, located in one of Jesselton's new commercial buildings. He devotes less and less time these days to his newspaper. He has been spending almost as much time in Malaya or Singapore as in North Borneo, and has been several times hospitalized for illness complicated by fatigue. He lived in Singapore for a while before the war, working as an office employee at the British military base, and he traveled into Malaya as a sight-seer. He now returns to Singapore and Malaya as a VIP, a state guest to whom all doors are open and toward whom all eagerly look for co-operation.

After living as a modest citizen of Jesselton, relatively conspicuous, to be sure, as a member of the Legislative Council and more recently of the Executive Council as well, he now finds himself suddenly achieving state-wide and regional prominence. He is known not only as North Borneo's leading politician and the organizer of its first and its biggest political party, but as the favorite candidate for top position in whatever new North Borneo government emerges. As yet, at least, his new prospects have not altered his way of thinking or of living, save of course, very greatly to increase the pressures.

Now that the Crown, in the person of Sir William Goode, prepares for a dignified exit one day soon, and North Borneo, in the person of Mr. Donald Stephens—or someone else—prepares for exercise of sovereignty, the people of Jesselton are beginning far more clearly than ever before to analyze their problems and prospects. As elsewhere in the area, some of the really big problems are race, education, and the cold war.

Of Jesselton's 22,000 inhabitants, 15,000 are Chinese—most of them far more advanced and privileged than any of the other racial groups. The city, like the colony as a whole, is obviously due for major readjustments when North Borneo becomes a sovereign state in which the two-thirds indigenous majority has the right to vote. The various racial elements are already beginning to jockey for position, and the beginnings of tension are as apparent as is the necessity to keep that tension from becoming disruptive.

Jesselton, like all of North Borneo, suffers from the relatively low level of education, not only of its indigenous inhabitants but of many of the Chinese as well. In all North Borneo, only about half of the children in the 5-15 age group are now registered in school; only about 4,000 students are registered in secondary school. The existing schools leave a great deal to be desired, and are considerably better and larger for the Chinese than for the indigenous peoples.

Educational advancement, nevertheless, has already in the past few years been spectacular. Total school enrollment has risen from 20,000 in 1950 to 51,000 in 1960. According to present plans, 1971 is the target date for universal free primary education. The year 1971 is none too soon if North Borneo is to have a citizenry capable of achieving the individual advancement which is essential for what is still one of the world's notably underdeveloped populations. It will be none too soon, either, if the people are to achieve reasonably good self-government, in which the interests of a highly diversified population can be reconciled without resort to gross discrimination or to violence.

Finally, the cold war has already come to North Borneo. The Malaysia proposal as much as anything else has served to precipitate it, probably a bit sooner than might otherwise have occurred, but in time perhaps that appropriate precautionary measures can be taken. Some of the North Borneo Chinese maintain their long-standing ties with mainland China; some of the North Borneo people who are of Malay and Indonesian origin—and there are many who do not distinguish between Malayan, Indonesian, and Bornean nationality—have ties with the Indonesian Communist Party. Whether these ties are or are not already a serious cause for alarm, they may soon become so. In any event, as the day approaches for North Borneo to become independent, either within or apart from a Federation of Malaysia, the agents of world communism are quite clearly beginning to turn their attention to this remote Southeast Asian outpost. It is, on the whole, rather a remarkable outpost of what has been an enlightened European colonialism and of what could prove in the future to be a workable Asian democracy—toward neither of which the Communists are partial.

CHAPTER
VI

BORNEO BOOM TOWNS

March 15, 1962

As the proposal for creation of a new Federation of Malaysia gains ground, political observers in Southeast Asia are devoting an unprecedented amount of attention to the potential member state of North Borneo, to its modern and thriving capital city, Jesselton, and to Jesselton's political leader, Mr. Donald Stephens. North Borneo, Jesselton, and Stephens may prove to be decisive factors in the success or failure of the merger plan. But to gain real appreciation of what North Borneo may actually mean as a member state of Malaysia, the observer must proceed beyond Jesselton. An anthropologist would insist, with justice, that to understand North Borneo one must first know the 300,000 of its 450,000 inhabitants who belong to the Malay or other indigenous racial groups, many of them still jungle tribesmen. The less venturesome observer, however, must content himself with a visit to the larger coastal towns and villages, most of them predominantly Chinese populated. Labuan, Sandakan, and Tawau provide diversified examples of the new North Borneo, which often seems almost as exotic as the old.

Labuan

The 36-square-mile island of Labuan (population 15,000) is to North Borneo what Penang Island is to Malaya—a onetime British Straits Settlement built up into a prosperous free trade enclave. The British have recurrently entertained great expectations for Labuan and have recurrently been disappointed. In 1846 they claimed possession of this flat little island commanding the approach to Brunei Bay and set about building it up as a coaling station and naval base on the China trade route. Labuan coal deposits proved inadequate in quality and quantity. The value of the Labuan naval base dropped to near zero with the swift improvement of navigation and the even swifter rise in importance of nearby Singapore and Hong Kong. Labuan's own trade potentialities seemed meager. The British government, with evident relief, in 1889 handed the island over to the British North Borneo (Chartered) Company, which then seemed content to lose money on Labuan along with the rest of North Borneo—but in 1905 handed it back again.

As the British contemplated the gradual dismantling of their empire in Southeast Asia after World War II, they eyed Labuan speculatively as a last alternative to their Singapore and Hong Kong bases and entrepôts. Few realists, however, placed much sustained faith in Labuan's mid-20th-century potentialities, and British moves to develop Labuan as a military and commercial base have therefore been both tentative and intermittent. The colonial government did decide, nevertheless, when it began rearranging its Borneo territories in 1956, to give Labuan special free port status. It drafted and executed a set of plans—grandiose ones, in a miniature sort of way—for port, urban, and rural development, industrialization, rehabilitation of the island's few rice fields, coconut groves, and rubber plantings, and improvement of its social services. It even planned and carried out expansion of Labuan's military base facilities so that today the port can service more and bigger vessels than are ever likely to visit it in trade; the airport can handle the newest and biggest of jet planes; and the island has a transient hotel in which the air-conditioned VIP suite can be reserved for US$12 single, or US$19 double per day.

Despite all this effort, Labuan remains notable today not as a Little Singapore, in accordance with British dreams, but as a very modest Penang, in accordance with their calmer expectations. It is far less a gamble on the future than a lasting memorial to the past and a tranquil retreat in the present. Labuan Island and Victoria Town, its small "capital" (3,000 inhabitants, mostly Chinese), are something out of a stage set, say, for a Harvard Business School production of South Pacific. The distant green headlands, the tropical sea and sky, the white sand beaches, the waving palm trees—all are there; so too are a 400-foot concrete wharf, a Shell installation, handsome new Chartered Bank and Hong Kong and Shanghai Bank buildings, rows of trim two-story shophouses, Harrisons and Crosfield's and the Borneo Company's business and shipping agencies, and a tree-shaded sea-front drive with the inevitable clubhouse and playing field, crowded in the later afternoon with British, Chinese, Malay, and Indian sportsmen.

Victoria Town is not only a Little Penang but a Little Jesselton, for it is a new town, rebuilt since the war, now provided with modern facilities, including a fleet of taxis and buses which go whirling about the island's expanding road system. But the noteworthy sights of the town as of the island are its memorials. A couple of miles from Victoria, in one of the most beautiful gardens in all of Southeast Asia, is a military cemetery. In it are buried thousands of victims of the Pacific War. Along its cloister walls are inscribed the names of those whose bodies were never recovered, including the 1,500 victims of the Mt. Kinabulu death march perpetrated by the Japanese in 1945 when they moved Commonwealth prisoners of war through the jungle from Sandakan toward Jesselton. Near the War Cemetery in a little plot of land close to the beach are buried some of the earliest British visitors to the island. In front of the government complex on Victoria's shore drive stands another group of memorials, a collection of remarkable incongruity. One commemorates the British claim to possession in 1846; another bears a long Japanese inscription in memory of one General Maeda (d. 1942), after whom, for a brief time, the island was renamed; a third celebrates the British return on June 10, 1945. Four trees, planted by the European, the Chinese, the Malay, and the Indian communities on the occasion of Queen Elizabeth's coronation, symbolize the hopes for new and harmonious development. It is just possibly symbolical that the British tree, which two years ago had developed a premature stoop and spread, is now shapely; that the Indian tree, which then seemed somewhat stunted, now seems even more so; that the Malay tree, then rather spindly, is now thriving; and that the Chinese tree has always been the sturdiest of them all.

Just as three of the four trees have prospered in the last two years, so too has the Labuan economy shifted from a tranquil sort of bustle into modest boom. Labuan's main economic function since the war has been to serve as a transshipment point for the supplies which are sent to the Brunei oil fields, and this service has ensured for it a steady source of employment and of income. Labuan's auxiliary function has been as entrepôt for consumer goods for Brunei, for the West Coast of North Borneo, and sometimes for more remote areas as well. In the last year or two this last function has expanded to such an extent that Labuan today is realizing windfall profits of very comfortable proportions. The reason is twofold. Copra barter traders—smugglers, that is—from the southern Philippines and the eastern Indonesian islands have run into such serious difficulties with Philippine and Indonesian government sea patrols, Filipino pirates, and Indonesian informers that they have begun to shift their trade from the East Coast port of Tawau. At Labuan they enjoy, as compensation for their longer voyage, the advantage of free port prices on the textiles, watches, cameras, and household goods with which they load their vessels for their return.

In addition to this new copra trade, Labuan has also enjoyed in the last few years a build-up of business in transshipping North Borneo timber. Now that its own small copra and rubber producers are beginning to make progress, all in all Labuan is beginning to experience economic boom of the sort, if not of the degree, which less realistic Britons had long anticipated.

With prosperity, fortunately, has not as yet come grave increase of political and social problems. North Borneo's political squalls over the Malaysia issue have as yet stirred up few crosscurrents in Labuan. The island's 30% Chinese and 70% indigenous population seems as yet almost unaware that North Borneo's racial tensions are mounting. One major factor is that even by North Borneo's standards, which are high for Southeast Asia, they enjoy a good life. They do not have enough schools, to be sure, but existing schools now offer education through the junior secondary level and are constantly expanding. They do not have enough medical services, but they do have a 100-bed "cottage hospital" which, for a Southeast Asian island of 15,000 people, is practically metropolitan. Their homes are all too often small wood and thatch shacks set on stilts above muddy tidelands, but such as they are, they are not congested, they are not squalid, and the economic system makes it possible for the tenants to accumulate capital and rebuild.

In brief, Labuan Island is no tropical paradise but it is about as close to it as is to be found in Southeast Asia—and that under a British colonial regime.

Sandakan

Twin and rival city to Jesselton, Sandakan (population 29,000) shoestrings between a spectacular tropical sea front and steeply rising hills. It preserves some of the spacious bungalows and gardens of prewar days and exhibits a high degree of concentration on trade and industry. Downtown Sandakan, like Jesselton, is notable mainly for its reduplicative blocks of new office and business buildings, its modern port facilities, its new hospital, schools, hotels, banks, movie theaters, and public buildings. The citizens of Sandakan complain that Jesselton absorbs far too much of the government outlay for reconstruction. But if Sandakan's residential suburbs are smaller, its public utilities rather less generously planned, its airport much less pretentious, its beach development delayed, none of this, to the visitor from, say, rural Thailand, Burma, or Indonesia spells real neglect and hardship.

Sandakan is the center of the flourishing North Borneo timber industry. In the vast jungle areas of Sandakan's hinterland are some of the territory's most highly developed timber concessions, and on the outskirts of the town are North Borneo's two big lumber mills. In Sandakan Harbor and nearby bays are collected the huge rafts of logs which are either fed into the mills directly or loaded aboard freighters that carry the logs to Japan for processing prior to re-export as lumber to the United States. It is thanks largely to the Sandakan timber exports (M$90 million in 1961) that the town has far more than the usual quota of Chinese millionaires and that the North Borneo revenues are much more than sufficient to meet the normal operating costs of the state—although not yet adequate for its special development expenses.

The North Borneo government, it may be noted, collected in 1961 about M$58 million in total revenues, and spent about M$47 million on ordinary expenses and an additional M$20 million on development. It made up the difference mainly with loans and grants, the largest single source being a Commonwealth Development Fund grant of over M$10 million. Its heavy development fund expenditures are occasioned by an extremely ambitious new communications program (M$13 million in 1961, mostly for new roads) and swift expansion of education (M$2 million for new schools in 1961). Previous development programs —including those involved in rehabilitating the timber industry—having already resulted in tremendous economic improvement and hence increase in government revenues, the continuing effort may confidently be expected to have the same result. The road program, which will bring vast new lands into production, and a rubber planting program, which will modernize and expand the territory's second most important industry (M$50 million in rubber exports in 1961), can be expected to pay back the original investment in a very few years. To the general observer of the Southeast Asian scene, the most impressive thing about the North Bornean development program is the fact that it is efficiently and honestly administered, and that it is largely self-financed and self-amortizing. In 1950 North Borneo was still impoverished and in 1955 struggling, but in 1962 it is as close to being a guaranteed gilt-edge, capital-growth, high-yield investment as is to be found in Southeast Asia.

North Borneo has not as yet, however, attracted much outside investment interest or activity, partly, to be sure, because the government and people are ambivalent about whether or not they really want it. The British are in a delicate position in inviting other outsiders to compete with both the British and the local population; the Chinese are far from enthusiastic about admitting even kindred Chinese capitalists from Singapore; the indigenous people are beginning to feel and to say that North Borneo belongs to them, and that any commitment made now may be subject to reconsideration after independence.

British firms long established in the area are nevertheless busily at work expanding their Borneo interests—Unilever, for instance,
within the last year laid out a 10,000-acre palm oil estate. The most
important newcomer among the non-British investors is the American-
owned Kennedy Bay Lumber Company, which now operates a large timber concession on Wallace Bay. The newest foreign investment comes
from the Philippines. The Soriano interests have established a new
shrimp and prawn fishing industry based on Sandakan. They have built
a M$1.5 million plant capable of handling a ten-ton daily catch, process-
ing it, and shipping it in a frozen state. They have brought in Chinese
fishermen and small fishing vessels from Hong Kong and have begun
to remedy the deplorable situation that in Sandakan waters uncounted
millions of the world's largest and most succulent shrimp have been
dying of old age. They have not as yet managed to remedy the almost
equally deplorable situation that indigenous fishermen prefer to remain
self-employed and to dip the shrimp each morning out of their shore-
line traps, rather than accept an open invitation to adopt regular working hours and learn deep-sea fishing techniques on the company's boats.

Sandakan is the headquarters for North Borneo's most important road construction operation—the building of a 150-mile stretch of
road through the jungle, skirting Mt. Kinabulu, to connect Sandakan
with Jesselton and to open up huge new tracts of land for development.
Starting two years ago from Mile 15, the end of the existing road, the
North Borneo Public Works Department engineers have pushed through
to Mile 57 and now, after being held up for some months by the monsoon
season, are starting to move again. In the West Coast area, meanwhile,
minor road building projects are under way to join the 50-mile stretch
out of Jesselton to the new Sandakan segment.

The newly opened land along the Jesselton-Sandakan highway
will be parceled out among applicants on the basis of demonstrated
need for land and ability to develop it. Indigenous applicants can qualify rather easily for free-hold "Native Title" assignments of 15-acre
tracts subject to payment of M$0.50 per acre per year. Indigenous per-
sons, Chinese, or others can qualify with considerably greater difficulty
for tracts of varying size—possibly 100 acres, possibly 1,000 acres, or
even more—on renewable 30-year leases. The annual rental is M$1.00
per acre for the first 6 years, M$4.00 per acre for the next 4 years, and
M$6.00 per acre thereafter. The investor will pay in addition a "pre-
mium" of up to M$50 per acre—but generally not more than M$25, a survey fee of M$0.75-M$4.00 per acre, an education tax of M$0.50 per acre
per year, and perhaps a few other charges. For 1,000 acres, then, his
outlay in 30 years will average out at about M$200,000, plus M$1.5 mil-

lion to plant the total acreage in rubber. It would be a very incompetent operator indeed who could not clear M$200,000 in timber alone, almost as soon as he could get machinery onto his land, and begin to net M$300,-000-M$500,000 each year in rubber about ten years later.

Not unnaturally, considering the terms, the government has been quite unable to keep up with the demand for new land. At the end of 1960, there were on file 17,836 applications, the great majority of them for the small "Native Title" tracts. At the same time that it was pushing forward with the big schemes to open whole new regions of the territory, it was pushing forward also with a few pilot projects of land settlement, projects in which landless families were assigned 12-15 acre plots in government-supervised centers and given assistance in establishing themselves as self-supporting farmers. The most extensive project to date is one in the fertile Kengingau highlands, where about 250 out of a prospective 1,000 families are now settled, each with about ten acres of dry land and three of rice land.

On a smaller project near Tawau, about 50 families, mainly Chinese, have now been settled. On another tract of land near Tawau the government is experimenting with controlled grants of larger plots, some of about 100 acres, a grant being provisional upon the recipient not only developing the land but building a road through it so that additional backlying areas can be opened up.

The land development policy is still in process of clarification and is complicated by the existence of concessions granted back in chartered company days to some of the most readily accessible territory. It is complicated also by pressures to designate greater areas as forest reserve and as mining land, timber being a known quantity of great volume and minerals being a speculative probability.

With the local emphasis upon land development, it is ironical that the town of Sandakan itself should be plagued by a shortage of available real estate and by difficulty in draining and reclaiming nearby swamplands. Almost all the available urban land is already taken up, prices are rising fast, and even the most enterprising of real-estate operators are unable to carve out new suburban developments. Notwithstanding this hardship, Sandakan is obviously making out very well.

Tawau

At the remotest point on North Borneo's East Coast, just two miles from the Indonesian border and 35 miles from the nearest Philippine island, is located the town of Tawau (population 10,000, 70% Chinese). In comparison with other North Borneo towns, Tawau is jerry-built, obviously a makeshift job, some day, perhaps quite soon, to be renovated almost in toto. Tawau can afford to do the job twice. It is a frontier boom town where smuggling, piracy, border crossing, and various other irregularities compete for attention and capital investment with agricultural schemes in the fertile lands nearby.

The Tawau of the future is probably a town of sober, steady rural industry, and both the colonial government and the local citizens are making strenuous efforts to promote it as such. In the adjacent countryside are some of North Borneo's finest coconut plantations. In the nearby uplands, where in prewar years the Japanese had developed rubber and abacá (hemp) estates, now again rubber and abacá are thriving. What is more, in the remoter highland is some of the richest land in all Borneo. Here the planters are now producing cacao, which may be the answer to the government's search for a new "miracle crop."

Whatever may be the Tawau of the future, however, the Tawau of the present is the rather shabby little port town where a few Chinese merchants, chief among them one Teck Guan, have developed the highly lucrative international barter trade, conducted upon somewhat loose free enterprise lines. Teck Guan, an illiterate fisherman when he immigrated from Hong Kong a few years ago, is today a multimillionaire pillar of the Tawau and North Borneo community. A territory-wide chain of Teck Guan Company branches operates out of Tawau's first skyscraper, whose four floors provide for a shop displaying all the merchandise favored by the coastal traders, office space, guest quarters, and a private penthouse residence. Teck Guan and other Tawau merchants finance Filipinos and Indonesians to acquire motor or sailing vessels for an adventuresome business venture. These operators surreptitiously pick up copra or other goods in the southern Philippines or eastern Indonesia, where it is sold cheaply in inflated currencies. They smuggle the cargo out of the Philippines or Indonesia and take it to Tawau where, in open trading, it commands high prices in hard currency. In Tawau they reload with such low-duty foreign consumer goods as textiles, watches, cameras, bicycles, sewing machines, and cigarettes. They then smuggle this new cargo back to the Philippines or Indonesia where it commands a very fancy markup.

The most lucrative of the patterns of operation is for a Filipino to acquire in the Philippines a kumpit (a boat of about ten tons), sail it full of copra to Tawau, and there sell the copra for enough money to in-

stall an inboard diesel engine. He then loads the vessel with trade goods,
smuggles them into Indonesia, sells off, reloads copra, and smuggles
the copra out of Indonesia and back to Tawau. He invests his copra profits in a long, slim canoe powered by two 40-horsepower outboards, loads
cigarettes ex-bond, and smuggles them back to the Philippines, easily
outrunning any pursuit. Profits can run up to 500% on a single complete
cycle, provided, of course, one's luck holds out.

The Tawau international barter trade has perhaps seen its best
—or its worst—days. The Philippine peso has recently been decontrolled,
Philippine copra has been brought more realistically into line with world
market prices, and Philippine coastal patrols have become tougher about
issuing or accepting false documents. Indonesian patrol craft have gained
in speed, their crews have improved in marksmanship, and their commanding officers are less given than before to the practice of towing
the smugglers in return for a cut in the profits. Besides, the whole
business has been getting to be almost prohibitively complicated by reason of infighting. Some of the Filipino Moros, finding piracy more
agreeable than trade, have become a grave hazard as they lie in wait
to hijack smugglers. The Indonesian regional rebels, who encouraged
the trade for their own supply purposes, have now been nearly liquidated.
Ordinary Indonesian operators who sometimes sailed for a month or
more through dangerous waters to carry only a ton or two of produce
to Tawau, have now become either intimidated or, as seems less likely,
indoctrinated by their own government. The North Borneo government,
which has adhered on the whole to the antiquated British trade practice
of cutting red tape, simplifying documents, holding down tariffs, and
maintaining laissez faire, has begun to develop bureaucratic impediments—one of the most recent being the imposition of quarantine regulations as a result of a Philippine cholera epidemic. Furthermore, the
government now makes trade rather more difficult, partly in order to
appease the Philippine and the Indonesian governments, partly because
the influx of Filipinos and Indonesians has threatened to create serious
problems.

The case of the Filipinos is partly social, partly political. Filipino copra traders—Moros from the Sulu Archipelago—have acquired
the reputation of being tough characters, all too likely to combine piracy with trade and pilferage with piracy. (Filipino operators were recently apprehended near Sandakan loading a stolen station wagon into
their kumpit.) They have staged recurrent raids on isolated coastal
towns and villages, and they are commonly thought to view Borneo's
crammed shop windows with larcenous eyes. Besides, there is the
long smoldering, now perhaps about to blaze, Philippine irredentist
claim to all of North Borneo.

Baron Overbeck, as has elsewhere been noted, ensured his lease from the Sultan of Brunei by acquiring an overlapping lease from the Sultan of Sulu, and the British rulers of North Borneo have all these years since been making annual payment to two reluctantly absentee landlords. The heirs of the late Sultan of Sulu have recently become alert to the new prosperity of North Borneo and to the old validity of their claims. They are now seeking to gain Philippine official and public endorsement of their residual sovereign—and financial—rights. The historical and legal facts of the case are proving extremely difficult to determine. The political fact, however, is that just as North Borneo is about to become independent of the British, a "North Borneo Is Ours" campaign is developing in the Philippines, and a retort of "Nonsense," is being made in Jesselton. Just to make things even more diverting, an "All Borneo Is Really Ours" sentiment exists and is beginning to be acknowledged in Indonesia.

Just as the Indonesian claim to North Borneo may eventually prove to be much more disruptive than the Philippine, so the case of the Indonesian immigrants to North Borneo is more immediately serious than that of Filipino visitors or residents. Some 7,000 Indonesian laborers are now domiciled in North Borneo, most of them remaining for a year or two at a stretch and then returning to Indonesia, perhaps later to return once more to North Borneo. Many of them originally rode, if indeed they did not man, the Indonesian smuggler craft which converge upon Tawau. Driven from Indonesia not just by craving for profit and adventure but by sheer economic necessity, they found in North Borneo an abundance of food and clothing, which in Indonesia are in desperately short supply. Even more important, they found an opportunity to get ahead by honest means. It is a severely limited opportunity, since only estate and day labor is open to them, but still a much better opportunity than exists in Indonesia.

In North Borneo these Indonesian newcomers are welcome for their industry. They are suspect, however—at least among the British and the Chinese—for their politics. Wherever Indonesian laborers go, Indonesian political intrigue is not far behind. They are suspect also for their personal temperament, for some of the Buginese—men from the eastern Indonesian islands, famous not only as hardy seafarers but as men of hair-trigger tempers—have given their countrymen a bad name. Tawau in particular has experienced tragic cases in which Indonesian laborers—Buginese drifters, single men separated from their homes and families and evidently overwhelmed by personal problems —have run amok and committed murders.

British justice at this point takes over. The spectacle of one Tawau amok trial warrants report. The sessions took place in the little white frame courthouse, set on the green in Tawau's water-front administrative center. The British judge, his wig laid on his desk during the heat of the day, conducted a most meticulous inquiry into every circumstance of the crime. Two Chinese lawyers appointed by the court, one for the prosecution and one for the defense, marshaled the facts and the witnesses. Two "assessors," one representing the racial group of the accused (Buginese), the other that of the victims (Chinese—there were six victims), sat beside the judge, took part in the interrogation, and at the end of the trial advised the judge on the verdict which, they agreed, was guilty as charged. The witnesses included a New Zealander Chief of Police, an Indian Sikh police officer, several Chinese police officers, and various Chinese and Malay witnesses to the crime. Court translators kept the whole proceedings intelligible in English, Chinese, and Malay. The spectacle was one of British justice, scrupulously and efficiently at work to uncover any possible grounds for mercy.

*   *   *   *   *

Despite the incidence of violence, its fixation on smuggling, and its episodes of piracy, Tawau, like the rest of British Borneo, is an oasis of strong and just government in an extremely troubled section of the globe. The unanswerable question, of course, is this: Whatever its future status, is North Borneo likely to remain so? The Bornean answer is: With any luck at all, yes! Certainly!

CHAPTER
VII

PROTECTION OR PROVOCATION IN SINGAPORE?

September 10, 1962

For how long and for what purpose is the Singapore military base likely to remain tenable to the British armed forces? This perennially urgent question has been revived by the Malaysia proposal.

The formula[1] at present agreed upon among all parties to the Malaysia arrangement is that Britain shall retain the Singapore base along with its other military installations in the region, for purposes of assisting in the defense of Malaysia, defending the Commonwealth, and preserving the peace in Southeast Asia. It is further agreed—whether to be explicitly stated in a new defense treaty remains to be seen—that Great Britain will not make use of these facilities contrary to the wishes of the Federation government. Most explicitly: it will not use them for "SEATO purposes."

The distinction between "SEATO purposes" and "preservation of the peace in South-East Asia" is one which is extremely difficult either to define or to apply. It is intended, perhaps, more to placate the powerful Singapore and Malayan opponents of SEATO than to redefine self-imposed British restraints upon freedom of action. The British have given formal assurances, perhaps incautiously, that all remains virtually as before. The Malayan Prime Minister has stated, perhaps quite incautiously, that "the Federation would not, in fact, if the security of

---

[1] It is stated as follows by the British Minister of Defence: "We have agreed with the Malayan Government that in the event of the creation of the proposed Federation of Malaysia the Agreement of 1957 [providing

Malaysia demanded it, oppose the use of Singapore for SEATO purposes."
The fact remains that Great Britain is conceding to the local government greater and greater control over the use which may be made of
British military installations. This concession is inevitable and desirable, but it indicates that the question regarding the status of the Singapore base might perhaps better be reformulated: How and for how long
will the Singapore base serve whose purposes?

The future as indeed the present status and utility of the Singapore base involves much more complicated considerations than those of
formal or informal agreement among the parties to the Malaysia negotiations. Current world history demonstrates that Western military
forces on Asian or any other soil are critically vulnerable not only to
a single bomb but to a single politician. Any informed discussion or
speculation regarding the Singapore base, furthermore, must introduce
underlying questions which seldom are even asked, let alone answered,
among them: Just what is the Singapore base? Just what is the role
which it is really expected to play? What are the forces which back-
stop it? What are the actual or potential forces which threaten it? What
are the factors which make for its retention, curtailment, or expansion?
To none of these questions, obviously, is there any quick, easy, satisfactory answer.

To begin with, the Singapore base can never be dissociated from
its disastrous past. It was built up between 1923 and 1942 at a cost of
£50 million as a grudging gamble—or, more accurately, a combination

---

for British assistance in defense and training, in return for base rights]
and its annexes shall be extended to all territories of the Federation of
Malaysia, subject to the proviso that the Government of the Federation
of Malaysia will afford to the Government of the United Kingdom the
right to continue to maintain the bases and other facilities at present
occupied by their Service authorities within the State of Singapore and
will permit Britain to make such use of these bases and facilities as
Britain may consider necessary for the purpose of assisting in the defence of Malaysia, for Commonwealth defence and for the preservation
of peace in South-East Asia. The new state would of course become responsible for internal security throughout its territory and this would
in due course relieve Britain of a considerable responsibility in respect
of Singapore for which a number of major units of the British Army are
at present stationed in Malaya and Singapore . . . ." Statement of Defence. 1962. The Next Five Years. Presented to Parliament by the
Minister of Defence by Command of Her Majesty. February 1962.
London. Her Majesty's Stationery Office. Cmd [Command paper] 1639.

of military bluff and blooper. It was an "impregnable" sea, land, and
air "fortress" whose ships were ordered but never built, whose planes
were never even ordered, whose guns were aimed in the wrong direction, and whose troops were never efficiently equipped, deployed, or
commanded. It fell in three days of confused fighting, the tragic prel-
ude to three years of mounting tragedy for Singapore's military and
civilian population, and indeed for all of Southeast Asia. It has now
been rebuilt and expanded at immense cost as a stabilizing factor in
Southeast Asia, even though practically everyone concedes that stability,
like impregnability, is a delusion, that an armed camp within a civilian
area is a trap, and that empire, for whose benefit bases were created
in the first place, is only a memory. Still, the Commonwealth must
have its armed services; it must station them somewhere; it must
assume that self-defense, or at least determent of attack, is militarily
feasible; and the new Singapore base is one of the results.

The Singapore base is what the old was in fact as contrasted
with its fiction—not a strategic gridiron but a grid, less the military
bastion than the military bastard. Singapore has its ships, planes, and
batteries, to be sure, and it has tough men trained for sea, air, and
jungle warfare. Nevertheless, its iron fastness is greatly extenuated
and deeply cushioned; its weapons and arsenals are scarcely as impressive as its parking lots. The Singapore base, in brief, is no bulwark.
Rather, it is an immense command, service, traffic, and billeting complex scattered so promiscuously over 10% of the land area of so congested a 225-square-mile island as to require the most indefatigable
espionage to plot out.

The Singapore base is not, but sometimes seems to be, General
Headquarters, Land Forces Far East, better known by its happy abbre-
viation, FARELF. Here, on a landscaped hilltop in Singapore's best
residential area, surrounded by concentric rings of ever more cautiously
screened military and civilian staff, patrolled by splendidly trained guard
dogs, is to be found by those armed with the necessary passes, Lt. Gen.
Sir Nigel Poett, K.C.B., D.S.O., Commander in Chief of British Army forces
in Singapore, Malaya, and Hong Kong, these forces totaling respectively
about 10,000, 15,000, and 4,000 men. Directly under Lt. Gen. Poett falls
the Singapore Base Command, with headquarters in old Fort Canning on
the scenic downtown hilltop which Sir Stamford Raffles in 1819 chose for
his official bungalow and Singapore's first botanical garden. Associated
with Lt. Gen. Poett are Admiral Sir David Luce, K.C.B., D.S.O., O.B.E.,
Commander in Chief of the Far East Station of the Royal Navy, and Air
Marshal Sir Hector McGregor, K.C.B., C.B.E., D.S.O., Commander in
Chief of the Far East Air Force.

Each commander carries responsibility for Malaya and Hong Kong as well as for Singapore. Actual headquarters for the Royal Navy is located at Woodlands Naval Base on the Johore Straits at the north of the island. At Woodlands there have again been built up first-class dock and repair facilities for anything from an aircraft carrier to a sampan. The tremendous facilities of the Singapore Harbour Board are also on call, should the Royal Navy's Far East Fleet, its Indian Ocean Task Force, or any other integral or friendly seafarer have need of them. Headquarters of the Royal Air Force for Far East is located at Changi Air Field on the East Coast of Singapore Island, practically within sight of the Singapore International Airport. Under FEAF come also two other major airfields on Singapore Island itself, one in the west at Tengah, one in the north at Seletar, not to mention the RAF-RAAF base in Penang some 500 miles distant. In connection with these various headquarters there proliferate, in the manner of military installations everywhere, transport and communications centers, quartermaster and supply depots, engineering outfits, and related military, paramilitary, and quasi-military adjuncts too numerous even to mention. On Singapore's remotest beach and byroad and on the off-lying small islands, there pop up big and little units which may or may not be communicado via the military telephone circuit, but are all, in some indefinable military way, interrelated and essential.

The three major Singapore commands are scheduled in November of this year to be consolidated into a unified command under Admiral Sir David Luce. The change, it is hoped, will make for greater military efficiency but not for either uniformity or monotony. Today, quartered in old tropical colonial or new modern-style barracks and bungalows, surrounded by city and jungle, palms, rubber trees, mangrove swamps, Malay fishing villages, and Chinese slums, the Singapore armed services display all the macaronic variety of the Commonwealth. There are Gurkha guards, Iban jungle trackers, British frogmen, Australian paratroopers, Scottish bagpipers, Chinese machinists, and Malay drivers. There are walrus-mustached officers who still say "pip-pip," play polo, eat tiffin, and drink stengahs; duck-tailed young privates whose sport is the jukebox; housewives in flower-print frocks who compare notes about the shortage of good servants; sun-tanned blond children of whom a few—a very few—still have "nannies" instead of "amahs"; and other more or less normal specimens performing more or less standard military support functions, from running electric lawnmowers to tracking satellites. They operate and patronize NAAFIs, schools, clubs, hospitals, churches, charities—all the standard fixtures of a military welfare state whose population, finding itself assigned for three years or so to an unfamiliar area, seeks to make it as much like home as possible, only more comfortable. Both on and off the military preserve, with or without many of its amenities, live some 40,000 local employees of the armed services—some 9% of Singapore's working population, earning approximately 5% of the national income—whose dependence upon the base for a livelihood is a compelling argument for permitting the British to retain it indefinitely.

The Singapore base, as its British proprietors point out, is neither an isolated strong point nor a static garrison nor both, but rather a base in the true sense of the term: "a place where troops, ships, aircraft, heavy equipment, supplies, and facilities for maintenance and repair can be kept for military operations elsewhere." (Cmd 1639.) It fulfills, on the whole, the essential requirements of having "good communications by sea and air, adequate harbourage and docks, facilities to handle heavy traffic for freight and trooping, an efficient network of local road, rail and telephone communications, a large labour force for a multitude of technical and non-technical tasks, and last but most important, a condition of security," although, to be sure, "it has from time to time had internal security problems, and the Communist threat of subversion is still real."[2] Since it is meant primarily for the support of operations elsewhere, but at the same time is so small, crowded, insecure, and exposed that it may require swift reinforcement from without merely to survive, the Singapore base must be considered also in relation to other British installations in the region, mainly in the adjacent Federation of Malaya.

The British retain today numerous military complexes and facilities in the Federation. They do so partly as carry-over from the military build-up during the 1945-1957 colonial and Communist Emergency period, partly in discharge of their treaty responsibilities for assisting in the defense of Malaya and in the formation and training of Malaya's own armed services, partly as a deployment area for the Commonwealth Strategic Reserve. Since Malaya achieved its independence in 1957, the British have been following a policy of withdrawing and consolidating local British forces.

The most important British military installations in Malaya today are a huge new M$80 million Terendak Cantonment, near Malacca, now home of the Commonwealth Strategic Reserve; an RAF-RAAF air base at Butterworth in Penang state; a barracks on Penang Island; plus installations for Gurkha troops in northern Malaya, a military hospital in Kuala Lumpur, and various scattered transport, ordinance, and other

---

[2] *Singapore: A Guide for Servicemen and Their Families.*

depots, some of them just across the Straits from Singapore in the State of Johore. At the Malacca Terendak Cantonment are stationed some 10,000 Commonwealth troops and their families, occupying an almost completely self-sufficient complex which includes 3,000 acres of jungle training grounds, seashore clubs, a supermarket, 1,000 homes, three churches, two schools, a 120-bed hospital, a beauty parlor, and a community center. At Butterworth are stationed two wings of the Royal Australian Air Force, flying Sabre jets equipped with Sidewinder air-to-air missiles, cannon, and rockets. On Penang Island at present is quartered a battalion of British Green Jackets. On Penang Island are also to be found a leave center for Gurkha troops stationed in northern Malaya, a seashore holiday hotel for army officers and their families, a "Little Australia" suburb which includes a new school for 600 RAAF children, and various other installations.

The Commonwealth Strategic Reserve in Malacca and other British forces are prepared to move fast to support the Singapore base or, in case of grave civil disorders in Singapore, to restore the peace. The Singapore troops, similarly, are ready to move fast to the defense of Malaya and presently Malaysia. The British authorities, however, alert to the potentially incendiary results of using British troops to put down local insurrection, now place increasing reliance on the indigenous armed services for maintaining the peace and as a national defense force as well.

Most important by far of these indigenous armed services are the Royal Malayan Army, Navy, and Air Force. To help build, equip, and train these forces, the British have supplied tremendous technical, material, and financial assistance, and have seconded British personnel of all ranks and grades. A British or Commonwealth officer, in fact, is still in command of each of the three services; other British officers and technicians are still to be found in virtually all of the units. But the RMA, the RMN, and the RMAF have long since passed the stage of mere apprentice services. Malayan officers—many of them trained in England or in Commonwealth countries—are rapidly taking over from the British. Malayan troops have reached a high point of training, particularly in the difficult operations through jungle and swamp.

The oldest and the largest of the Malayan services is the Royal Malayan Army, now composed of seven Malay and three mixed battalions, with a total strength of 10,000 men. The Malayan battalions trace their origin to 1932 when the British first experimented with local recruitment and selected 25 out of 1,000 eager volunteers to form the first Malay unit. The Malays, then as now, displayed a marked aptitude and enthusiasm for military service. To the ordinary Malay, the Army represents a highly respected, well-paid, well-fed, well-clothed career, offering plenty of parade and excitement along with leisure and privilege. The Malay battalions have now become crack units for which there are always far more volunteers than openings. The three mixed battalions which originated in 1952 during the Communist Emergency are recruited on the basis of 25% Malay, 50% Chinese, and 25% other races. They have gained rapidly both in military precision and prestige and have lately begun to overcome even the traditional Chinese reluctance to enter military service. Both the Malay and the mixed battalions have had actual field experience, first in Malaya during the Emergency, more recently in the Congo. The Malayan soldiers—especially the members of the Malay battalions—proved themselves both tough and effective in fighting the Communist jungle guerrillas. The mixed Malayan Special Force of 450 to 700 has earned strong commendation for its recent performance in the Congo. One much publicized episode of being surprised by raiders and several others of insubordination may fairly be considered, under the chaotic circumstances in the Congo, indicative more of the times than of the troops.

The Royal Malayan Navy and the Royal Malayan Air Force are as yet token units of very recent origin. The RMN is an 800-man navy which operates a fleet of about 20 small craft, some transferred from the British Navy, others, such as fast new 200-ton to 400-ton patrol boats, built to order in England. The RMN is gaining experience these days and nights by chasing pirates, smugglers, and illegal immigrants, all of whom abound in Malayan coastal waters. The RMAF, which came into being four years ago with 12 men and one plane, is now a 500-man air force with a fleet of about 40 planes. The RMAF is gaining experience by performing photo-reconnaissance, emergency airlifts, and VIP transport flights. Twenty-six of the pilots are Malayans; the others are seconded Commonwealth officers.

Both the RMN and the RMAF are sending a high proportion of their officers to Commonwealth countries for advanced training and are vigorously recruiting into the ranks new candidates of exceptionally high physical and mental qualifications. The RMAF operates out of a M$15 million air base in Kuala Lumpur, transferred several years ago to the Malayan government as a British grant-in-aid. The RMN operates out of the Singapore Woodlands Naval Base where it rents barracks and training facilities for M$400,000 per year from the Royal Navy. It recently proposed to build a M$13 million base at Lumut, midway up the Malayan West Coast, but the imminent advent of Malaysia has led to a decision to remain at Singapore.

To the apparent total of 13,200 in the Malayan armed services must be added some 22,000 well-trained police who until very recently were under the military command. There must also be included the Malayan Territorial Army, a volunteer reserve of 5,200 members, most of them Malays who train generally in the evening, go to camp for two weeks each year, and undertake in return for a M$100 annual stipend to provide local defense at the village level.

The State of Singapore, anticipating the achievement of independence in one form or another, began in 1957 to build up an armed service of its own. It started with 22 local Chinese, Indian, and Malay recruits under the command of seconded British officers with training assistance of seconded British "other ranks." The First Singapore Battalion has now grown to full strength of 800 men, the majority of them Chinese. The Second Singapore Battalion is now being organized, and the defense budget is being doubled accordingly from M$1 million to M$2 million per year. The service is still heavily dependent upon seconded British personnel, but local officers and technicians are rapidly increasing in number and competence.

The First Singapore Battalion of the Singapore Infantry Regiment is now well trained and well equipped to move in fast to help the 5,000-man Singapore police force put down riots or other disorders. In case of really serious local trouble or threat of trouble, the Singapore government is still dependent upon help from the British and the Malayan forces.

To the potential total of Singapore—and Federation—armed strength must be added the 600-man Malayan Royal Navy Volunteer Reserve, based on and largely recruited from Singapore Island, and a small Federation Air Force Reserve. To it must also be added a highly complicated lot of National Service, Civil Defence Corps, Reserve, and Army, Navy, and Air Force Cadet Corps groups, a total of several thousand Singapore men who receive military training on a part-time basis.

With the advent of Malaysia, Malayan and Singapore armed services are clearly due for integration. They are also due for augmentation. Sarawak will no doubt contribute its Field Force of 175 men, the successors to the proud Sarawak Rangers. Brunei will supply a few hundred recruits, most of them already in training in Malaya. North Borneo has no armed service of its own, but does have British military training grounds and an air and navy base potential on Labuan Island. The real build-up will come, however, when and if the government of Malaysia proceeds with the expansion program already contemplated in Kuala Lumpur. It has announced its intention of decreasing its dependence upon British forces and its willingness to increase its own military effort and outlay. The present budget for defense and security, which comes to M$180 million annually in recurrent expenditures, or about 20% of the national budget, is due therefore for a sharp increase. The taxpayers of Malaysia, the low-taxed Borneo territories included, are bracing themselves for the added expense of independence.

The new Federation of Malaysia will have the facilities and the experience for rapid build-up of its own military services, thanks in great part to the British who have transferred whole installations intact and have provided the funds to build others. The showpiece installation is the brand new 500-square-mile, M$22.6 million Armed Forces Cantonment at Sungei Besi, near Kuala Lumpur, now nearing completion and already partly occupied. This cantonment, described locally as a "Sandhurst and Aldershot all rolled into one," was built with a British M$49 million grant-in-aid. It is a recruitment, training, and billeting center for all of the Federation's armed services. It provides all the facilities required for a military and civilian population totaling 8,000—housing, sports fields, drill grounds, training area, an assembly hall, a mosque, a clinic, and a primary school. Within the cantonment is located also the M$7.5 million Federation Military College, comprising a Cadets School for 80 officer candidates, and a Boys' School for 300 select secondary students.

The Sungei Besi Cantonment is indicative of the privilege and inducement which Malaya and presumably the new Malaysia offer to the military recruit. The monthly base pay is good—about M$250 plus marriage allowance (M$125) for the new recruit, about M$550 plus allowances for the second lieutenant. The standards of service loyalty and honesty and of public approbation are correspondingly high. The profession of soldiering is one which offers a future, and one to which, from present indications, the climax need not be the political coup.

The changing role and status of the Singapore base must be interpreted in relation to the changing role and status of the armed services of the region. The British are now increasingly reliant and hence dependent upon the indigenous forces. They seem assured of loyal cooperation and support, but only so long as they make it clear that the British forces and the British bases themselves serve a local and not an exclusively British purpose. This means more emphasis upon the second of the three stated objectives—"assisting in the defence of Malaysia," such assistance to be provided not just "as the British consider

necessary," to quote the British version of the new agreement, but "as
Malaysia sees fit to request," to quote the Malayan. It means less
emphasis in the future upon "Commonwealth defence" and "preservation of the peace in South-East Asia," just as it has meant in the last
several years less and less emphasis upon the third objective of "defence of South-East Asia against Chinese Communist aggression," i.e.,
use for SEATO purposes. Whether the attainment of objectives two and
three will be seriously prejudiced by a shift of emphasis or even outright redefinition of purpose may turn out, as many British now seem
to believe, more a matter for semantic than strategic concern. By de-
terring aggression from without and subversion from within, the British
can obviously help build up a stable new Malaysian nation which will itself have some stabilizing influence upon the region and thus serve
British, Commonwealth, and other enlightened world interests.

In maintaining the Singapore base and the other British installations specifically for Malaysian security and defense, the British elicit
warm support from the present government of the Federation of Malaya,
cool support from the present government of Singapore, and bitter criticism from the many political factions that seek cause for agitation. The
Federation government, while it officially deplores SEATO and Western
military "intervention" in Southeast Asia, welcomes British military
"cooperation" within Malaysia and the British stabilizing influence in
the area. The Malayan government freely acknowledges, furthermore,
that without British bases, troops, technical assistance, and grants, it
would be quite unable to defend itself or to contemplate merger with
the potentially insurrectionist State of Singapore. The Singapore government both deplores and acknowledges the military necessity for
British bases—for the next 10 to 15 years, at least; it realistically
admits that Singapore's economic viability depends upon the annual
M$95 million British base payroll for local employees, plus an addi-
tional M$65 million British military outlay for contractual supplies
and services, plus another M$100 million paid to British service per-
sonnel and most of it spent locally.

Thus, the Singapore base, which must be viewed as part of a
much bigger military complex, is not only a Singapore but also a Malaysian fixture. It commands not only British but also Commonwealth
support, including support of local armed services. Correspondingly,
it calls up not only local but also regional and world-wide opposition.
The obvious threat is from Moscow and Peking, most possibly via Indochina or Indonesia. Direct armed attack is much less likely than indirect political attack which has, in fact, long since been mounted. The
island city-state of Singapore, as rich and shaky and hence as inviting

a target as exists in Southeast Asia, affords a natural cause and arena
of agitation to the Singapore Chinese extremists and Communists, the
reactionary Pan-Malayan Islamic Party, the Indonesian Communist
Party, the agents of Peking, and all other opponents of Malaysia, the
British, and the smoothly changing status quo.

Possibly the most critical question regarding the Singapore base
concerns not its actual strength and stated role but whether the mere
existence of the base serves more to deter or to attract trouble. The
capacity of "peace-loving peoples" to let themselves be "provoked"
into "anticolonial" campaigns for a neighbor's "liberation" has been
illustrated by regional condemnation by Communists, quasi-Commu-
nists, and others—among them some men of good will—of the "neocolonialistic" Malaysia proposal. It is the judgment of the British authorities—and one with which it is difficult to quarrel—that the effort by
military and other devices to strengthen Singapore and Malaysia as a
whole is both necessary and desirable. It is as good a military gamble
as one can make in Southeast Asia today. But gamble it is, even though
it is one attended by a far greater degree of realism than the tragic
gamble of 1941.

CHAPTER
VIII

BILLETS FOR BALLOTS

September 11, 1962

Can a Southeast Asian government successfully cope with a population explosion? Can it, for instance, provide shelter commensurate with the demands of a huge slum and squatter population? Can it in so doing also provide shelter against the political, economic, and social evils which result when too many too expectant people are packed too tightly into too little space? Can it, to pursue the matter to its melopolitical climax, barter billets for ballots to bolster itself long enough to see its program through?

In Singapore, where the world's youngest population, as well as one of its most restless, is increasing at the world's highest rate of 3.6% per annum, where not only homes and schools and hospitals but also space and jobs and tempers are short, the official answer is, "Yes." Even though the program is speeding ahead at an astonishing rate, the official "Yes" is not so confident a "Yes" as it was two years ago when a vast Five-Year Development Plan was announced, or one year ago when it could be clearly demonstrated that the program was taking hold.

As a major part of its M$871.02 million five-year plan, the Singapore People's Action Party government is laying out M$194.1 million for low-cost housing for workers—51,031 new units to house 300,000-400,000 people. The PAP government had the good fortune, to begin with, to inherit from previous governments a total of some 20,000 government-built housing units plus a deep reservoir of experience and blueprints. It had the ill fortune, on its assumption of office on June 2, 1959, to stall its own expanded program on an in-party feud, so that newly completed housing units dropped from a record high of 3,841 in 1958 to 1,611 in 1959, and 1,517 in 1960. It managed, presently, to "clean up the mess" into which its own "deviationist" Minister for Housing had thrown the whole program. In 1961 it built 7,300 units; in 1962, if it maintains its present pace of one new flat every 45 minutes and one new block of 120 flats every four days, it will complete a total of 13,000. By the end of the project period, some 25% of Singapore's population will be living in government housing.

The main question now seems to be not whether the PAP government can actually make good on its tremendous housing scheme—as many once doubted; nor whether the scheme will actually come close to meeting the demand—as the PAP itself doubted at the outset; but whether the PAP itself, or its rival and splinter party, the extreme left-wing Barisan Sosialis, or some other party, conceivably the United People's Party of the ex-PAP, ex-Minister for Housing, will reap the political profits. The government today is making tremendous and readily apparent strides toward rehousing major segments of the 250,000 people who now occupy Singapore's worst slum and squatter areas and of the 400,000 others who occupy substandard buildings; it is redistributing the urban population—and the votes—and hoping that, contrary to the political pattern of its own early period, benefits bestowed will weigh more heavily with the electorate than grievances agitated.

Singapore's new housing program spreads itself out most spectacularly on view in the new satellite area of Queenstown. Here, several years ago, the rolling countryside supported only a tropical scrub growth dotted by Chinese tombs and a few squatter shacks and gardens. Today, whole hilltops have been sliced off and swampy valleys filled to provide space for new industrial, business, and residential development. Groups of small one- and two-story detached bungalows, most of them put up by private builders, occupy some of the residential land; rows of two-story "terrace" houses, some privately built, some government built, predominate in other sections. But most impressive of all, stretching row on row across the landscape, are blocks of seven-, nine-, eleven-, even fourteen-story apartment buildings, their simple architectural lines emphasized by clear-standing outside stairways and galleries, wide, open balconies, and bright paint work.

Here in Queenstown, if you are a Singapore citizen, aged twenty-one or over, married, encumbered with a family of at least four members, yourself and your family earning a total income of no more than M$800 per month, you can qualify for a new home, in all probability a flat. For a one-room flat with about 250 square feet of floor space—a combined living room-bedroom with kitchen, bath, toilet, and balcony—you will pay M$20 per month. For a 375-square-foot two-room flat you will pay M$40; for a 500-square-foot three-room flat, M$50. Your rent, you will be informed, covers only about two thirds of the actual cost of a one-room flat, about 80% of a two-room flat, but practically all of the

actual cost of the three-room flat. You will have to pay moderate additional fees for electricity and water, but you will be provided with free
caretaker service for the building grounds, even automatic elevator service to alternate floors if you live in a building more than six stories high.
You will have to provide your own furniture—but you can do so on a particularly hard austerity basis for M$300-M$600 if you copy the prize-
winning models turned out by the architecture students of Singapore Poly-
technic. You can rent at a nominal fee both stove and refrigerator from
the city government, but most people settle for no refrigerator at all and
for one or two simple gas burners at a rental of M$0.25 each per month.

There are certain building regulations which you will be required
to observe. You may do all the laundry you wish on the premises, and
the builders have thoughtfully provided slots into which can be inserted
bamboo poles on which the laundry can be hung out to dry, giving the whole
building every day of the week the effect of gala decorations. You may
not keep dogs, cats, chickens, ducks, or pigs on the premises or place
flowerpots on balcony ledges, but you are free to indulge in tropical fish
or birds and well-anchored plants. You may not install a ceiling fan—
the ceilings are too low for safe operation. Neither, unless you have a
doctor's certificate, may you install air conditioning—an air conditioner
at a minimum of M$750 cash seems unduly luxurious for a M$20-M$50
flat. You are free, however, to install a telephone, to keep and park a
motor scooter, a motorcycle, or—as many do—even a car. You may
not sublet the flat or operate a business on the premises, but you may,
as some do by devices more ingenious than comfortable, pack in as
many as 11 or 12 bona fide relatives, all contributing to the rent.

Your apartment, obviously, is a far cry from the "luxury"
M$500-M$750 per month apartments of Singapore's Tanglin district
about two miles distant. Nevertheless, it is undoubtedly a bargain,
even if you calculate that the units cost the government approximately
M$2,000, M$3,700, and M$4,700 to build—exclusive of high costs for
land purchase, clearing, and pile driving, and that full rental payments
over a 20-year period will return the government M$4,800 to M$12,-
000 per unit on its investment. Nobody expects, of course, that the
government is actually going to make money on this venture. But the
government subsidy, on careful scrutiny, proves merely to cover government taxes, and the amortization period is quite certainly rather
less than the 60 years which government spokesmen cite. If you have
any real doubts about the deal, you may dispel them, perhaps, if you
approach one of the private builders who advertises an easy rental-
purchase plan whereby you can actually own your own home. He will
want a minimum of M$1,500 down and M$80 per month for a unit some-

what bigger and better, but by no means that much bigger and better
than the government's, and you will pay an additional M$20-M$50 per
month in taxes.

Notwithstanding the bargain rates, there are some fairly common and basic objections which the tenants register against these new
quarters. The multiple-story buildings in particular give rise to serious apprehensions on the part of prospective tenants and sometimes
require a particularly long period of acclimatization. A one-room
flat on the 13th story may seem to the city planner to be vastly brighter,
cleaner, airier, and more scenic than a windowless tenement cubicle
or a squatter's hut, but it does not provide planting space for a papaya
tree and a banana palm, a run for a pig and a duck, or safe play space
for small children. Nor does it afford easy, friendly access to the peddlers who vend all sorts of tempting foodstuffs from portable stands
and save one not only the trouble but even something of the expense of
cooking for the family. A flat, furthermore, regardless of through ven-
tilation and open balcony, strikes many tenants as being breathlessly
hot. They prefer the thick-walled, high-ceilinged rooms of the old tenements, where rats scamper when one turns on the ceiling fan, or palm-
shaded, rain-washed thatched huts where one can feel and hear the night
breeze stirring the mosquitoes.

Apartment house living, furthermore, involves an uprooting of
all of the old patterns of life and resettling in a strange new neighborhood among strange new neighbors. It means the effort of forming new
associations for mutual comfort, frequently with persons of a different
racial and cultural background. Chinese, Indians, and Malays—but few
Malays, since they stick resolutely to their kampongs—are mixed both
deliberately and by chance in new buildings to a degree much greater
than occurs in the established settlements. Furthermore, as some tenants become accustomed to apartment living and grow even to prefer
its amenities, they become increasingly conscious of its drawbacks.
Electricity and water bills are far less welcome than electricity and
water. Wiring and plumbing require expensive repairs. "Someone
else's" carelessness results in blocking of the incinerator, stopping
of the elevator, cluttering of the corridors, damage to stair wells, rail-
ings, and paint work; windows get broken and water meters get discon-
nected and sold as scrap. Small children sometimes mistake the elevator for a public convenience; small boys regard smashed-up light bulbs
as an essential to kite decorating; children and adults alike are given
to throwing bits of refuse from high windows. An occasional flowerpot
tipped off a balcony makes it advisable to gaze upward as one follows
the walks. Strangely enough, the noise level is seldom a subject of com-

plaint, even though the proliferation of children, traffic, and radios means that during major portions of the day and night Queenstown lives in pandemonium.

Singapore's low-cost housing program seems for the moment at least to be overtaking demand. The government has an official backlog of 30,000-40,000 applicants, many of whom have been on the books for years. It also has plenty of flats which could be occupied tomorrow, and in the Queenstown area, at least, it is sometimes waiving its former minimum requirement of five members per family. Government officials report with some dismay that only about one half of the families to whom they offer new housing now actually accept it. Prospective new tenants are becoming more and more "fussy" and "choosy." They want new and better housing, to be sure, but they want it in the immediate area in which they now live and work, they want it of a type with which they are already familiar, and they want it at even lower rent than it is now being offered.

At the same time that it is experiencing unexpected new troubles filling the buildings that are already completed, the government is encountering a reintensification of old troubles in getting new buildings actually under way. Singapore squatters occupy great tracts of government land on which the new housing developments are to be located. In Toa Payoh, one special problem area, some 2,300 squatter families have been established since the war years on land now scheduled to house 250,000 people. They have built their own shacks—some of them fairly substantial and expensive; they have established businesses, including bean-curd making, pig farming, and poultry raising; they have planted gardens for the commercial production of vegetables and orchids. The government, rather than evict the squatters outright, prefers to buy them out. Negotiations between government and squatters, however, frequently result in prolonged delay and great additional expense. The squatters have now organized—on the instigation of the political opposition, the government charges—and have made demands for compensation running as high as M$9,000 per acre of vegetable land and M$30,000 per acre of orchid land. The government has had to keep increasing its offers and now makes settlement on the basis of one or more of the following: compensation of M$1.00 per square foot of building land and M$2.00 per acre of farm land; provision of substitute farm land worth up to M$4,000; provision of a substitute home worth up to M$5,000; free transportation to move from old to new location; and government assistance in re-establishing a business or a farm.

In its dealings with squatters—who, it need scarcely be mentioned, are also voters—the government runs into the baffling sort of policy conflict which occurs also in its dealings with labor. The government is attempting not only to provide new low-cost "housing estates" for laborers, but to provide new jobs for them as well. It is engaged, therefore, in an immense program of opening up adjacent "industrial estates" in which private investors, both local and foreign, may establish new factories which would offer new employment possibilities. As yet, new industry has been slow to take advantage of the urgent Singapore invitation. The reason: the Singapore labor force in the last several years has proved far more articulate in its demands for emancipation from colonial and capitalist "exploitation" than willing to acquire new skills or new capacities. Labor unions have made demands which employers find not merely excessive but whimsically subject to retroactive reinterpretation once settlements have been almost completed. The PAP, now vigorously competing with the Barisan Sosialis for domination of a labor movement split almost equally between them, has had to compete also with the Barisan Sosialis in support of labor demands against the very employers it is eager to persuade to expand operations.

Government effort to expand job opportunities at the same time that it provides improved housing entails also a complicated program of co-ordination in community development. As an adjunct to housing and industrial estates, it is building schools, hospitals, playing fields, swimming pools, markets, community centers, and all the other necessities of new urban and suburban complexes. It has not yet demonstrated, however, that it is creating a healthful new spirit which will inspire citizens of widely different racial background to participate in integrated community activities.

The new Singapore housing-industrial communities are being populated today by a potentially dangerous mix of semidisplaced, semi-integrated persons of widely diversified racial, cultural, social, political, and economic background. In these new communities, at least according to the evidence available prior to the recent referendum, not the PAP but its enemy the Barisan Sosialis seemed to be making the greatest political gains—winning, it seemed, the allegiance of the very persons whom the PAP has itself done the most to help. The very fact, however, that these new communities have remained orderly during a period when the Singapore population as a whole has felt itself increasingly encircled and compressed, indicates that the government is at least gaining time in which, just as the PAP hopes, investment in quick physical benefits may begin to pay off in long-range political dividends. In any event, the Singapore housing experiment, by far the boldest in Southeast Asia today, is likely for good or for ill to produce truly dramatic results.

CHAPTER
IX

TAKE-OFF POINT IN HIGHER EDUCATION

September 14, 1962

The prospective Federation of Malaysia will escape one of the urgent problems of many new nations: how to establish a national university. It will encounter, however, at least three other problems of comparable magnitude: what to do about three universities—two state and one private—already established but overlapping, incomplete, and competitive. These three, the University of Malaya, the University of Singapore, and Nanyang University, might better, some say, have concentrated their resources upon one campus, one faculty, one student body, and one curriculum. Qualified faculty members, it is now evident, are hard to get or to keep; student preparation and performance are uneven; standards leave much room for improvement; theory and method of advanced education are being debated; faculty and student politics includes extramural as well as intramural conflicts. Nevertheless, three universities already in being is no small educational endowment for a small new nation. There are money and enthusiasm enough, fortunately, for all three, and each has already proved itself a vital entity.

The present universities of Malaya and Singapore came into separate and official existence only on January 1, 1962. They share, however, an inbred academic pedigree which goes back to the establishment in Singapore in 1905 of a colonial medical school serving the Malayan area. This school, presently known as the King Edward VII College of Medicine, enrolled only 23 students the first year; it now enrolls 600 and has produced during its history a total of about 1,000 medical doctors and 200 dentists. The King Edward VII Medical College in 1928 sired a separate Raffles College of arts and sciences. Raffles College, housed on a handsome campus in Singapore's best residential district, was born just as the world-wide depression caught up with the city and through the mid-1930's it had a total enrollment of only about 80 students. It had begun to prosper mildly by about 1940 and even to entertain ambitions of becoming a university. Then came the Pacific War, the fall of Singapore, and the Japanese Occupation, during which Raffles College was converted into a military headquarters and King Edward VII College into a serological institute.

By March 1946, as soon as British military occupation units could be persuaded to vacate the premises, Raffles College and King Edward VII College reopened and by the following year had a total of 650 students. What Singapore really needed, almost everyone then agreed, was a full-fledged university. In 1949, accordingly, after lengthy investigations, reports, and debates, all complicated by a swiftly changing political situation, the British colonial government created the University of Malaya. It did so, however, mainly by redesignating Raffles and King Edward VII colleges — then, as now, physically separate — a single institution which would presently be moved across the causeway to Johore, expand, and serve the needs of the prospective new Malayan nation. But the Communist Emergency, the independence movement, and complicated considerations of colonial and postcolonial policy altered the plans. The various transitional governments in Singapore and Kuala Lumpur were both unable and unwilling to proceed with the move-to-Johore scheme. They did appropriate enough money to build up the University in Singapore, but stalled on all other important decisions. In 1957 came political divorce between Singapore and the Federation, leaving the University of Malaya anomalously outside the boundaries of the Federation of Malaya. Custody of the infant University became an important factor in the post-divorce settlement, but for a period of years it was unclear whether the University of Malaya was to be an orphan or a twin.

Responding to intense political pressures, in 1957 the University of Malaya put out an offshoot University of Malaya in Kuala Lumpur. Between 1957 and 1960 the branch took root so deeply and flourished so luxuriantly that it threatened soon to overshadow the parent institution. The Federation and Singapore governments, which had been contributing first at the rate of 60:40, then at 2:1 to the general financing and arguing over the control, in 1961 passed separate but complementary education acts providing for separate institutions. On January 1, 1962, accordingly, the offshoot University of Malaya in Kuala Lumpur became the acknowledged University of Malaya, while the parent institution became simply the University of Singapore. The two undertook to co-operate rather than to engage in such rivalry as had in the past led to a serious suggestion — fortunately disregarded — that the University librarians get together and divide up the excellent collection of books on a one-for-you-and-one-for-me basis.

While the University of Malaya was going through this period of genesis and fission, the Singapore Overseas Chinese community was hatching its own private Nanyang University. Nanyang is the precocious third party to an adolescent educational triangle whose benefits and problems the new Federation of Malaysia will inherit.

The University of Singapore, the most deeply rooted of the three, has been in the past a distinctively British type of institution, colonial, of course, in many of its aspects. It was staffed to a very great extent by the conservative British or British-trained. It was attended by a small, privileged, English-speaking student body, mainly Chinese. Although both faculty and students sought to create the atmosphere of a tropical Oxford or Cambridge, the curriculum was limited; the method of instruction was a rather rigid combination of the formal lecture and the tutorial; the faculty was aloof; the students were dedicated to the passing of examinations on which depended not only their academic but their future professional advancement. Recent years have brought swift but not yet complete emancipation from the restrictions of British colonialism in education as well as in politics, and a wide range of related conflicts and rivalries.

The key University conflict a few years ago was between factions seeking to bind the institution more closely to the British tradition and those seeking to cut it loose to develop along lines more characteristic to the area. It was a conflict, one might say, between the educational colonialists and the educational nationalists, although the colonialists and the nationalists alike were remarkably flexible. As was inevitable, the old school-tie clique lost ground. As time passed, a majority of the senior British faculty members retired or resigned and were replaced by British newcomers or by newly promoted local citizens, most of them disposed to favor a fresh approach.

About 1955, just as the University was gathering new strength and embarking upon a major program of construction and expansion, the intramural conflict shifted to outright political grounds. The State of Singapore at this point was moving into a period of left-wing Socialist political domination. One University group opposed, another applauded the political swing. More personnel changes occurred; more time passed; the People's Action Party staged an election victory; and the University conflict, rather than clarifying, became more complicated. The PAP created consternation by attacking not only the "excessive privileges" of the "expatriates" (foreigners), but the "sterile intellectualism" of the "English-educated" (Westernized Chinese and Indians), and by seeking to curtail academic salaries and freedom. Presently, however, the PAP, fearing betrayal by its own extremist elements, sought reconciliation with the intellectuals. It found the University staff

a bit cool on politics as such but more approachable on the basis of
making common cause to restore the institution's standards and prestige, particularly in relation to the new Kuala Lumpur branch by which,
simultaneously, some of the staff were being wooed, some repulsed or
repelled. The University's attention now has reverted from political
rivalry to academic matters—including some rather bitter jealousies
—and with the reversion has come a pronounced swing on the part of
the faculty to favor the now politically chastened and academically lib-
eralized PAP.

Politics as such still consumes a very great deal of energy, of
course, upon the University campus, most of all these days among the
students. The University of Singapore's student body which several
years ago was strongly pro-PAP has swung farther to the left at the
same time that the PAP has been veering a bit to the right. The Singapore campus today, consequently, is one of the PAP's toughest and
most critical political forums. Nevertheless, University student politics, like faculty politics, falls short of being the major avocation that
it becomes on campuses in Rangoon, say, or Djakarta. Singapore University student groups, while they take up every local issue and voice
resounding statements of Afro-Asian solidarity regarding Goa, Irian
Barat, Cuba, and Algeria, still seem to look with more dismay than
envy upon the practice of demonstrations and riots. Singapore's really
rough student politics is for the Chinese high schools, not the University.

The University of Singapore today comprises Faculties of Medicine (including Dentistry and Pharmacy), Law, Arts, and Sciences,
plus a School of Education. It has a teaching staff of 200, a student
body of 2,400, and in 1962 turned out 334 graduates, including 65 doctors and 18 dentists. The student body is approximately 70% Chinese,
15% Indian, 5% Ceylonese, 5% Malay, and 5% other races. The teaching staff is about 50% foreign (mainly British and Commonwealth citizens) and 50% local. The staff is seriously under strength and has been
so for years, but is slated for rapid increase—500 by 1969—to provide
a much more diversified program for a much larger student body which
is expected to number 5,000 by 1965.

With regard to curriculum, students, and faculty, the University
of Singapore obviously runs into some very special difficulties. The
curriculum—merely to begin the itemization of special problems—is
Western style, the instruction is in English, the students and staff are
predominantly non-Malay in a Malayan country. The objective of the

institution, naturally, is to prepare young men and women for constructive roles in the new nation—a nation which may or may not be part of
Malaysia, may or may not remain Western oriented, may or may not
offer relatively equal opportunity to all who are academically well prepared.

The various University departments, which are uneven in quality
and quantity of academic resources and sometimes uncertain in emphasis—as is not uncommon elsewhere, of course—are under heavy pressure simultaneously to improve and to expand, with counsel divided,
naturally, regarding the method. The Faculty of Medicine, for instance,
even though it has suffered serious personnel losses in recent years,
is now proposing rapidly to increase the number of its graduates in order to meet the Singapore doctor shortage (one doctor per 4,118 of population). There are already many critics who say standards should but
do not come first and numbers second. The University of Malaya, incidentally, is planning to establish its own new medical college in 1963;
and this question arises: why not strengthen the Singapore college instead? The University of Singapore has directed its Board of Asian
Studies to take steps to make sure that the institution becomes a major
center of area research, as, indeed, Singapore's location and its multiracial, multilingual population immediately suggest—but the University
of Malaya is planning to do almost exactly the same thing. Whatever
the charges of overexpansion and empire building, however, one hears
less and less these days of the old charges of ultraconservatism.

In recruiting a new teaching staff for its swiftly expanding program, the University of Singapore is faced with the fact that qualified
personnel is in short supply, not only in Singapore but everywhere else
in the world. The University gives preference to local candidates, when
and if local candidates are available. It advertises regularly in the
London Times and other Commonwealth papers, yet it has serious problems merely in filling vacancies, let alone building up the big, new,
strong staff it wants. One reason is that terms of service in Singapore,
although extremely good by general Southeast Asian standards, are not
so attractive by strictly local or by international standards. A Singapore professor draws about M$1,700 per month in salary and allowances;
he is provided at a low rental with university-owned living quarters; if
recruited abroad, he draws travel money and an end-of-contract bonus.
But a foreigner is inclined to wonder about his long-term career prospects in Singapore. A local citizen is inclined to wonder about more
attractive offers in Malaya, either in the University at Kuala Lumpur

or in booming new business concerns. Each is inclined to wonder whether, qualification for qualification, the other is not now or will not in the near future be getting by far the better deal. In any event, university teaching in Singapore, as elsewhere, often seems a career more for the dedicated than for the ambitious, and this is an ambitious new country.

The Singapore student body, like the faculty, is distinguished most of all, perhaps, by its interracial character and outlook. Just as this fact makes for exciting new educational possibilities of combining the best features of many cultures, it makes also for present problems of diversity of educational, economic, and social background and opportunity. The Malays, who have heretofore been the underprivileged minority, are today coming into their inheritance. They receive special encouragement which involves waiving of tuition fees; they can be sure of attractive job offers; they may or may not, however, display the industry and ambition which characterizes, for instance, the great majority of the Chinese. These Chinese students, traditionally the economically and educationally privileged, today face tougher competition than ever before—a great deal of it, to be sure, from each other. Some educators who think that the Malays at times exhibit a dearth of drive, sometimes think that the Chinese are as likely to exhibit an excess. The Indians, Pakistanis, Ceylonese, and others constitute articulate, colorful minorities determined to excel. The academic competition at the University of Singapore, although it is far from being racial in base, is racial in many of its overtones. This makes the present Singapore academic achievement to date particularly noteworthy for being one of harmonious blending of interests—which is exactly what the University and the state seek to achieve.

Among the strictly educational problems which preoccupy the student body, one is especially noteworthy. The university system stresses the formal academic lecture as background for first year examinations, on the basis of which the minority of the students in arts are privileged to qualify for an "honours" degree but the majority are doomed to work merely for a "pass" degree. The adverse effect of this early selection process upon academic enthusiasm and achievement is apparent both before and after the examination. The professional and monetary difference between the two degrees is evident on graduation day. The "honours" graduate qualifies almost automatically for a beginning government salary of M$554 per month, the "pass" graduate must compete for a mere M$324 job, and both find private employers guided by government standards.

        The Singapore University administration, with worries enough
regarding other matters, has its share of financial woes as well, but
perhaps not quite as many as the great majority of universities elsewhere. It has no very impressive endowment—only about M$5 million,
which it has to split with the University of Malaya, and no very great
expectation of more. It does have confidence, however, that the government of the new Malaysia will prove at least as solvent and as generous
as the British, the Federation, and the Singapore governments have been
in the past. The three, among them, have provided for an impressive
collection of new buildings and equipment—an administration building,
a library, a science building, a men's dormitory, a women's dormitory,
each at the M$1 million-M$1.5 million level, and other additions as
well. They have provided adequate if not abundant operating expenses,
the grant from the Singapore state government for the current year being M$8.4 million. The University calculates, incidentally, that each
student costs it from M$3,000 (arts) to M$8,000 (medicine) per year,
while it charges only M$450-M$540 in tuition fees (plus M$330 per
ten-week term for room and board). A good third of the students are
on government "bursaries" of M$750-M$1,500 per year, and Malay
students, as already noted, study free.

        The University of Malaya in Kuala Lumpur shares virtually all
of the problems and prospects, as discussed above, of the University of
Singapore. One major problem which the University of Malaya distinctly
does not face is that of moral and financial support. Seven years ago
it seemed a forlorn academic foundling, housed in a borrowed building,
provided with a loan staff, attended by a hastily recruited and trans-
ported student body of about 320 that could choose only among first-
year subjects of extremely limited range. Today, the institution occupies an entire new M$15 million complex built on a landscaped 400-
acre tract of land in Pantai Valley on the outskirts of Kuala Lumpur.
It is provided with half a dozen big new buildings, all of them handsomely
designed and built in bright and airy tropical modern style, with air
conditioning laid on in the library, auditorium, offices, and various
lecture halls. It has a M$34 million budget for still more new buildings
in 1963, and a 1962-63 operating budget of M$7 million. Although the
Chancellor deplores the dearth of Malayan philanthropists willing to
provide an endowment, the University enjoys practical expressions of
good will on the part of foreign governments. The British, for instance,
contributed M$2.6 million through the Colonial Development and Wel-
fare Fund; New Zealand put up M$2,142,000 through the Colombo Plan
to build and equip a School of Agriculture. The University enjoys also
the immense good will of the general public. Although there are mut-
terings at times about "extravagance" in building a "luxury" institution

where "scions of the rich" create parking problems with their shiny
little British sports cars and devote far too much time to "ragging"
and to the twist, there are even more insistent statements of pride
in what is truly a remarkably swift achievement.

The University has a student enrollment of 1,400 and in 1962
turned out 132 graduates. Of the student body, more than 50% is Chinese, about 20% Malay, 15% Indian, 5% Ceylonese, and 5% other races.
The University seems committed to a policy of Western-style education
in English, with increasing emphasis, however, upon development and
use of the Malay language and special encouragement of the heretofore educationally underprivileged Malay students. It aspires to the
fast build-up of all University departments and emphasis upon local
and regional studies. Its aspiration perhaps frequently exceeds its
grasp, as, for instance, with regard to the establishment in 1963 of
a medical faculty, in addition to the present faculties of arts, sciences,
engineering, and agriculture. Nevertheless, there is nothing static
about the University program. The really basic question is whether
with a good start and the good intentions already evident, the University can develop quickly into a first-class institution in which both
staff and students will be secure against racial and political favoritism.

Of the three universities in the new Malaysia, Nanyang is the
real problem institution. It is a Chinese type of university offering
education in Chinese on a self-consciously racial basis, but forced to
deny that it does and forced to attempt to do otherwise. Theoretically,
there is a very important place for a good Chinese education at the
university level in a multiracial state in which the Chinese have dominant interests. Practically, as Nanyang has demonstrated, there are
extremely difficult hurdles.

Nanyang began instruction in March of 1956 as a result of the
efforts and gifts of a group of Singapore Chinese businessmen, outstanding among them the multimillionaire industrialist and philanthropist, Tan Lark Sye. It was envisaged by its founders as an institution
serving the higher educational needs of the Chinese language-trained
Overseas Chinese of all of Southeast Asia, many of whom were dis-
criminated against in their home countries and confronted with a choice
between going to Communist China or to Nationalist Taiwan if they
wanted a university education. It was greeted by the general public,
however, with almost as much suspicion as approbation. To practically
everyone of any political persuasion, Nanyang seemed a prime objective for manipulation. Communists, anti-Communists, neutralists,
nationalists, colonialists, and isolationists maneuvered for influence

and accused each other of conspiracy. The University might have foundered in its politics had it not been so preoccupied with its academic
and financial problems.

The stated academic purpose was to assemble a first-rate staff,
to enroll a first-rate student body, and to provide a first-rate education
in a first-rate institution, but at almost every turn Nanyang had to settle
for second best—its critics say third or fourth. The University imported
Lin Yutang to be its first chancellor and proposed to assemble about
him a faculty of equal prestige. The Lin Yutang appointment was can-
celed by mutual consent at the end of about one year to the accompaniment of recriminations which have not yet died down. The first-rate
educators have never shown up in substantial numbers, partly because
of bureaucratic difficulties in recruiting abroad and in gaining local
resident status, partly because salaries are low—about 50% of what the
University of Singapore pays—and partly because word has spread that
Nanyang is in trouble.

Troubles regarding faculty and administration were matched by
troubles regarding the student body. Many of the best qualified potential
students preferred other institutions. Most of the potential students from
abroad ran into insuperable difficulties getting out of their home countries
or getting into Singapore. The build-up of the Nanyang curriculum on a
year-to-year basis, with some departments lagging seriously behind
others, and required courses for a degree being difficult to dovetail,
led to both confusion and discouragement. Furthermore, the Nanyang
students proved susceptible to political intrigue, particularly to the
machinations of the extreme left, and to academic confusion was added
political conflict. The fact that the basic language of instruction is
Chinese led to continuous debate both within and without the University
regarding the preservation of and the threat to Chinese culture in the
new Malaya, and the desirability of creating a new group of Chinese-
educated when many of the old are notoriously anti-Malayan, pro-Com-
munist, and nonco-operative.

Nanyang's finances have proved particularly vexatious. The
original and later gifts of the sponsors, particularly those of Tan Lark
Sye, were sufficient to allow for construction of a M$12.3 million com-
plex of classrooms, laboratories, offices, dormitories, and faculty residences, but for operating expenses the institution has to depend mainly
upon student fees—M$720 per student per year. The Nanyang physical
plant has come in for a great deal of criticism on the basis that the
buildings do not conform to good principles of design or construction
and that the 500-acre grounds are grown up with weeds and brush. The

Nanyang budget, furthermore, has been inadequate to provide attractive salaries for the teaching staff or to keep library and laboratories up to good university standards. Government funds are always in prospect, but always contingent upon concession to the government of a degree of control which the University authorities have been unwilling to grant.

Nanyang has repeatedly requested full "recognition" by the government of its degrees, such recognition being an extremely valuable asset to the graduate in the Singapore job market. The government has repeatedly refused, and in conjunction with its refusal has run two full-scale investigations of the institution. The consensus of the investigators is that Nanyang needs to improve its facilities, its faculty, its student body, and its standards. Nanyang University authorities argue that it is all very well to talk of improvements, when what the institution needs is encouragement. Instead, they say, it has experienced constant criticism and indeed antagonism, not only from the present government but from the British colonial administration in the past, from the Federation, and from many segments of the press and public; it has experienced the multiplying effect of doubts repetitiously—and unjustly—cast upon faculty, students, the institution, and its politics.

To the surprise of many observers who expected Nanyang to be overwhelmed by its problems, it has managed, regardless of complex misgivings about its policies and its politics, to enlist such widespread support on the part of the Overseas Chinese community as a whole and such determination on the part of faculty and students that it seems assured of survival. The Singapore government, after much wheeling and hauling, now recognizes Nanyang degrees as equivalent to "pass" degrees from the University of Singapore; it provides an increasing number of "bursaries" for Nanyang students—in 1961 a total of 700 with a total value of M$716,000. The government seems prepared at present, provided long-debated plans for reorganizing the University really work out, to assume a considerable part of the operating costs, perhaps a 55% share of its present M$2 million-plus budget. Nanyang's troubles are far from over, but at least they seem reduced, and whatever its academic achievement to date, its record of survival and growth must command admiration.

Nanyang at present has a teaching staff of 110, about 65% of them from Taiwan, 15% from Hong Kong. It has a student body of over 2,000, 56% of them from the Federation, most of the others from Singapore, and a few from Borneo. It has graduated 1,200 students, 385 in the class of 1962. Under the leadership of Tan Lark Sye and quite independently of its expectations from the government, it is embarking

upon a new building and fund-raising program and is planning for a
total enrollment of 5,000 in 1965.

The relative and growing prestige of the various institutions,
as well as something of the racial accommodation which education en-
courages and the new Malaysia demands, is indicated in the new line-
up of chancellors and vice-chancellors. Sir Malcolm MacDonald, onetime Governor of Singapore and High Commissioner for Southeast Asia,
formerly held the position of Chancellor of the University of Malaya,
for both the Singapore and Kuala Lumpur divisions. On June 13, 1962,
in a ceremony at the University of Singapore, Sir Malcolm inducted
into office as new Chancellor the multimillionaire "rubber king" and
philanthropist, Dato Lee Kong Chian. Dato Lee, now sixty-eight, China
born, and China and Singapore educated, is a self-made man of no academic pretensions but of academic pride and drive. On June 16, in a
similar ceremony in Kuala Lumpur, Sir Malcolm inducted his successor
at the University of Malaya, namely, the Prime Minister of the Federation of Malaya, Tengku Abdul Rahman. The Tengku, like Dato Lee, is a
man of modest academic achievement but possessed of tremendous enthusiasm for education. He proposes to keep out of University administration but to throw all of his tremendous influence behind the institution.
The Vice-Chancellor—that is, the administrative president—of the University of Malaya is Sir Alexander Oppenheim, a British mathematician
long associated with the University of Singapore and more recently with
the University of Malaya. Singapore's Vice-Chancellor is Dr. B. R. Sreen-
ivasan, a Singapore-born Ceylonese, a graduate of King Edward VII
Medical College, and a long-time member of the University Congress.
Nanyang University, since the departure of Lin Yutang in 1955 has
risked no new chancellor. The Vice-Chancellor is Dr. Chuang Chu-lin,
formerly the principal of Singapore's biggest and most troubled Chinese
high school. Without the prestige of the position, Dr. Chuang has had to
cope with a chancellor's as well as a vice-chancellor's responsibilities.

The three universities of the new Malaysia, while they do not
serve three different academic needs and might in combination better
serve one, have proud if brief traditions of their own and show every
indication of proposing to enhance them. The University of Malaya
signifies the determination of the Federation of Malaya swiftly to achieve
a first-rate national university. The newly expanded University of
Singapore signifies the determination of the island city-state not to
suffer any diminution of prestige in educational or other matters in
comparison with its late-starting but now hustling neighbor. The sep-
aration of the two reflects the rift between the Malay-oriented Federation and Chinese-oriented Singapore, a rift which the creation of the

new Federation of Malaysia is calculated to heal, but not by any such
device as bringing the two institutions back together again. Meanwhile,
the existence and expansion on Singapore Island of Nanyang University
signify the determination of the Overseas Chinese of the region to maintain their traditional culture. It reflects also the difficulty of modifying
that tradition to conform to the composite Malaysian pattern in which
in Kuala Lumpur the Malayan and in Singapore the Chinese element now
predominates. Singapore, Nanyang, and Malaya universities may not
as yet, either singly or in combination, constitute a top-flight institution
of high international prestige. On the other hand, they do provide the
emerging Federation of Malaysia with such varied and extensive university facilities that at the very moment of its birth, the nation may already be approaching the take-off point in higher education.

CHAPTER
X

THE MALAYANIZATION OF PENANG

September 15, 1962

The island of Penang, from the time of its peaceful acquisition
in 1786 from the Sultan of Kedah by the British East India Company,
has stirred many sober persons to flights of rhetoric. "Penang rivals
anything that has been fabled of the Elysian Fields," wrote Mr. J. John-
son in The Oriental Voyager (1807). "The brightest jewel in the impe-
rial diadem" is the way the British residents liked to describe it. "Dear
Penang," wrote America's Townsend Harris in his Journal on May 21,
1855, "a part of the primeval Paradise not altered at the Flood: here,
an everlasting spring reigns; fresh flowers scent the air on each morning . . . . It is a land of delight, and the people are simple, warm hearted
and hospitable."

Penang, to be sure, has also occasioned its periods of misgiving.
One of them was on October 28, 1914, when the German raider "Emden"
paid a sudden call and sank a Russian cruiser and a French torpedo boat
in Penang Harbor. Another was on December 9, 1941, when the Japanese
dropped enough bombs to shake not only Penang but even those Singapore
pillars of empire who nonetheless went right on declaring, although with
slightly less conviction than before, that Singapore itself was impregnable. Another was in mid-1957, when the Federation of Malaya was preparing for independence and the Crown Colony of Penang was preparing
to join it. As a wealthy Chinese island city-state, a colonial enclave, and
a free port, Penang lived by entrepôt profits which were dependent not
only upon Malay tolerance but upon Indonesian caprice. Many of its leading citizens were split between Anglophilia and Malayaphobia; its lower
elements, including some obstreperous Chinese students, were spoiling
for riots. But Penang in 1962, five years after merger, is more prosperous than ever before in its history and if not more tranquil, certainly
more exciting.

As Malaya prepares to be transformed into Malaysia, and as not

just Penang but Singapore too prepares to join, it seems a useful exercise to draw the parallel between the situation of Penang five years ago
and that of Singapore today, and even further, to extrapolate from the
Penang situation today some conjecture regarding that of Singapore five
years hence. In 1957, then, there were many who predicted that Penang
would experience political deterioration or eclipse, economic depression, and race riots when it attempted to merge with the Federation,
and that the Federation itself would be weakened by involvement in these
miseries. In 1962 there are many who predict that Singapore will experience political disruption, economic dislocation, social disequilibrium
—some say if it does, although most, to be sure, now say if it does not,
join the Federation of Malaysia. The Federation itself, conversely, may
be critically weakened if it assumes Singapore's problems—or if it does
not. The parallel obviously is not exact, and analogy proves nothing.
Nevertheless, the experience in merger of one Overseas Chinese island
city-state may have some relevance to the experience of another.

        The most conspicuous outward sign of Penang's change in status
when it ceased to be a British Crown Colony and became a member of
the Federation of Malaya was the replacement of the British Resident
by a local governor. Penang, of course, had its favorite sons, all of
them Chinese. The Federation government made its own choice: Raja
Tun Uda bin Raja Muhammad, a member of the royal family of the State
of Selangor, English educated, an experienced but retired civil servant,
decidedly an outsider, and a Malay. The appointment, although it is to a
position of little importance save prestige, was a sensitive political issue in Penang at the time. Penang quickly made its adjustment—as
quickly in fact, as Singapore four years ago made its adjustment to the
selection of a Malay from Kuala Lumpur, as Yang di-Pertuan Negara,
replacing the British governor, and could adjust again, no doubt, to a
Federation of Malaysia Malay prime minister.

        The actual administration of Penang state is the responsibility
of the Chief Minister, working with a Legislative Council of seven members, themselves elected from and by a popularly elected 24-member
Legislative Assembly. The present Chief Minister, Dato Wong Pow Nee,
is a Penang Chinese and his deputy, Inche Aziz Ibrahim, is a Penang
Malay. The two are leaders of the Penang branch of the Alliance Party,
a coalition of the Malay (UMNO), Chinese (MCA), and Indian (MIC) parties, which controls the Federation's national government and all but
one of the state governments. The Alliance holds at present a majority of 17 seats in Penang's Legislative Assembly. The opposition,
made up of Socialist Front members and Independents, claims growing
support in the state and accuses the Alliance of dictatorial, communal
(racially-biased), inefficient, and extravagant practices.

```
STATE OF PENANG


                        AREA

        Penang Island          108 sq. mi.
        Province Wellesley     280 sq. mi.

            TOTAL              388 sq. mi.



                    POPULATION

                      Chinese   Malaysian   Indian   Other    TOTAL

George Town           171,272    26,759     32,023    4,876   234,930
Rural Penang Island    58,431    33,933      8,623    2,961   103,968
Butterworth            41,088    56,246     13,269    2,238   110,842
Rural Province Wellesley 56,486  19,143      9,116      648   122,393

   TOTAL State of Penang 327,287 165,081    69,031   10,733   572,132


Note: Figures are from the 1957 census. Discrepancies between components and
      totals are owing to residents of some outlying suburban areas having been
      included in both urban and rural count. Over-all totals are correct.
```

The really flamboyant political conflict on Penang Island is
staged, however, not in the Alliance-dominated State Legislative Assembly but in the Socialist Front-dominated George Town City Council.
The City Council, reflecting the political sympathies of the urban Chinese laboring class, has an Alliance minority of one to the Socialist
Front's majority of fourteen. It has also a Socialist Front mayor,
elected from and by the Council members. Mayor Ooi Thiam Siew,
described by his admirers as "Humble Thiam Siew," was a labor union
leader before he became City Councilor and Mayor, and is a gentleman
who enjoys controversy, the more public and prolonged the better.

Mayor Ooi and the Socialist Front maintain what Chief Minister
Wong and the Alliance term an antigovernment vendetta. Sometimes
the provocation seems petty. The Mayor and the City Council refused,
for instance, to fly flags, drape bunting, or make speeches when Malaya
celebrated the end of the Communist Emergency in 1961. The occasion,
they said, was one not for "merriment" but for "mourning" since laws
were becoming ever more "arbitrary," and regulations ever more "re-
strictive." Sometimes the quarrel seems significant. The City Council, for instance, has long since embarked upon low-cost housing programs for George Town and has appealed to the Federal government
for big loans with which to finance them. The state government, by
failing to support loan requests and by failing also to make necessary
state lands available, has obliquely reprimanded the Council for bypass-
ing approved channels. Furthermore, it has announced similar — the

Council says identical—housing programs of its own. The Council accuses the Assembly of "legislative plagiarism" when occasionally it "awakens" from its "sleeping beauty act"; the Assembly accuses the Council of "juvenile" and "disloyal" behavior and seriously proposes to persuade the Federal government to "scrap" it.

Somehow, despite mutual recrimination, programs eventually are planned and implemented, and harmony occasionally prevails. The Legislative Assembly, for instance, just recently achieved the first unanimous vote in its history when it endorsed a new City Council plan to borrow M$900,000 from the Federal government for one of the disputed housing schemes.

Penang politics immediately evokes national politics and the vigorous effort on the part of a newly coalescing Penang-centered opposition effectively to challenge the Alliance grip upon national, state, and local government. The UMNO-MCA-MIC Alliance has in the past suffered less from the opposition's strength than from its own internal weakness. It has suffered, specifically, from friction between the UMNO (Malay) and the MCA (Chinese) factions and the effort of a rebel element within the MCA to revise the terms of MCA-Alliance co-operation in a manner to decrease UMNO dominance and to enhance MCA prestige. The Alliance has faced its major outside threat in the past from the Pan-Malayan Islamic Party (PMIP), a race- and religion-based party which combines far-leftist with far-rightist politics. The PMIP, which has commanded its strongest following in the less-developed East Coast states, now seems to be experiencing a sharp decline in influence. The Alliance is encountering today what may prove a much more formidable threat on the part of the Socialist Front, a heretofore unstable confederation of the Socialist Party, the Labour Party, and various other left-wing parties and groups in the Federation, especially in Penang, Singapore, and British Borneo. MCA rebels, furthermore, and Independents have begun to cohere in a new Penang-organized United Democratic Party (UDP), which itself shows some slight indications of being willing to co-operate with the Socialist Front.

The UDP and the Socialist Front both claim to be multiracial, anticommunal, and anti-Communist. The Alliance accuses both of being in fact communal in base and of stirring up racial and extremist agitation. It accuses the Socialist Front in particular of intrigue with the Communists and with the "Communist front" Singapore party, the Barisan Sosialis (also, in English translation, the Socialist Front). Since the Labour Party and the UDP both maintain their headquarters in Penang and the Socialist Front is centering more and more of its activities there, Penang rivals Kuala Lumpur as a national—and now a Malaysian—forum.

The nature of the UDP and the Labour Party opposition is likely to be obscured rather than clarified by any brief summary of their announced principles or analysis of their actions. Their stand on Malaysia, for instance, is that they approve of the concept in principle but reject the procedure and regard the outcome as a victory for British colonialism and a "sellout" by the Alliance and the PAP. The best introduction to the UDP and the Labour Party is probably an introduction to their leaders.

The founder and chairman of the new UDP is Dr. Lim Chong Eu, a prosperous Penang medical practitioner, a long-time member and onetime president of the MCA. Dr. Lim is the son of a prominent Penang family; he is English educated and philosophically minded, partial to long, rather rambling public and private speeches in polished English in which the arguments are subtle and the conclusions vague. He was regarded a few years ago as one of the most capable and dynamic of the young Chinese political leaders. He was then elected president of the MCA to succeed Malacca's venerable Sir Cheng Lock Tan. He was expected to revitalize the party, to transfer control from the cautious Chinese towkays (wealthy merchants) to the daring younger men who could better stand up against Malay leaders to achieve Chinese rights. At a critical point in the 1959 election campaign, Dr. Lim Chong Eu was shocked to have a major crisis precipitated upon him when the young MCA rebels attempted in his name a fait accompli of take-it-or-leave-it terms to Tengku Abdul Rahman. Dr. Lim at that point experienced a sudden breakdown of health; he resigned the MCA presidency and presently departed on a round-the-world trip. On his return he resumed his practice of medicine and devoted a good deal of spare time to denial of rumors that he was about to form a new party. In April of 1962, just after a new spate of denials, he suddenly announced the formation of the UDP. There are those, like Dr. Lim, who declare that the old MCA is dead and the Alliance derelict; and others, like MCA leader Tan Siew Sin, son of the late Sir Cheng Lock Tan, who say that the UDP is stillborn.

The prime mover of the Labour Party and Joint Secretary of the Socialist Front is Mr. Lim Kean Siew, son of an extremely wealthy Penang family, himself a successful lawyer and a conspicuous Member of Parliament. Mr. Lim is a man of undoubted intellectual brilliance and—when he chooses—of attractive personality. He took double first honors at Cambridge University in law and English literature, thus tying

Singapore's Prime Minister Lee Kuan Yew, who likewise took double
first honors. He has long had the reputation of being a political radical.
His close friends report that upon graduation from Cambridge he would
have gone to Peking to teach but was unable to get an entry visa. His
brother, in case this is relevant (as his political supporters deny), is
a prominent left-wing leader who has for years been on the Singapore
black list. His wife is an American citizen. She is the organizer of a
new sociological research institute which now publishes in Singapore
a magazine of political as well as sociological significance.

Mr. Lim Kean Siew has the reputation of being the one Chinese
politician whom the ordinary Malay admires and trusts. He defends
the special Malay rights which most Chinese oppose. He proposes, however, to extend these rights to "the masses of Malay fishermen, farmers, and laborers," not just to the "rich and privileged" who, he says,
now monopolize them. He has made it a major point of policy and action to align himself with the Malay Socialist political faction and its
leaders, particularly with Inche Ahmad Bustamam, a Malay politician
of Indonesian origin and Indonesian ultranationalist proclivities and together with Mr. Lim, Joint Secretary of the Socialist Front.

With Dr. Lim Chong Eu and Mr. Lim Kean Siew in residence,
Inche Ahmad Bustamam a frequent visitor, and Mayor Ooi Thiam Siew
making weekly statements that by 1964 the Socialist Front will control
not only the city but also the state and after that the nation, Penang
politics is always a lively show. The current city-state conflict and
the threat of future State-Federation conflict are reminiscent and perhaps also prognostic of Singapore. In 1956 the Singapore City Council
was engaged in a gaudy feud with the Singapore state government; in
1959 this same clique was greatly instrumental in achieving the PAP
victory in state elections; in 1960 the clique and other even more extreme elements split off from the PAP and formed two dangerous opposition groups which have threatened to overthrow the state government.
At the very least they can cause Singapore acute embarrassment in its
relations with Kuala Lumpur, and Kuala Lumpur acute misgivings regarding Singapore.

Penang Island's free port status, which in 1957 seemed a potentially unworkable anomaly, remains unchanged today—the long-standing
imposition of duty on tobacco, liquor, gasoline, and motor vehicles serving as a reminder, however, that even an official "free port" is only relatively and temporarily free in the mid-20th century. Penang is experiencing no serious new difficulties regarding free trade, only variations
and continuation of the old ones and notwithstanding all of them, an unprecedented degree of prosperity.

Penang's trade rose from M$819.1 million in exports and M$551 million in imports in 1957 to M$1,191,300,000 and M$638,900,000 in 1961, its total tonnage rising meanwhile from 1,957,190 to 3,973,159. Its entrepôt trade with Indonesia, the least predictable item on its statistical tables, rose proportionately, Indonesia's stifling export-import regulations serving still to make Penang a port of emergency need that serves nearby Sumatra's government, private, and smuggler purposes.

Penang's rubber exports, dependent in large part upon re-export of Sumatra rubber, experienced a boom last year in spite of a brief crisis brought on by Federal government action taken without due regard for the special situation obtaining in Indonesia. Kuala Lumpur ordered that rubber grown on Penang which had heretofore been exempt from the Federation's export cess, would be subject to that assessment as of January 1, 1962, and that Penang rubber growers would qualify thereafter, as they had not before, for the Federation's cess-financed replanting subsidy. It was necessary, therefore, to determine how much of Penang Island's export rubber was actually Penang grown, and hence subject to the cess. Customs officers ordered that all Penang imports and exports of rubber be delivered, weighed, evaluated, and checked at designated points in the George Town port area. The difference between imports and exports would obviously be the taxable Penang-grown total.

The rubber dealers protested publicly that the inconvenience, delay, and expense of such a procedure would be almost as bad as payment of the cess. At the same time they pointed out privately that the rubber imports originated mainly from Indonesia, and were covered by quite fictitious Indonesian shipping papers. Any public record of the true amount and value of the shipments would lead to Indonesian government retaliation against the shippers and demands for refund of a generous share of the hard currency proceeds. Shipments of Indonesian rubber, in actual fact, dried up at the mere prospect of weighing and evaluating in Penang customs. The upshot of the matter was a reasonable settlement whereby Penang rubber growers and Malayan customs authorities agreed merely to estimate the approximate amount of Penang-grown rubber and to arrange payment of cess on that amount. The import-export trade has now been resumed without tedious customs formalities.

Penang's tin trade and its tin smelting industry, continue also to benefit from Indonesian government inability to deal effectively with its own economic problems. The Indonesian government has attempted to alter the whole pattern of its exports of tin as of other commodities and has proposed also to set up its own tin smelters. To date, it has failed to do either. It has been impelled, therefore, as an emergency measure, to ship increasing quantities of Bangka tin to Penang for smelting and re-export. No one really expects the arrangement to last, but while it lasts, Penang's tin smelters, like its rubber mills, enjoy quite a welcome volume of business.

Free port status raises other problems. The increasing number of small George Town manufacturers—processors of meat, fish, and fruit—would like, naturally, to enjoy the best of two worlds. They want to combine duty-free import of factory supplies and equipment with duty-free export of products to Malaya's protected markets. Federal officials point out that eventually, and why not soon, Penang must make some major readjustments. Minister of Finance Tan Siew Sin, has formally proposed that Penang voluntarily forgo island-wide free port status and create a small bonded area instead. Penang's response has been unenthusiastic, since everyone knows that in the rest of the Federation there is a 20% tax on virtually everything and that living costs but not wages are higher.

Penang's prosperity today remains linked to its free port status and to its long experience in providing shipping, warehousing, banking, insurance, and various merchandising services to its neighbors. Save for its tin smelters and its rubber mills, both now greatly dependent on Indonesia, it has not had any very rewarding experience with industry. A new fisheries company operating as a joint Penang Chinese (51%) and Japanese (49%) venture has been experimenting since February 1960 with four 100-ton to 150-ton Japanese fishing boats which operate out of Penang, process the catch in two local canning plants, and are attempting to build up a profitable local and foreign market for its product of about 7,000 cases of tuna per month. Company officials and local residents report indifferent results to date. The company is proceeding with an expansion program which involves acquisition of four to ten ships of up to 300 tons each and installation of its own storage and processing facilities, but no one is very sanguine about prospects.

The State of Penang's really important economic development seems slated for the Butterworth-Prai area on the mainland just opposite George Town, already included, as is the rest of Province Wellesley, within the Federation customs area. At Prai the government is developing new port, rail, road, and industrial facilities in anticipation that George Town's capital and enterprise will find room for expansion onto the mainland and that foreign enterprise will either lead or follow.

The Penang economic experiment since 1957 suggests that Singapore's economic well-being, just as practically everyone says, lies in merger with Malaya. It suggests also, however, that the problems of free port status, common market, industrialization of Singapore Island, and others which now seem critical, may not, after all, demand swift and decisive resolution. Singapore, like Penang, may find the answers, if any, to its long-range economic problems not in intensive new development of the island but by expansion onto the mainland—a proposal which the adjacent State of Johore, for instance, is not at this point prepared to welcome.

Social development in Penang between 1957 and 1962 has been marked by no readily discernible achievement in merging and blending of social and racial strata. Neither, however, has it been marked by any single outbreak of social or racial conflict. Penang has continued with development of the social program in which it has traditionally specialized and in which it seems likely to specialize even more in the future: education. Already the site of some of Malaya's oldest, biggest, and best secondary schools, Penang was selected five years ago as the site of the pioneer Malayan Teacher Training College. It is nominated today as the site of a proposed University of Malaya branch institution which its more enthusiastic local proponents hope will develop into a full-scale university.

Penang's most famous school is the Penang Free School, generally conceded to be the best secondary school in Malaya, the alma mater of an impressive number of local leaders, including Tengku Abdul Rahman. In the last few years, Penang Free School has expanded and progressed in keeping with its tradition. It now registers more boys than ever before, including an increasing percentage of Malays, but it has to turn away as many qualified candidates as it accepts. Mission schools, both Catholic and Protestant, are equally flourishing and congested, and like the Free School, attract students not only from Penang but also from all parts of the Federation.

The big Chinese high schools have been in the past the focus of much of Penang's social and political problems. In 1957 they were the scene of Communist-inspired student strikes and riots. In more recent times they have been the center of vigorous resistance to government proposals to impose certain academic controls which seemed to a great part of the Chinese community seriously to jeopardize the preservation of Chinese culture. Today, the schools have accepted the controls— along with the subsidies which the government was shrewd enough to attach to them. The schools have graduated or retired the superannuated students who were professional agitators. They now seem to be competing with each other not in putting out protests, as in the past, but in putting up bigger, showier buildings to accommodate the bicycle-riding relays of students who congest Penang's traffic.

The distinctively Malay schools remain today, as they have been in the past, inferior to the other Penang schools in physical and academic facilities. As a result both of new official encouragement and of new private initiative, the Malay schools are now beginning to build up fast. An increasing number of Malay students, furthermore, are attending the non-Malay schools and some of their records will bear comparison with those of the Chinese.

The Malayan Teacher Training College is Penang's most significant new educational departure. The college, which is located on a scenic hillside outside George Town, was built a few years ago with a M$6 million grant from the British Colonial Development Fund. It has modern classrooms, offices, laboratories, dormitories, faculty residences, a theater, a sports field, also special facilities for training in domestic science, arts, and crafts. It is financed by Federal government funds and administered by a British principal working with a combined British and local staff and most recently, one American Peace Corps member. The school enrolls some 360 students of Malay, Chinese, and Indian race; it gives them a two-year training course to prepare them for higher primary and lower secondary level teaching. All students receive free tuition, room, and board, plus a monthly allowance of M$75. They undertake in return to serve as government teachers for at least three years on monthly salaries that will start at about M$300.

The college has been faced with some ticklish if not, from the outsider's point of view, any very critical problems, not all of them strictly educational. One has been that of cuisine. The school has to cater to four different dietary systems—Muslim Malay, Chinese, Indian vegetarian, and general. It was confronted early on with a demand on the part of the Malay students that the cooks refrain from cooking or serving pork on the premises. The demand has been met by voluntary abstention from pork on the part of all concerned, pork-hungry Chinese included.

The history of the Penang experiment between 1957 and 1962 also suggests that just as Penang itself looked with undue apprehension upon the prospects of merger with the Federation—apprehension which many in the Federation shared—so too apprehensions regarding merger of Singapore, whose problems are bigger but similar to those of Penang, may be unduly exaggerated. Singapore, like Penang, has already become the center of a strong and even dangerous political opposition but may still be able to carry on peacefully and constructively, as a Federation member. It may find economic development not just less spectacular than it hopes but less difficult than it fears. It may find Malayanization of its Chinese population and transformation of all others through education and similar devices producing not so much a new sense of identity, as might be hoped, but a new sense of respect for the identity of others which may prove almost as good.

This paradisiacal Penang outlook on Singapore's prospects is not one which is likely to recommend itself automatically to the Southeast Asia observer conditioned to expect only deterioration. There is plenty of evidence to be collected today that Singapore's troubles are really bad and swiftly worsening, that Malaya next door—including Penang—is far less happy than it seems on the surface, and that British Borneo is due for typhoons. Nevertheless, a new Federation of Malaysia, including Singapore, just like a new Federation of Malaya five years ago, including Penang, seems to be what the stockbrokers call a growth, not a speculative, issue—and like any other growth issue, not to be left for long periods without re-examination.

50916

CHAPTER
XI

THE MODERNIZATION OF PENANG

September 21, 1962

Penang Island manages to combine something of Singapore's
traditional drive, Kuala Lumpur's calm, Malacca's charm, Hong Kong's
scenery, and Hawaii's social climate as a South Seas melting pot.   It
has always been a bit remote and generally more than a bit neglected
and has never entertained any very grandiose concept of its own importance.   It has been the milieu of colonial officials who generally
felt themselves on the road down, not up; of not a few Malay, Thai, and
Javanese royalty who knew that pleasant as might be their exile, it was
also permanent; of Chinese towkays who rather doubted whether they
really did want many more millions; of British businessmen who decided to mark time and retire on the spot; not to mention its ordinary
Chinese and Indians, tirelessly industrious, and its ordinary Malays,
traditionally presumed to be indolent, whose general behavior did little
to disabuse their detractors.   Penang all the same had plenty of what
19th-century visitors called "grit" and "pluck," and then as now a business deal could, if absolutely necessary, intrude upon tea or cricket.

Penang, then, never really aspired very high, but its aim was
good and it generally hit the mark.   The mark, for better than a century, ever since Penang gave up its rather forlorn notion of competing
with Singapore, has been to live up to its billing as Empire's Brightest
Jewel, now Federation's Precious Gem, the "Emerald" and "Holiday"
Isle, "Paradise of the Far East" and "Free Port Entrepôt," featuring
sandy palm-shaded beaches, cool scenic hills, temples, mosques, and
churches, along with tax-free watches and cameras.

Survival even as a paradise isle naturally means also keeping
in step with progress.   Without being heavy-footed about it, Penang is
marching steadily onward.   There are those who would alter the pace
and the direction and tamper more and more drastically with the backdrop, but the first reaction of the ordinary visitor to Penang today is

to wonder why. The reasons, few of them compelling, however, may in fact occur to anyone who goes beyond the tourist circuit of the capital city of George Town into the island's rural area, and onto the mainland stretch of Province Wellesley.

Province Wellesley, which few visitors bother to explore, is a narrow 45-mile strip of mainland leased to the East India Company in 1800 by the Sultan of Kedah in consideration of an annual payment of M$10,000 for Penang and Province Wellesley. In 1800 merely an under-populated tract of seacoast swamp and jungle, Province Wellesley today is planted almost solid with rice, coconuts, and rubber. It is so intensively developed, in fact, that the state is at a loss for new land to open up for its growing population and has to export its surplus farmers to other states.

The northern part of Province Wellesley forms a segment of the Kedah-Perlis "rice bowl," the richest of Malaya's few stretches of land suitable for rice farming. In recent years this part of Province Wellesley has been the scene of a major drainage and irrigation project, undertaken both to extend the scope of the paddy fields and to permit double cropping. Bridges, dams, canals, pumping stations, and other installations give visual support to recent statistical claims that Province Wellesley's rice production has doubled, tripled, and quadrupled since the project started. Delegations of visitors from British Borneo now come to view Malaya and to preview Malaysian prospects. What they see generally persuades them that with more projects like this one—some are already under way—the Malaysia of the future can grow as much rice as it consumes.

The urban center of Province Wellesley, just opposite George Town, is the town of Butterworth and the adjacent area of Prai. On the seacoast, just north of Butterworth, is located a Royal Australian Air Force base. This installation has as yet given rise to very little of the familiar controversy about Western bases on Eastern soil. It has recently featured, however, in a maneuver which raises a very delicate question. British bases in the new Malaysia, according to recent understanding, may not be used for SEATO purposes. In early June of this year RAAF planes from Butterworth took off to join SEATO forces in Thailand. The question arises whether such an action, involving not the actual use of local bases but the transfer of forces from them, will constitute in the future a violation of the agreement.

Just south of Butterworth, in the Prai area, the Penang state government is engaged in a complex economic development scheme.

At a cost of M$1.8 million, it is clearing and filling 320 acres of land, most of it at present mangrove swamp, and providing all the facilities and utilities which should serve to attract local and foreign industry. The expectation is that this Prai project will rival the Petaling Jaya development outside Kuala Lumpur, which in the last five years has proved spectacularly successful. At a cost of an additional M$50 million, the government is proposing to build by 1970 six new deep-water berths capable of handling one million additional tons of cargo each year and adding a good 25% to the present capacity of Penang Port. When and if the project is complete, Penang will be able to maintain its position in relation to its new rival, Port Swettenham, 150 miles to the south, where three new deep-water berths are being completed this year with US$10 million in American aid. The Federal government, meanwhile, is building a new railway center at Prai and plans to build a new highway to connect Prai with the as yet underdeveloped East Coast of the Malay Peninsula. The indirect results of these development plans are beginning to be apparent in the Butterworth-Prai region—new industrial establishments such as a foam rubber factory and a biscuit factory, new godowns, new shops and offices, and lots of new homes.

Stretching southward from Butterworth are rich rubber estates which peter out in the Nibong Tebal region into small-holder plantings of rubber and copra. Some 13,000 of these Chinese- and Malay-owned plots suffer from poor maintenance and poor drainage and are seriously threatened by coastal erosion. The government has now undertaken the construction of a 21-mile sea wall, plus auxiliary draining, road building, and replanting programs, together with other miscellaneous projects such as school building, midwifery centers, low-cost housing, power lines and water mains adequate for the needs of the area's 75,000 population. The new Nibong Tebal developments are matched by widely scattered developments elsewhere in Penang state.

The trip from Butterworth to Penang Island is a scenic cruise by fast car ferry across the two-mile channel. To the east rise the low hills of the mainland, and to the northeast is the 3,978-foot Kedah Peak, the landmark of many generations of sailors. At anchor in the channel lie a dozen or more big freighters, often including Russian vessels loading rubber. Dead ahead are the green hills of Penang on which one can discern the vacation bungalows of Penang Peak, the course of the cable car, and the pagoda of the rococo Ayer Hitam Chinese temple. George Town comes into focus as a row of two- and three-story buildings on the water front, half a dozen taller bank and office buildings beyond, a fine new ferry terminal, and most conspicuous of all, the new

M$3.2 million 13-story government building featuring much aluminum, glass, and a gaudily colored façade.

At close range from the ferry landing, George Town looks rather like an older China coast port. The water front is cluttered with hundreds of junks and small craft which, if the tide is low, rest on an evil-smelling mud flat. The water front is lined with commercial buildings. It is populated mainly by yellow-, brown-, and black-skinned dockworkers, their bodies gleaming with sweat as they haul bundles or bales or squat alongside the vendors' stands eating rice or noodles.

A three-minute drive from the ferry landing brings the visitor to another George Town. At one end of the northern sea-front esplanade stand the well-preserved walls of Fort Cornwallis, named for a general whose later Indies record was rather more successful than his American. Across the parade ground under huge rain trees stand Victorian-style city government buildings. If it is early evening, hundreds of the city's Malay, Chinese, Indian, and British inhabitants will be strolling along the sea wall, enjoying the breeze and the sunset and sampling the snacks offered by the hawkers.

The fine Penang residential district lies to the west, stretching a couple of miles along the coast and a mile inland. The approach passes more big old government buildings, the graceful Doric facade of old St. George's Church, an assortment of schools, hotels, car dealers, and the cemetery where lie buried generations of Penang's British residents, among them founding father Captain Francis Light (d. 1794). The residential area is one of splendid trees and of British and Chinese mansions set in broad gardens an acre or more in extent. The classical colonial house, of which Penang has hundreds, is an airy, spacious two-story structure whose immense windows and galleries can be shuttered against the noonday glare. The ground floor is given over to reception and dining rooms; while the drawing room, on the second floor, is built out over the porte-cochere, opened wide morning and evening to catch the breezes. Whereas this extraordinarily comfortable and elegant colonial style has been aptly described as "tropicalized Regency," the Chinese mansion is more likely to be vaguely Victorian and of semi-Newport dimensions. It features much stonework, stucco bas-relief, ironwork, marble, crystal, tile, redwood, stained glass, and 19th-century Italian statuary. It can be quite handsome.

To the northwest of the old Penang residential area, along the hilly coastal road facing Kedah Peak, stretch the new suburbs, whole hillsides of efficiently bulldozed modern real-estate developments built for air conditioning, not for shaded breeze-cooled comfort. The standard model is a three-bedroom, two-bath, ranch-rambler number, its outer and interior walls preferably painted in raw, contrasting colors. The package is complete with fully equipped modern kitchen, carport, and just enough garden space for a hibiscus or croton bush or two. It is built to sell fast at US$7,500 to US$15,000 on a 15-year easy-payment plan. The new suburbs blend and alternate with week-end cottages and resort centers along the sandy beaches, and Penang's ten-mile northern coast drive, once a miniature Corniche, is rapidly being beset by the jukebox and transistor blight.

South of George Town's residential area lies the main part of the city. Street after street is lined with two- and three-story "shophouses," the ground floor given over to small industry or trade, the top floors serving as family quarters. The covered arcaded "five-foot way"—the sidewalk—usually serves more as overflow space for the shops and small industries than for foot traffic. Interspersed among the blocks of shophouses are a phenomenal number of Chinese temples and guildhalls, a few Indian temples, and an occasional mosque. There are also an increasing number of large modern buildings designed for banks, offices, hotels, and apartments. The area was overcrowded 50 years ago and is packed even more tightly today. Indeed, parts of the older town seem literally to have sunk under the sheer weight of its population for the gurgle and smell of high tides rise from gutters many blocks from the water front. The city is confronted with a major need for slum clearance. It has recently made a beginning by the construction of a few blocks of low-cost flats (rental about M$20 per month) in what has for many decades been the most impoverished and most crime-ridden Chinese market area.

Along the water front to the southeast, beyond the junk anchorages and repair yards, are to be found the more important of the urban Malay kampongs, collections of shacks of wood, bamboo, and thatch. The shacks and their rickety plank connecting runways are supported on stilts above the reeking tidal flats or over marshy land which floods with every rainstorm. These Malay kampongs are squalid beyond belief for being located near the heart of a major modern city which, for all its congestion, is elsewhere basically clean and usually sightly. The very existence of the kampongs is evidence that the Malay sector of the urban population is lagging dangerously. Government programs of rehabilitation for this Malay community have been as yet slow and inadequate, having bogged down in political and jurisdictional disputes between the City Council and the State Legislature.

Four years ago the City Council initiated a program to rehabilitate Kampong Selut, one of the worst of these areas. In Kampong Selut live 209 Malay families, totaling 1,260 persons, with family incomes averaging M$100-M$150 per month. The city purchased the property for M$212,681 from the owners, a British business firm. It ran up two rows of low-cost housing, a total of 24 family units. It proposed to move a group of families from their old homes into the new units, demolish their derelict shanties, build modern replacements, move the displaced families into the new quarters, and repeat the cycle until the whole site was cleared and rebuilt. There arose, however, a long series of unanticipated difficulties.

Government and tenants could not agree upon a fair system for selecting which families should move first. In any case, the prospective tenants decided that they disliked the design of the new houses— they were not the detached Malay-style houses, raised on stilts, but the ground-level, brick-walled, cement-floored row houses favored by the Chinese. Occupancy turned out to entail payment of rent and of electricity and water bills. Additional government funds to continue the project were not forthcoming. Consequently, most of the new houses have stood empty for the last four years while the project has been debated again, replanned and refinanced. The City Council has just recently been granted a Federal government loan of M$900,000 to get the project going again. This time, the plan is to build Malay-style houses to be sold at M$20-M$30 per month on a 15-year payment plan and to keep with the program until it is actually completed.

If major areas of George Town itself prove on close inspection to be overcrowded and depressed, if not downright slum areas, the city does enjoy conspicuous amenities: a tremendous general hospital, and a dozen or more other big hospitals, clinics, and dispensaries; dozens of public and private schools; many well-run markets; adequate transportation, electric power, and water supply, all being constantly improved and enlarged. To the water system, for instance, the city is adding new reservoirs and pipelines calculated to meet the needs of the population ten years hence. It has recently installed, among many other improvements, a new underwater pipeline to carry fresh water to the leper colony on the off-lying island of Jerejak. The city transportation fleet has just been fully converted from trackless trolleys to diesel buses. To the hospital facilities have been added such embellishments as a snake serum laboratory. Here, poisonous land and sea snakes are kept and milked; the venom is flown off to Melbourne to be processed into a newly developed serum, some of which is then flown back to Penang to treat the occasional fisherman or swimmer who encounters one of Penang's lethal water snakes, the ular selempat, or the person who blunders into a cobra or viper, statistically a total of about 60 patients per year.

Beyond George Town lies rural Penang, bits of it reminiscent of the early days when a few British and Chinese owned great estates on which they grew nutmeg and cloves for the European markets, supervising operations from comfortable estate houses, at least one of them quite the equivalent in size, beauty, and landscaping to a stately home of rural England. Of the great houses only a few wrecks and ruins remain, and of the original properties only a few small patches are now planted in spices, although clove is now being replanted with new stock under government subsidy of M$5 per tree. Most of the old estate land is given over to housing or institutional development. A British barracks, for instance, occupies a whole hillside at Glugor, one of the finest of the old estates; the Malayan Teacher Training College occupies another. Both command splendid views of the seacoast, the shipping channel, the small islands, and mainland Province Wellesley.

Most of rural Penang is given over not to large-scale foreign or Chinese developments but to small-holder Chinese, Chinese Malay, and Malay settlements and tracts of rubber, copra, and spice plantation. Most picturesque and at the moment the most significant are some of the small Malay fishing villages built in what have been until recently the most out-of-the-way parts of the island and the most neglected. What is now happening at the fishing village of Telok Kumbar may be indicative of a new spirit stirring in rural Malay Penang.

In or near Telok Kumbar on the southeastern shore of Penang Island the government has undertaken the following construction projects: a recently completed 1,000-foot fishing jetty costing M$150,000; a M$4,000 "fisherman's halting bungalow," soon to be started; a small belachan (fish paste) processing plant, soon to be started; widening and straightening of an old road leading from the main highway some few miles along the coast to the remotest fishing settlement of the region, a project on which construction is now well advanced. The government also contemplates a low-cost public-housing program to provide new homes for some of the fishing families, a good 25% of whom already own neat and attractive little Malay houses. No school is being built, incidentally, for existing school buildings are adequate for the present population.

The catalogue above does not exhaust the list, and similar projects are being undertaken for other fishing villages. Mere enumeration

of projects does not suffice, of course, to appraise them.   There is
ground to argue, as many do, that the long-range prospects of the fishing industry do not justify the big outlay of funds, that the villages were
already adequately served by the existing road, and that the fisherman
today might find better employment for his spare time than joy riding
along the new blacktop on his new motor scooter.   The fact remains
that along with other improvements the government is operating a fisheries training and research station nearby which may instill new incentive along with new skills.   At the station, Japanese experts are helping
trainees in modern fishing methods, and a Canadian Chinese biologist on
FAO assignment has made a scientific breakthrough that may prove of major importance.   He has succeeded in breeding, under controlled conditions,
a gigantic and luscious local prawn which may one day populate every paddy
field and enrich every dinner table.   Accomplishments like this, some are
confident, will someday, somehow, add up to a greatly improved life for
the Malay fisherman and rice farmer and for everyone else.   If there is a
somewhat extravagant do-everything-for-everybody approach now, the nation can afford it; better, perhaps, actually to go to work on a pragmatic
basis now than to wait for all the theoretical analyses to be reanalyzed.

The real vantage point from which to view Penang is from the as-
cent to 2,270-foot Penang Peak.   Here, from a comfortably trundling cable car, one can look out over George Town, the channel, and the mainland.
The view is the most splendid perhaps in all of Malaya, and the air is
cool and invigorating.   The spectacle is one of almost unmarred peace,
progress, prosperity—and beauty.   It is also a spectacle of change, but
not so swift a change as to upset all calculations and to deface the landscape.   True, according to present government plans, it will not be many
more years before a road will lead up to the peak and a new residential
area, perhaps including a new university campus, is laid out on the hillside.   Quite a lot of unsightly bulldozing and construction may soon be going on and quite a lot of traffic may soon be roaring along the road.   But
it is going to take quite a lot of concrete, tasteless modern bungalows,
diesel fumes, and picnic litter really to spoil Penang Peak or Penang Island, and neither British, Chinese, Indian, nor Malay is now attempting
by political devices deliberately to spoil it for the other.

If anywhere the process of gradual revolution is to have a chance
of success, that is, if orderly amelioration of serious social, economic,
and political difficulties can forestall an outbreak of violence, Penang appears to be one of the most hopeful experiments.   Although Penang is far
from being typical of Southeast Asia as a whole, it is typical of much of Malaysia; and it is one of the spots where it is easy—and hence, perhaps, delu-
sive—for the observer to focus mainly upon evidences of progress.

CHAPTER
XII

THE PANGKOR EXPERIMENT

September 22, 1962

        Pangkor Island, a half-hour's ferry ride into the Strait of Ma-
lacca from the river mouth port of Lumut, Perak, conveniently encap-
sulates almost all Malaysia's problems. Into its six square miles of
land, Pangkor crowds over 8,000 people. They live in two small Chinese towns, one Indian settlement, and numerous Malay kampongs.
They earn their living by tending a lot of shops, a few acres of rubber
and coconut, and one important industry—sea fisheries. In simplified
miniature Pangkor runs the gamut of Malaysia's races, religions, and
cultures; its political, economic, and social stratifications and tensions;
its urban agricultural dichotomy; even its international relations.

        Three years ago Pangkor Island was the scene of a short-lived
race riot which served as a preview of what might happen throughout
the area if Chinese Malay animosities flared into violence. The riot
served also as a test of the determination of police, military, and other
official agencies to take the vigorous measures necessary both to restore order, as they did after some delay in arrival, and to prevent re-
currence, as they are now doing, with some little diffusion of effort.
Pangkor Island three years later is an example of a government program
of community rehabilitation and reintegration such as is being undertaken throughout much of rural Malaysia to remove the sources of potential conflict, particularly the economic and social handicap of the
Malays in relation to the Chinese. The example is one which leaves
still in doubt the proposition whether the program is either quite appropriate or adequate to the need.

        The 5,890 Chinese, 1,322 Malays, and 191 Indians of Pangkor
Island[1] are dependent primarily upon fisheries for their living. Many

------

[1] 1957 census. The population presumably is increasing at a rate
of 3.3% per year.

of the Chinese combine fisheries with trade; the Malays, with agriculture; and the Indians, with day labor. The Chinese operate the powerboats; the Malays, the one- or two-man canoes; the Indians, the inshore dragnets.   The Chinese, who also monopolize the buying, processing, and selling of fish, obviously have by far the best of the deal. But this season no one is happy. The catch has been almost unprecedentedly large, but the price has dropped to the point where it is sometimes not worthwhile for the fisherman to put out to sea—even though the ordinary Malay fisherman hopes for no more than M$3.00 for a good 30-pound catch.

The present crisis in the Pangkor fisheries industry is just one variant of the problems which occur every year or two—sometimes too many fish, sometimes too few, sometimes too much trouble with poachers from nearby areas, sometimes too far to travel to the best fishing waters. The situation today, which is basically a failure of long-range effort to co-ordinate supply and demand, seems particularly deplorable because it recurs after certain important remedial measures have already been taken. The government has undertaken in the past few years, not only for the benefit of the people of Pangkor Island but for some 50,-000 other Malayan fishermen scattered among some 350 coastal villages, to improve collection, processing, storage, transportation, and marketing facilities. It has attempted also to encourage fishing co-operatives so that the little man—particularly the Malay—can compete on more favorable terms with the big, wealthy Chinese operator.

In some areas of Malaya—on the East Coast, for instance—the combination of government and private effort seems to have made the fisheries industry far sounder than before. On Pangkor Island, too, the fishing fleet has now been expanded; equipment has been improved; several new processing plants have been opened; an old ice plant has been enlarged and a new one built. Local communications, including shipping service to the mainland, have been improved, one contributing factor being the completion by the government of a new jetty. But somehow—nobody can or will say quite why—all this has not added up to an answer.

On Pangkor today there is a glut of locally worthless fish; in the urban markets of the Federation, while there is no shortage of fish, there is most certainly no excess of either fresh or processed fish irresistibly priced for the ordinary consumer. Frozen and canned fish and other sea food from abroad, meanwhile, continue to command good markets both at the luxury and the austerity levels. Nearby Indonesia, an important but fickle market, has once again clamped the door closed on imports from Pangkor, and no substitute foreign outlet has been found. Under the circumstances, it is difficult to say just what has not been done which should have been done, or vice versa, especially since economic surveys show that the Pangkor deep-sea fishing industry is the most efficient in Malaya—perhaps at the moment just too efficient for its own good.

Local government officials think that development of fisheries co-operatives would do a lot to improve the Pangkor fisheries situation. That would not solve the problem of supply and demand, however, and in any event on Pangkor Island the co-operative idea has not caught on. Generous government loans, equipment, and advice are available, but so far no real co-operative organization has appeared. The commonest explanations, whether true or false, are equally unfortunate: (1) that the Chinese towkays have unscrupulously obstructed the plan; and (2) that the Malay fishermen cannot be bothered to change or improve their ways.

The Pangkor fisheries industry may yet retrieve itself. It is not alone among island industries, however, in having failed to establish conspicuous advances in the last few years. The minute Pangkor rubber industry is in a sad state despite a generously subsidized, nationwide drive that has been under way for over ten years to achieve 100% re-planting of all old stock with new high-yield trees. Most of Pangkor's rubber trees, some Chinese-, some Malay-owned, all superannuated small-holder property, are badly tended and unskillfully tapped. A few small plots of land have been or are being cleared and replanted but not according to the most efficient methods. Coconut trees are almost as badly neglected as rubber, although, to be sure, they demand relatively little attention to go right on producing. Of new agricultural crops on the island or improved methods for the scanty fruit and vegetable plant-ings there is no readily discernible evidence.

If neither fisheries nor agriculture signals the dawn of a new day for Pangkor, a remarkable physical transformation of the island is nevertheless already well under way and scheduled for acceleration. For the most part it is the result of government effort. The most note-worthy project is one of road building. Three years ago Pangkor had a single one and a half mile stretch of sandy road leading across the island from the smaller of the two villages to a little beach resort area. Today that stretch is being straightened, widened, and paved. Along the greater part of the seven-mile length of the island, connecting the two East Coast villages and extending beyond each of them, runs a brand new and partially paved road which will presently be extended around the island. Island motor traffic, which consisted three years ago of one semiderelict taxi, has increased to the point where there are at least 30 cars and trucks, dozens of motorcycles and motor scooters.

Most of them are piloted in a manner which emphasizes the utility of
two new island ventures—a driver's school and the beginnings of a
motor and body repair industry.

Along Pangkor's new speedways a new Pangkor exurbia is being
built up. It features a post telephone and telegraph building, a small
Chinese school (the island's third), a small Malay school (the second)
several Chinese guildhalls, and many Chinese shops and homes. Government plans call for construction in the near future of a "subclinic"
to be visited weekly by a doctor from the mainland, a community hall,
and at least two new villages for the Malay fishermen. A privately-
financed electric power plant has been completed and electricity services extended throughout both towns and to some of the outlying houses.
The water supply has been improved by the digging of a couple of dozen
new artesian wells.

All these changes underscore how much remains to be done. The
larger of the Chinese towns is one of the most squalid in the whole of
Malaya. It is one straggling strip of dank little houses and shops set
in badly drained land, the whole town pervaded by the smell of fresh,
dried, and processed fish, the lanes serving also as runs for pigs,
chickens, and ducks. The smaller of the Chinese towns is clean and
spacious by comparison and is favored, not unnaturally, as the site for
new homes and shops. The Indian settlement is much smaller but only
slightly less squalid than the main Chinese village. In the Malay areas,
by contrast, neat little nipa palm huts—some of them new—are set on
stilts under the palm trees, a scene which leads one to the old speculation whether raw new government-built villages are going to make life
more agreeable as they make it more modern.

On Pangkor today the material evidences of a higher standard
of living are already visible. There is a better selection of higher
quality merchandise in more shops than ever before. More people
than ever before, Malays included, are buying not only rice and cooking oil but electric fans, radios, refrigerators, motor scooters, and
motorcars. Increased consumption and construction, however, have
not brought a commensurate increase in local initiative. Nor have they
brought integration. The racial communities still lead their distinct
if sometimes overlapping lives, segregated in effect in homes, schools,
shops, and boats, on the land and on the sea. Social and economic gra-
dations remain sharply contrasted; renewal of race conflict remains
almost as great a hazard as before.

It is dangerous from any brief observation and quick analysis of the Pangkor experiment to draw firm conclusions regarding Pangkor's prospects or the prospects of the Malayan and presently the Malaysian nation as a whole under a rural development program of which Pangkor provides but a glimpse. Nevertheless, a few general observations seem relevant. The Pangkor projects and their counterparts elsewhere were conceived not on the basis of a carefully blueprinted nationwide master plan but as a crash program on a project-by-project basis, adding up in theory to a master plan but in fact to something more like a montage. The individual projects have been developed and implemented by local officials who may or may not be experienced in routine administration but are definitely not experienced in economic development and frequently lack any special ability or drive. The nationwide program is supervised from a military-type command post in Kuala Lumpur. There the major incentive is to keep things rolling and to demonstrate that a bewildering assortment of projects in widely scattered areas is being kept strictly on schedule.

This procedure is to be justified and quite possibly to be applauded in view of the special circumstances obtaining in Malaya. The nation has already enjoyed the advantage of big, blueprinted economic and social developments, including a monster program for the replanting of rubber, others for roads, power, telecommunications, and schools. It is now undertaking equally impressive programs of resettlement, housing, and health. What may be most urgently required at the moment is a huge total of scattered projects to plug the gaps, most particularly to remedy many of the obvious shortcomings of the colonial and Emergency periods, and to bring to the remote little Malay kampong the benefits which all too often stop short at the urban limits. These benefits may well include the training of local officials as well as ordinary local citizens to think, plan, and act for themselves.

The most compelling consideration of all, however, is that the Malay-dominated Alliance Party government of the Federation experienced a major shock in the 1959 elections. The Alliance turned out to be by no means as popular in rural Malaya as its leaders had assumed. It determined, therefore, for political as well as numerous other reasons, to start making deliveries fast on long-promised benefits and to accept the end of the Communist Emergency (July 31, 1960) as the beginning of a new era of national reconstruction. The rural development program, which on Pangkor had the even earlier incentive provided by the 1959 riots, is the result. Rural Malaya is now being offered an opportunity which, whatever the motivations and the shortcomings, is almost unique in Southeast Asia. The question is yet to be answered, and to it Pangkor does not as yet give any clear guidance: will rural Malaya passively accept the benefits or actively compound them?

CHAPTER
XIII

THE STRATEGY AND TACTICS OF MERGER

September 28, 1962

On September 1, 1962, the State of Singapore voted 71% in favor of the PAP government's formula for merger into the prospective Federation of Malaysia. Thus, the September 1 referendum represents a major move closer to realization of the Malaysia plan; a major victory for Singapore's left-wing People's Action Party; a major reinforcement of the government's position vis-à-vis the extreme left wing of the Barisan Sosialis; and a major personal triumph for Prime Minister Lee Kuan Yew. It does not, however, even in the opinion of the most innocently idealistic, constitute a good clean victory for free democratic principles. Rather, it constitutes a very illuminating demonstration of how basically democratic objectives can be achieved, in the face of extremist agitation, by realistic left-wing politicians who recognize, utilize, and counteract standard Communist tactics. Whether unavoidably or unnecessarily tricky—and there is some little debate as to which it was—the conduct of the referendum constitutes a virtuoso performance in counter-Communist one-upmanship.

"I say this without the slightest sense of moral embarrassment," Prime Minister Lee Kuan Yew told the Legislative Assembly when the referendum was over and he was still under attack for a "heads I win, tails you lose" stratagem. "We were meeting cardsharpers and we were not going in like spring chickens."

"A crook for a crook," suggested ex-Chief Minister David Marshall of the Workers' Party, who had publicly denounced the referendum as "dishonest" and "immoral," "an act of political prostitution."

"No. A blow for blow. An intelligent move against another intelligent move," retorted Mr. Lee. He had just referred to Mr. Marshall as a "vestal virgin" wandering through "a brothel area, crying out for the freedom of men and women," and had referred frequently during

THE SINGAPORE NATIONAL REFERENDUM ORDINANCE 1962
(No. 19 OF 1962)
SECTION 18.

A

Saya sokong perchantuman yang memberikan kapada Singapura kuasa oto-nomi dalam perkara buroh, pelajaran dan perkara2 lain yang di-persetujui, sabagaimana yang terkandong dalam Kertas Perentah No. 33, Tahun 1961, dan dengan sendiri-nya warganegara2 Singapura menjadi warganegara2 Malaysia.

我支持合併，星加坡應根據一九六一年所發表講院文件第三十三號白皮書所開列的建議，獲得勞工、教育及其他議定事項的自主權，同畤星加坡公民將自動成為馬來西亞公民。

கூட்டாட்சிக்குப் பட்டினையர். இதுவே தொழில், இ௭க்களவியாளர் துறை, இன்னும் ஒப்புக்கொள்ளப்பட்ட ௧ல்வி, சுயவியர்கள் தைலண்யகூறும் ௧ண்ணா கட்டடேர்கள்........

I support merger giving Singapore autonomy in labour, education and other agreed matters as set out in Command Paper No. 33 of 1961, with Singapore citizens automatically becoming citizens of Malaysia.

Bendera Negara Singapura
新加坡邦旗
சிங்கப்பூர் தேசியக் கொடி
Singapore State Flag

B

Saya sokong perchantuman penoh bersharat bagi Singapura sa-bagai negeri yang sama taraf-nya dengan sa-belas buah Negeri2 Bahagian menurut sharat2 Perlembagaan Persekutuan Tanah Melayu.

我支持全部及無條件的合併，星加坡以一州的地位，根據馬來亞聯合邦的憲法，與其他十一州在平等的基礎上進行合併。

கூட்டாட்சியின் அரசியலமைப்புப் பத்திரங்களுக்கிணங்க மலேயாவின்........

I support complete and unconditional merger for Singapore as a state on an equal basis with the other eleven states in accordance with the Constitutional documents of the Federation of Malaya.

Bendera Negeri Pulau Pinang
檳城州旗
பினாங்கு தேசியக் கொடி
Penang State Flag

C

Saya sokong penyertaan Singapura ka-dalam Malaysia dengan sharat2 yang tidak kurang daripada sharat2 yang di-berikan kapada wilayah2 Borneo.

我支持星加坡加入馬來西亞，條件應不遜於婆羅洲地區所獲予者。

போர்ணியோ பிரதேசங்களுக்கு அளிக்கப்பட்டதை விடவும்........

I support Singapore entering Malaysia on terms no less favourable than those given to the Borneo territories.

Lambang2 atas bendera Sabah dan Sarawak
北婆羅洲及砂勝越旗幟上的徽章
வடபோர்ணியோ சரவாக் கொடி.கௌலஙளின் சின்னம்
Badges on the Flags of North Borneo and Sarawak

This government referendum poster was the basis of an opposition accusation that the

the campaign to the Barisan opposition as "Communists taking orders from the PKI [Indonesian Communist Party]."

We were steam-rollered, said in effect the Barisan Sosialis and the United People's Party opposition, charging that the PAP had won only by raising the "ogre of communism" and resorting to "intimidation." Whoever is right—and only the opposition insists that it is virtuous—the Singapore merger referendum may give some clue to Singapore and Malaysia politics and prospects.

On September 1, 1962, Singapore's 625,000 voters, more than half of them illiterate, were asked—indeed, according to the state's mandatory voting law which imposes a penalty of M$1.75 for noncompliance, they were ordered—to express a preference not for or against merger but for one of three rather complex merger alternatives. They were handed a ballot on which were printed oversimplified explanations in four languages with three flag symbols laid on to load the choice still further. The government had just staged an all-out campaign for Alternative A, to which—at almost the last moment—had been added what might seem to be the clinching attraction: the privilege of Federation citizenship, exactly what almost everyone was hoping for, or said he was hoping for. The opposition had staged an all-out campaign for a blank ballot. It rejected not only Alternative A, but also Alternatives B and C, which had presumably represented opposition preferences; it demanded repudiation of the PAP, of all of the alternatives, and of the referendum itself. But a blank or a spoiled ballot, according to the referendum ordinance, would actually be counted as a vote for merger in accordance with the will of the Legislative Assembly. This "shameful" provision, said the opposition, meant that the blank ballot would count as a vote for Alternative A which, opposition spokesmen thereupon either intimated or admitted outright, was by far the best. No, said the PAP, suddenly adding a new dimension to the uncertainty; if more people voted for B than for A, then the Assembly might vote the blank votes for B. In that case, some 340,000 voters not born in Singapore would lose Federation citizenship rights.

"Trumpery," "treachery," and "treason" were the epithets which some of the more literate and less profane applied to a considerable part of the campaign, and nobody's totalizator could work out the odds. On referendum day, out of Singapore's 625,000 registered voters, 561,-559 showed up at the polls; 377,626 voted for Alternative A; 9,422 voted for B; 7,911 voted for C; 2,370 cast spoiled ballots; and 144,077 cast blank ballots.

Then, after the results were in, the State Legislature debated the referendum all over again and acted out an anticlimax worthy of the crescendo of climaxes which had preceded it. The Prime Minister moved that the blank votes be counted in accordance with the will of the opposition Assemblymen. He challenged them to cast the 144,077 unmarked ballots—or even one of them—in favor of Alternative A, thus to "extend their hand in friendship to the Federation and Borneo" and to save themselves from "blank minds." The Barisan proposed an amendment that the votes be counted as "protest ballots," failed to gain acceptance of the amendment, and thereupon staged a walkout. As the bell began ringing for adjournment, the disposition of the blank votes was still undecided. At this point David Marshall made a stagy exit, and the Prime Minister demanded a vote on few knew quite what. Everyone abstained except United People's Party leader Ong Eng Guan and his one Assemblyman adherent who voted "no."

The battle of the Alternatives was over, but the battle for Merger was not, and little was quite clear except what had been perfectly obvious all along: that most people in Singapore wanted merger on the best possible terms. It had also become fairly clear that quite a lot of people were almost equally as unwilling for the Barisan to dissuade or the PAP to persuade them by specious devices. The PAP had gained a resounding victory, but it had not demonstrated that it could easily win a new general election which may soon be forced upon it. The Barisan had lost an important battle, but it still has the potential to block or to sabotage the actual implementation of merger, to the accompaniment, possibly, of violence. The Singapore public, not one of the more naïve if one of the less literate voting bodies, had been witnesses to and participants in a brilliantly strategized political campaign in which, to borrow the Prime Minister's figure, the government had played politics as an expert practices judo.

Singapore's PAP government had in fact from the very first exploited for its own ends the strength of the big extremist opposition. The PAP utilized the strength of the Barisan and the UPP, each quite capable of instigating riots among Singapore's inflammable labor and Chinese secondary-school organizations, to persuade the Federation of Malaya government first to concede the possibility of merger, then to grant relatively attractive terms, then to improve upon the terms already granted. It used the opposition's strength to work up a degree of British, Federation, and Singapore vigilance against violent outbreak which served to make the strategy of violence unattractive. It used it to convince the Legislative Assembly to pass an ordinance providing for a virtually undefeatable referendum. Then, finally, it used it to

frighten the opposition itself by confronting it with the possibility of its
own blank ballots being counted for Alternative B, which it wanted even
less than Alternative A, forcing it to admit that Alternative A was, in
fact, what the people of Singapore if not of the Barisan and the UPP
wanted. While exploiting the strength of the big extremist opposition,
the PAP also exploited the strength of the small moderate opposition.
It smoked out David Marshall into an unequivocal declaration that Alternative A was in fact fair and workable, that it met all his previous objections, but that he would not vote for it. It netted former Chief Minister Tun Lim Yew Hock and his Singapore People's Alliance into a
brief and unaffectionate PAP-SPA alliance in which the SPA, while con-
demning the PAP, strongly supported the merger referendum and eventually even Alternative A.

To complete its triumph, the PAP need only have accomplished
the really impossible: itself to assume genuine humility in the hour of
its victory. Far more than the strategy and tactics of the PAP, which
almost everybody has to admire if not approve, what really puts people
off about the PAP, even in its hours of adversity, is its arrogance. They
deplore also the contempt and ridicule which its top leaders lavish upon
their opponents, who, to be sure, are never at a loss for expert invective of their own, but rarely, like Prime Minister Lee Kuan Yew, masters of almost equally polished English, Chinese, and Malay.

The arrogance of the PAP and its own insistence upon recognition
of the inspired, indeed, the Machiavellian brilliance of its strategy and
tactics, serves to obscure what may in fact be the most important point
about the merger referendum: that democratic processes were truly if
obliquely at work. The PAP was not required by law to submit the merger
proposals to the electorate at all; yet it did so, and it risked crushing
repudiation if a majority of voters actually had cast blank ballots. The
PAP could have drowned out if not muzzled the debate; but it did not, and
day after day, the opposition spokesmen broadcast through high-decibel
amplifiers in Singapore's equivalent to Hyde Park and everywhere else
whatever political message occurred to it, even going so far as to hint
at violence and to charge treason. The voting could have been fixed;
but in fact the elections procedures were scrupulously honest and even
the most demagogic of the opposition leaders found it profitless to pursue formal charges of falsification. The whole referendum went off so
peacefully and successfully that the question now arises: could not the
same result have been achieved without the fuss about freedom only to
vote "yes," and without leaving behind a residue of hatred?   The answer, practically everyone agrees, although for wildly varying reasons,
is "no." The explanation involves a recapitulation of the major events
leading up to the referendum itself.

*   *   *   *   *

By the time merger negotiations opened in mid-1961, the PAP had been critically weakened numerically by defection of its own extremist elements. It had seen its Legislative Assembly majority of 43 out of 51 members whittled down to a bare majority of 26. It had experienced frightening and humiliating defeat in two important by-elections. It was confronted by sobering evidence that among labor and youth, the two most important and potentially dangerous Singapore activist elements, the Barisan and the UPP, were making increasing headway.

Prime Minister Lee Kuan Yew undoubtedly felt his personal prestige and popularity dwindling by reason of competition and, even more important, vilification on the part of the opposition leaders. He was subject to incessant attack by such ex-PAP colleagues as Lim Chin Siong, the Barisan's labor leader, S. Woodhull, Barisan's theoretician and tactician, and Dr. Lee Siew Choh, Barisan's spokesman—the first two having been detained by the British on grounds of subversion and released on Lee Kuan Yew's own demand. He was subject to constant sniping from ex-PAP Minister Ong Eng Guan, whose United People's Party stronghold is in the most densely populated slums of Singapore's old Chinatown. The Prime Minister and the PAP faced also the opposition of the small but articulate Workers' Party, headed by ex-Chief Minister David Marshall, a flamboyant criminal lawyer; of the Liberal Socialist Party, headed by the crusading welfare-statist, Mrs. Felice Leon-Soh; and of the Party Rakjat, a rather mysterious Malay racial-based party of strong Chinese membership headed nobody knows how or where, for Singapore's Malays almost unanimously favor Malaysia although the Party Rakjat does not. The PAP could depend for support, if at all, and then only fitfully, upon the Workers' Party and upon the Singapore People's Alliance, the latter headed by ex-Chief Minister Tun Lim Yew Hock, upon whom the PAP had heaped abuse in 1959 for being London-, Kuala Lumpur-, and Washington-manipulated. It soon came to the point where it had to depend upon Tun Lim Yew Hock for the decisive vote in the Legislative Assembly.

The PAP, almost everybody said, could just barely maintain itself in government let alone win a new general election, and yet it had promised somehow to take to the people the decision on Malaysia. So when the PAP decided in January upon a merger referendum, the immediate problem arose: how to frame the question or questions? "Do you support the white paper proposals?"[1] would lead inevitably to an opposition referendum campaign on the basis of "Do you support the PAP?" The PAP, arguing that everyone professed to support merger anyhow and that support of the PAP was irrelevant to the major issue, devised the strategy of offering the electorate the choice: "Do you support Alternative A?", i.e., the PAP white paper plan already approved by the Federation; or "Do you support Alternative B?", i.e., the kind of merger demanded by the opposition.

Alternative A, to enumerate its drawbacks, involved surrender of Singapore's right to proportional representation in the new Federal Legislative Assembly in return for semiautonomy in labor, education, and finance; it meant acquisition of less desirable Federation "nationality," rather than Federation "citizenship" status, a distinction which only constitutional lawyers can clarify and then not briefly. The opposition promptly accused the PAP of attempting to palm off "phony merger" and "second-class citizenship" such as would make Singapore a "semicolony" of the Federation of Malaya in accordance with "nefarious" British schemes of "neocolonialism." It demanded instead "full" and "genuine" merger and "first-class citizenship." Its slogans proved much more memorable and exciting than the tame slogans and jingles with which the PAP government loaded Radio Singapore.

The following jingle, broadcast at frequent intervals by Radio Singapore, was equally inspirational in its Malay, Chinese, Tamil, and English versions:

> Unite through merger and we will stand,
> Unite through merger and we will stand,
> Happy and free in one strong band.
> Equal through merger citizens all,
> Equal through merger citizens all,
> Malaysia brings wealth to one and all.

---

[1] I.e., Memorandum Setting Out Heads of Agreement for a Merger Between the Federation of Malaya and Singapore. Cmd [Command paper] 33 of 1961. Presented to the Legislative Assembly by Command of His Excellency the Yang di-Pertuan Negara. Ordered by the Assembly to lie upon the Table: November 15, 1961.

At this point the opposition slipped up. While promoting its de-
nunciations of "phony merger" and "second-class citizenship," it attempted to make a deal with the PAP whereby the PAP would abandon
the merger plan in favor of retention of semicolonial status under the
British. Although the Barisan could and did deny the move, the PAP
had ammunition to use against the Barisan for advocating the very "neocolonialism" it deplored. It also had evidence that the Barisan, for all
its reiterated demands for "full" and "genuine" merger, actually hoped
to block any merger at all, presumably since continued British colonialism would be easier to agitate against than membership in Malaysia.

The opposition also slipped up in becoming too specific about
what it would accept as "full" and "genuine" merger. It cited the example of Penang and Malacca, former crown colonies now absorbed
into the Federation of Malaya. The PAP seized upon the definition and
framed Alternative B as a second choice. It pointed out, however, that
merger in accordance with the Penang and Malacca precedent would
mean that some 340,000 out of Singapore's 625,000 voters—the foreign
born—would have to requalify for citizenship. They had qualified originally for Singapore citizenship under regulations much more lenient
than those in force for citizenship in Malaya; obviously they would now
have to meet the tougher provisions which applied to Chinese in Penang
and Malacca. The opposition, naturally, repudiated Alternative B as a
fair statement of its position, but it was unable to conceal its real
embarrassment.

While the alternatives were being debated, Tun Lim Yew Hock
brought forward the proposal that if Alternatives A and B were offered,
then logic demanded also an Alternative C—merger on the model of
that applied to the Borneo states. The PAP pointed out that it was still
far from clear just what the Borneo model would be, but Tun Lim Yew
Hock was insistent, and the PAP finally accepted his amendment. Practically everyone it seems, overlooked the fact that the Kuala Lumpur
government had never openly or formerly committed itself to accepting
Singapore into the new Federation on any conditions other than those of
Alternative A; the assumption was that B or C would also be acceptable,
but this was only an assumption.

While the alternatives were being debated there arose an even
more animated controversy in which, once again, the Barisan slipped
and slipped badly. The Barisan brought forward the proposal that since
none of the alternatives on the ballot filled the specifications of the
major opposition, all ballots left unmarked by the voters should count
as votes against merger. The Barisan thus revealed what the PAP had

said all along would be its strategy—to sabotage the referendum by in-
ducing people to vote not against merger as such but against any feasible
formula for merger. The PAP proposed, therefore, to reverse the procedure, that is, to have all blank or spoiled ballots count as votes in
favor of merger. The assumption, said the PAP spokesmen, should be
that the voters actually wanted merger, just as everyone said, but being
confused and uncertain about the alternatives, consigned their ballots
in trust to the Legislative Assembly which would vote them for the good
of the state.

Not unnaturally, the debate proved prolonged and stormy. By
acceding to Lim Yew Hock's proposal about Alternative C, the PAP
gained his support on the blank ballot issue, support which it needed
desperately. In the course of the debate, one more PAP member defected, leaving the party one vote short of a majority. Nevertheless,
with SPA support the PAP won a 29-17 victory when the referendum
ordinance was finally put to vote on July 12. On July 13 it won a 24-
16 victory when it defeated a no-confidence motion. Tun Lim Yew
Hock, rising to heretofore unaccustomed heights of wit and urbanity,
took pleasure in tantalizing both the Barisan and the PAP by seeming
first to go along with a vote of no confidence—but on the basis of no
confidence in the PAP government for failure to put restraints upon
"Communist" and "Communist front" leaders "like those of the Barisan Sosialis."

The referendum ordinance was approved, the PAP was reconfirmed in office, and the merger campaign promptly took on a new dimension. The opposition of the extreme and of the moderate left came
together in a Council of Joint Action which appealed to the United Nations Committee on Colonialism. Prime Minister Lee Kuan Yew, paus-
ing only long enough to redeploy the PAP and to castigate the opposition,
took off in mid-July to defend himself in New York, where he satisfied
the UN Committee that the Singapore referendum was a domestic issue
quite within his competence to handle. From New York he proceeded
to London, where the British and the Malayan representatives were
working out the last details of the Malaysia plan, particularly with regard to transfer of sovereignty of Sarawak and North Borneo.

In London Prime Minister Lee Kuan Yew achieved a penultimate
victory which quite overshadowed the other achievement of the conference. The British and Malay officials had already hurdled a few "crises"
which, according to official and press reports, threatened to "wreck"
the Malaysia plan. Few onlookers, to be sure, could take these crises
very seriously in comparison, say, with concurrent crises over Laos,

Vietnam, Burma, Irian Barat—and Singapore. The negotiators had worked out their major differences, which concerned the timing of transfer of the Borneo states and the retention of British colonial officials for an interim period. They had agreed upon transfer of sovereignty by August 31, 1963, then an indeterminate transition period for readjustment of administration and retention for an indefinite period of "as many of the expatriate [British] officials as possible." Lee Kuan Yew then appeared upon the scene with what seemed to almost everybody like the far more serious crisis of Barisan and UPP determination to wreck the merger referendum. Whether it was Lee Kuan Yew's importunity, Federation generosity, British pressure, general apprehension over Barisan-UPP strength, or all factors combined which turned the tide, Lee Kuan Yew gained a major concession, one which everyone at the conference, with only slightly concealed satisfaction, called a "secret trump card."

"Federation citizenship" rather than "Federation nationality" was the "trump" which Lee Kuan Yew announced on August 14, six days after his return to Singapore. It was what the opposition had been demanding, he said. Now the PAP had delivered it. He called for a quick referendum on September 1, before the opposition had time to rethink its strategy.

The substitution of "Federation citizenship" for "Federation nationality," the Barisan and the UPP at once announced, changed nothing at all; it was a "shabby trick." The Barisan and the UPP stepped up their campaign against "phony merger," "sham referendum," and the "neocolonialist PAP." The change, said lawyer David Marshall, after taking time to examine it for any possible PAP trick, constituted in fact a "vital difference." Alternative A now meant merger on the basis of "equal rights and equal disabilities"—the lack even yet of proportional representation for Singapore being, he was willing to concede, a "workable compromise." But David Marshall refused nevertheless to vote for Alternative A. He demanded that the referendum be postponed so that the new terms could be adequately explained to the electorate. Tun Lim Yew Hock, however, now withdrew support from Alternative C and urged the voters to accept Alternative A. He also urged that in the next general elections they return the SPA, which would then gain even better terms from the Federation government. Mrs. Felice Leon-Soh asserted the referendum debate was a useless and expensive quarrel between the PAP and the Barisan, and demanded that the government spend the money on hospitals instead.

The Singapore referendum campaign opened on August 18. When

it closed on August 31 there had been some 600 rallies and forums, about 1,000 hours of major public speechmaking, including, say, about 50 hours each on the part of the top ten leaders. It was a marathon outdoor performance in which the politician confronted the voter almost face to face, generally with benefit of microphone and floodlights, to be sure, and the voter—including the messenger boy and the driver as well as the shopkeeper and banker—circulated from rally to rally to compare performances. The spectacle in downtown Fullerton Square each noon was indicative of the fact that the referendum involved not manipulation or coercion, as was variously charged, but free decision and free choice.

Each day the chief politicians of the party whose turn it was to appear lined up on a wooden platform set at the end of the Fullerton Square parking lot, just off the water front, drawing audiences of 2,000 to 10,000. Speakers and audience braved blazing sun and pouring rain and steaming heat, and enjoyed also a couple of cool, cloudy days. Behind the speakers were huge party emblems; hanging from a business building were party posters; on the balconies of the Fullerton Building there gathered a few dozen clerks from the government offices inside; on the balconies of the Hong Kong and Shanghai Bank Building stood commercial clerks and office employees. In the square itself gathered the downtown businessmen and office workers who had either hurried through their lunch to attend the show, or else ate on the spot, purchasing noodles, cakes, and fruit from the busy vendors, washing the food down with glasses of "lychee water," "sugar water," or "bird's-nest water." In the crowd were Chinese rubber brokers, Indian textile merchants, British office managers, also Malay and Indian and Chinese "peons," clerks, and students, and miscellaneous bystanders.

The speeches were in English, Chinese, and Malay—the English Oxonian, the Chinese generally Hokkien and occasionally Mandarin, the Malay an easy colloquial, but spoken more often by a Chinese or an Indian than by a Malay. The standard of speechmaking was distinctly good; the best of the speakers displayed a gift for language, logic, and psychology. Prime Minister Lee Kuan Yew carried off top honors in three languages—he was patient and cogent, skilled at producing the felicitous or the witty phrase, apparently quite offhand. He was evidently adjusting himself to the new image which his party seeks to impose upon him, for he succeeded not infrequently in combining an air of relaxation and friendliness with what both admirers and detractors describe generally as "cockiness." The Barisan speakers, in general, worked up more emotion than did the PAP; the UPP worked up more passion. But audience reaction did not, in general, encourage pyrotechnical forensics. There was much invective, veiled threat, and virtuous outrage; but there

were only rather mild cheers or boos from the audience, and only rather
indifferent response to repeated calls for the clenched fist salute and the
cry of "Merdeka" (Independence). The PAP called the Barisan and UPP
"clowns," "madmen," and "Communists"; the Barisan and UPP called
the PAP leaders "neocolonialists," "stooges," and "running dogs."
Claques were present, but they were rather self-conscious and generally, after a very short time, as the audiences grew, self-effacing.
There was no rowdyism and no violence.

What was true of Fullerton Square was also true in general of the
nighttime rallies which often drew more densely packed, more respon-
sive crowds into brightly lighted fields or parks. The amplifiers were
turned up higher, the food vendors were more insistent; at times a nearby
Chinese opera performance contributed to the din. But the only really
stirring moments came when the UPP tried on one occasion to drown
out a PAP rally with blaring loud-speakers, and on two occasions when
Mr. David Marshall showed up at PAP rallies and was challenged to
take the platform—once to decline, to the accompaniment of a good deal
of raillery, once to accept, to a greeting of both cheers and catcalls.
September 1, itself, was so serene that it was hard to believe that the
voters had actually visited the polls before they headed for the beaches.

                    *   *   *   *   *

Merger and referendum excitement began to die down as soon
as the referendum results were announced and was only briefly rekin-
dled when the Legislative Assembly met to vote—or rather to fail to
vote—the blank ballots. The PAP, although now reinforced, is still
shaky; the Barisan and the UPP, although shaken, are still powerful.
So far as Singapore is concerned, the road to merger now seems clear.
The state has surmounted, it now seems, the one great premerger crisis; it has overwhelmingly rejected the arguments of the extremist and
Communist elements; it has decided peacefully and overwhelmingly in
favor of merger on practicable if not perfect terms. The extremist opposition, which a very great many people feared might resort to violence, was successfully and peacefully circumvented. Its capability as
well as its disposition toward violence possibly decreases as merger
draws closer. It will probably decrease sharply when merger is
achieved and the new Federation government is in a position to take
fast, tough measures without raising an outcry over "outside interference."

It is still too soon, however, to assert with assurance, as newspaper headlines sometimes do, that merger is now a certainty. Merger

depends not only upon Singapore, but upon the states of Borneo as well.
The Tengku may change his mind, but he has said repeatedly that it is
an all or nothing deal: no admittance for Singapore unless the Borneo
states come in too, to counterbalance Singapore's preponderantly Chinese population and its risky politics and economics. In Borneo, the
day before Singapore voted for merger, the Sultanate of Brunei held its
first general elections. Merger seemed to be one of the most important
campaign issues. The Party Ra'ayat, which opposes merger into Malaysia but proposes a three-state Borneo confederation under Brunei hegemony and closer Brunei-Indonesian ties, won 51 of the 52 district
contests and thus gained all 16 of the indirectly elected memberships
in the new Legislative Assembly. The Sultan, who favors merger under not yet clearly defined conditions, appoints the other 17 Assembly
members. The political contest now shaping up in Brunei may be as
complex and possibly as significant to Malaysia as the Singapore referendum which has just passed.

CHAPTER
XIV

BACKGROUND TO INSURRECTION IN BRUNEI

January 8, 1963

At 2:00 a.m. on December 8, 1962, simultaneous armed upris-
ings broke out in the half-dozen population centers of the British-pro-
tected Sultanate of Brunei and in several nearby towns of the British
Crown Colonies of North Borneo and Sarawak. Conflict had long been
simmering between the Brunei Party Ra'ayat on the one hand, as typified by its leader, A. M. Azahari, and the government authorities on
the other, as variously typified by the Sultan of Brunei, his colonial
British advisers, his feudal Brunei Malay administrators, and his Federation of Malaya assistants. The conflict now turned suddenly, unexpectedly, but briefly violent.

Some 3,500 armed Brunei Malays and Kadayan tribesmen, including perhaps 1,000 from North Borneo and Sarawak, inspired by
Azahari and abetted from Indonesia, resorted to armed action for and
against exactly what no nonpolitician feels confident enough to say.
British military forces, airlifted from Singapore, managed in the course
of the next week to restore peace and order which will last nobody cares
to predict how long. The Sultanate of Brunei was revealed in the interval as a sadly troubled little state. Prospects for the stability and security of the newly emerging Federation of Malaysia, which have looked
more and more promising of late, began to darken. The Republic of
Indonesia was exposed as a belligerent and perhaps militant champion
of a highly incendiary thesis: the newly emerging nations, according
to Djakarta, should emerge not by way of peaceful evolution, as in Malaya, but by way of violent revolution, as in Indonesia. Indonesia will
offer all the assistance within its power to "freedom fighters" anywhere who feel themselves "provoked" not just by old memories of colonialism but by new images of "neocolonialism."

The full true story of the Brunei insurrection will not soon be
told, such is the present degree of mystification about developments in

Brunei in recent years as well as recent weeks. No one can yet satis-
factorily explain the motivations of Azahari and of the Sultan, who at
times have appeared to be challenging and at other times supporting
each other. Nor is it easy to explain the apparent obtuseness of the
British intelligence service and the local police, who virtually disregarded the danger signals, or to gauge the degree of involvement of Indonesia either before or after the event, not to mention the immediate
inducements which led some 2,000-3,000 Malays and Kadayans out of
the state's total population of 90,000 actually to take up arms and some
10,000 others—their most immediate family members—to condone if
not to abet the uprising.

Indonesia's President Sukarno says that the Brunei insurrection
is a manifestation of the "newly emerging forces" and that Indonesians
would be "traitors to their own souls" if they did not offer support. Malaya's Prime Minister Tengku Abdul Rahman says the insurrection was
fomented by local "traitors" and "subversives" with the connivance of
the Indonesian Communist Party as part of the effort of Communists
and their sympathizers everywhere to "sabotage" the Malaysia plan.
Equally sophisticated, less categorical observers say that Brunei has
been experiencing some very serious domestic problems in its transition from colonialism and feudalism toward self-government and independence, whether within or outside of the Malaysia context, and that
the very Malaysia proposal served both to intensify and to precipitate
domestic conflict just at the time when international rivalries were
converging upon all of what will soon no longer be British Borneo.

The Brunei story, then, is one which has long been asking to be
written and now becomes even more significant than before. The Sultanate of Brunei, to be sure, might seem a quite inconsequential bit of
Borneo real estate, only 2,226 square miles in area, inhabited by only
90,000 people, divided between two bulbous little enclaves that extend
into Sarawak at a point near to North Borneo and not far from the Indonesian border. But all real estate and all populations are potentially
strategic these days, and the smallest and most readily seized become
swiftly the most symbolical. The Sultanate of Brunei, additionally, is
even richer in oil than it is in domestic and international intrigue and
it has seemed until recently to be one shining example that to an underdeveloped nation, oil can do more good than ill.

Brunei, like all other nations, has its troubles, but it has
seemed also to enjoy progress to a degree unmatched in the region except in Malaya. The government has carried out a virtually all-purpose,
all-inclusive, M$100 million five-year plan (1953-58), carefully de-

signed to accomplish almost everything that a developer with unlimited resources at his disposal could dream up.   It has a M$900 million (US$300 million) reserve for programs not yet planned, and a M$125 million annual state income heavily outweighing a M$32 million expenditure.   The state has been moving rapidly in the direction of self-government and presumably also toward merger into the new Federation of Malaysia.

Swift economic, political, and social development—including shiny new schools with classroom space to spare—had resulted, not unnaturally, in new problems and conflicts quite a lot more complicated than those of Brunei's prewar days of impoverishment.   Some people in Brunei were unhappy about feudalism, colonialism, capitalism, and nepotism; others about communism, nationalism, and socialism; others about all of these, as well as inefficiency, corruption, lethargy and complacency, racialism, fanaticism, and tribalism.   The intrigues of the feudal court, the jealousies of the jungle tribes, the acquisitiveness of the Chinese minority, the improvidence of the Malay villagers, the machinations of the budding politicians, the instability of the Indonesian neighbors—each offered in itself sufficient cause for alarm that one cause seemed frequently to overshadow another.   All the same, anywhere one looked there were new roads, new schools, new clinics, new markets, new houses, shops crammed with reasonably priced goods, and pockets crammed with money.   Brunei Town, for instance, was once little more than a ramshackle water village built on piles over the river lagoon and a tacky Chinese business district on shore.   The water village, still built of wood, bamboo, and tin, but provided with amenities, serves now as a backdrop to the big lagoon in which is set a floodlighted M$2 million marble mosque; beyond it there has now grown up a new administrative complex scaled to a town and country of many times the present population, together with new shopping areas and new residential suburbs.   Under the circumstances, since there is always trouble everywhere and since nobody in Brunei was enduring real let alone intolerable hardship, it might seem that Brunei's multiple conflicts need not have led to violence.

Was it, then, basically the actuality or the agitation of grievances which brought about insurrection in what amounted increasingly to a welfare sultanate? Or, to update the local quip about Brunei's dependence upon oil, was it ills or shills in the Shellfare State? It is not a very satisfactory answer to say that it was both, for then the question shifts to one of proportion. The even more significant questions, then, emerge—questions, incidentally, which are not yet being very widely asked. Are relative peace, progress, and prosperity enough? Or is there some mysterious and irresistible urge which drives the "newly emerging nations" to purge themselves through violence of the very memories of the past and of the immediate present? If so, then what happens to the prevailing Western concept that by giving aid for carefully conceived national development projects one can ensure against precisely the sort of explosion which occurred in Brunei? Since Malaya too enjoys a remarkable measure of peace, progress, and prosperity, and Singapore enjoys progress and prosperity if not exactly peace, and both North Borneo and Sarawak, despite recent political furors, still look almost like oases of calm in a troubled area, the questions are as relevant to the Malaysia area as a whole as to Brunei itself.

Any meaningful report on the Brunei insurrection, then, must be complicated by consideration of political, economic, and social developments in Brunei in recent years, the leading personalities involved, and the domestic and international repercussions of the Malaysia plan, all of which and more besides are dealt with in the sections which follow.

*   *   *   *   *

The record of the Sultanate of Brunei between the years 1945 and 1962 is that of a Western-guided Southeast Asian national experiment in which, by comparison with conditions elsewhere in the area, the circumstances seemed almost unbelievably favorable and the difficulties seemed of modest dimensions. Resources were unlimited, the area was minute, the population was small and tractable, the Sultan was willing, the British had the authority and the experts, there was no emergency at hand or in sight, and there were few outsiders about to interfere or even to observe and criticize. The British decided, not without disagreement among themselves about method and timing, gradually to transfer authority to the Sultan and to encourage him to transfer it to the representatives of the people, and meanwhile to carry out a national development program designed to prepare the population for the way of living to which modern progress and their own national wealth entitled them. The British often bungled and botched, as they themselves admit; and the Brunei court was often far more eager to obstruct than to assist. The British muddled objectives, priorities, and follow-up programs in the fashion familiar in all bureaucracies; they manipulated too many, trained too few, trusted too much, got out too soon, and checked back in again too infrequently. By late 1962 they had reduced the British official "presence" to little more than a High Commissioner—absent on sick leave in England at the time of the insurrection—a British Commissioner of Police, and a few British contract personnel in the administration. The government service had greatly deteriorated in consequence, but the British were pinning their hopes on Brunei's entry into Malaysia to resolve many of the problems which they themselves had been quite unable to resolve. The British, as usual, bumbled as they bungled. Yet all the same, the Brunei political, economic, and social development program was probably better planned and better implemented by far than any similar program in Southeast Asia of larger or smaller dimensions. The inadequacies of the program signify not half so much incompetence on the part of the British as incomprehension on the part of the British and of everybody else of the devices whereby a backward area may be pushed—or led— forward.

Some of the dilemmas inherent in the Brunei national development program become apparent with examination of two of the key economic and social projects—the one to provide homes and jobs, the other to provide education. The Brunei Malay today, if he chooses to move ashore from the kampong ayer (water village)—and if he can clear the bureaucratic hurdles, can move into a new government-subsidized house. He can take up a piece of new land already cleared for him for planting and he can get government assistance in developing rubber or other crops. Or, if he prefers, he can get government assistance in setting himself up in some sort of trade or business. He can move up into the income bracket of the Chinese—who receive relatively little such assistance—and enjoy the Chinese standard of living or even better. The fact is, however, that an amazingly small proportion of the Brunei Malays do so choose—because, say some of their spokesmen, they do not know and do not like and do not hear any convincing arguments favorable to the new way of life that is offered them. They see that those who accept it are cut adrift from the Malay community. But even if the Brunei Malay remains in his kampong ayer, where the population is still increasing, he can now enjoy electric lighting, piped water, and other amenities, including such modern household goods as sewing machines and radios, including also the jewelry with which he likes to adorn his wife or wives, and the outboard motors with which he likes to power his boats. If he seeks employment other than the traditional fishing and small homecrafts, however, he finds little open to him except manual labor connected with the government construction projects, which have now tapered off very sharply, or estate rubber tapping, which does not appeal.

Any Brunei Malay child today can go all the way through school at full government expense. He can advance not just through the handsome new government secondary schools, where room, board, books, and equipment are free; if he exhibits any real aptitude and industry, he can go to Australia or England for further studies. The fact is, however, that few students exhibit as much enthusiasm or industry as one might expect, and that many parents feel little urgency about sending their children, particularly their daughters, to the secondary schools let alone beyond. On the other hand, the secondary-school students just now beginning to graduate in significant numbers complain that there are few white-collar jobs open to them and that they are not trained for the trades—vocational training, incidentally, having already been offered but having found few candidates. If a student does study in London there is only limited opportunity for him when he returns to little Brunei, especially if he should choose to study law or medicine, the prestige subjects.

In other words, the national development program, rather than serving as a catalyst to induce complete state regeneration, seems in some respects to have inhibited it and to have created more problems than it has solved. Both the government and its critics, naturally, are aware that something is amiss. The best that either can propose is a big new national development program to spend more of the huge reserve funds that are available and to duplicate a lot of what has gone before. As a result of one other major aspect of the development program—the encouragement of political change—the critics have been able to capitalize upon the defects of the program which has permitted them to emerge as critics in the first place.

The Sultan, Sir Omar Ali Saifuddin (age forty-seven), who came to the throne in 1950, has proved on the whole a liberal if alternatingly a hesitant and a headstrong monarch. He acceded to full executive control when the British relinquished it in 1956. He at once promised a Constitution which he promulgated in 1959. Under the terms of the new Constitution, which provides for gradual development of self-government in a constitutional monarchy, he then called for popular elections. The plan was to elect 55 members of four District Councils, and for the elected councilors in turn to choose 16 representatives in a new 33-member Legislative Council in which the other 17 representatives would be ex-officio and appointed members. The elections were first promised for 1961, then postponed, then actually held on August 30, 1962. The Sultan, furthermore, after prolonged hesitation, in mid-December 1961 announced his tentative decision to negotiate Brunei membership in Malaysia, which, he said, seemed to offer Brunei its best chance to achieve and to preserve self-government and independence.

In his program of democratic national development, the Sultan,

it appears, trailed and at times even opposed rather than led a popular
political movement. He relied upon the unquestioning traditional Malay
loyalty to the legitimate ruler rather than attempting to build up a political machine or a public personality. He found himself inadvertently in
competition with an adroit politician, one who knew the full potency of
the nationalist slogan, the mass movement, and the anticolonialist cause.

Inche A. M. Azahari, Brunei's key political figure, is an immigrant Brunei citizen, thirty-four years of age, the son of an Arab
father and a Malay mother. He was born and brought up on Labuan Island. After graduating from the Government Secondary School (English
language), he went to Brunei to enter government service. During the
Pacific War, he was selected by the Japanese for advanced education
and was sent to Indonesia to study veterinary medicine in Bogor. After
the collapse of Japan, Azahari, according to his own account, entered
the Indonesian revolutionary army, rose to officer rank (he was still in
his late teens), and associated with top Indonesian republican leaders.
After Indonesia achieved its independence in 1949, he returned to Brunei, where the British jailed him for a short time for undesirable political activities, then released him and permitted him to go into business
and to start organizing a political party. His Party Ra'ayat (People's
Party) was accorded authorization in the way of registration in August
1956. It began almost at once to hold big rallies and to claim virtually
the whole adult population of the state as its members.

Azahari, in his person, is short, slight, bearded, bespectacled,
much more Arab than Malay in physical appearance, not a very commanding figure, not a particularly good orator, and not in the past,
from all appearances, a totally dedicated revolutionary. He has seemed
to many observers, in fact, more the erratic and the fanatic than the
organizer, and rather easily diverted from politics to business, pleasure, religion, and matrimony. He has three wives and three families,
and at least two sets of rather serious marital problems. One wife in
Singapore has just sued for divorce on grounds of desertion; another
was arrested in Brunei soon after the insurrection broke out; and the
third accompanied him abroad. He has plunged in various businesses,
including motion picture production, construction firms, and a printing
establishment. He has found the Brunei government at times generous
in loans, at other times importunate about repayment, and for years it
has been an open question whether some hundreds of thousands of dollars in outstanding debts were to be regarded as a vote of confidence,
a bribe, or a bureaucratic accident. He has traveled repeatedly to Djakarta—on a "business-cum-pleasure" trip the last time, he reported,
when his visit coincided with a communiqué from the Indonesian Com-

munist Party denouncing Malaysia as a "colonial intrigue" and pledging Indonesian support for all "patriotic" anti-Malaysia groups. He has traveled elsewhere — to Cairo, for instance, for the Little Afro-Asian conference which many Afro-Asians repudiated. He professes a profound interest in religion and likes to be known as Sheik Azahari, a title which in Southeast Asia constitutes a claim to special religious attainment. After the recent Brunei elections, he informed the Sultan and announced to the public that he proposed to retire for a time "to pray to God after long and arduous work in the political field."

Azahari is not the typically hypnotic, magnetic, ultranationalist leader, yet he apparently has some of the qualities of charisma for he managed in an amazingly short time to rally virtually the entire Brunei Malay population about him, to make their vague grievances his own, and to translate vague grievances into a misty program which seems at once loyally nationalistic to the insider and recklessly opportunistic to the outsider, a great many of whom brand him as a Communist. Azahari denies repeatedly that he is a Communist or a Communist sympathizer, or even that he is a Socialist, stating categorically that he is a Brunei nationalist and adducing his allegedly unswerving loyalty to a feudal Sultan as proof.

The Party Ra'ayat had no very clear-cut program or policy during its first few years, at least none discernible in its public pronouncements. It seemed to stand for socialism, nationalism, and revolution, with emphasis upon nationalization of state resources (oil), provision of all manner of social services — such as the government itself was already providing — and some sort of revolution to achieve at once Brunei independence under the Sultan and restoration of Brunei sovereignty over Sarawak and North Borneo. It seemed also to stand for close ties with Indonesia, from which Azahari obviously drew his inspiration, to which he traveled repeatedly in search of support. Finally, from the moment the proposal was first made, the Party Ra'ayat opposed Malaysia, Azahari's own preference — all of his opponents and some of his onetime associates say — being for merger with Indonesia.

The Party Ra'ayat clarified its public platform to a greater extent than ever before at the time of the 1962 elections, when it issued a lengthy "manifesto" in which the following are some of the more significant items: (1) Opposition to Malaysia; (2) Demand for the creation in 1963 of a three-state Borneo federation under the Sultan of Brunei; (3) Opposition to a new Brunei Security Ordinance of July 1962 on the basis that its strict controls over publications, meetings, paramilitary activities, and arms were both unnecessary and "oppressive" in a state which was "a model of harmony, peace, and prosperity"; (4) Protection of Malay culture and privileges by measures which included maintenance of Islam as the state religion, suppression of "yellow culture," elimination of vice, and establishment of a pilgrimage board; (5) Development of a new "national" education system stressing mass adult education, vocational training, foreign scholarships, and provision of jobs for all graduates; (6) New programs of rural development, industrialization, improvement of communications, utilities, and social services; (7) Establishment of an anticorruption board, elimination of "political controversy, family privilege, and favouritism."

On this platform, the Party Ra'ayat on August 30, 1962, won a landslide victory. Lacking detailed study of the Brunei elections, which will not soon be forthcoming, it is extremely difficult to determine whether the population was voting against Malaysia, or for the three-state federation, or for a whole calendar of economic and social benefits, or all combined, or, for that matter, whether it was voting for Azahari or for the Sultan or for both. What the elections did prove conclusively, however, was that the Party Ra'ayat had taken the opportunity very firmly to consolidate itself and that the government had muffed the opportunity to build up any effective non-Party Ra'ayat political movement.

The Sultan, as already noted, had earlier postponed the elections for one year. He had given as his reason the difficulty of working out the mechanics of voter registration. His actual reason, according to the local grapevine, was to give the government time to promote a new political party. This new party never got itself organized. Government-backed political leaders, several of them defectors from the Party Ra'-ayat, organized a couple of forlorn little parties which never attracted a public following or achieved co-ordination among themselves. These parties could not even manage to enter candidates in 32 out of the 55 constituencies. Those of their members who did compete were overwhelmingly defeated, one drawing no votes at all, evidently not even his own; another drawing 13 out of a 411 vote total; another drawing 25 out of a 291 total. The Party Ra'ayat, accordingly, won 32 District Council seats by default, won another 22 by ballot, and immediately after the election persuaded the one other winning candidate to throw in with it. The Party Ra'ayat therefore gained also all 16 of the popular seats in the 33-man Legislative Council.

If the government seriously proposed to compete against the Party Ra'ayat, the elections constituted a political bungle of major proportions—just the sort of thing, said its critics, which was to be expected of the incompetent feudal aristocrats who monopolized most of the high positions. The critics of the government, who had been outspoken before the elections, became even more outspoken afterward, calling for thoroughgoing reform throughout the administration, more benefits for the people, less privilege for the gentry, and recognition of the thesis that since the Party Ra'ayat had won the elections virtually without opposition, it should have the controlling voice in the Legislative Council, not merely the 16-vote minority which could be outvoted on every important issue.

The Brunei political conflict came to a focus on the Malaysia issue, for the Sultan, it developed, still planned to proceed with his Malaysia negotiations despite Party Ra'ayat opposition. The Malaysia issue itself meanwhile had been exacerbated by conflict between Malays from Malaya and those of Brunei. The Sultan, at the time of the big exodus of the British administrators several years ago, had made a request to the government of the Federation of Malaya for the loan to Brunei of certain types of officials. The Federation government had acted favorably on the request, and "seconded" ten high administrative officers, 42 teachers, and a detachment of police. The Malay officials were soon reporting back to Kuala Lumpur that they were encountering resentment, interference, and even insult and threat. Brunei Malays in turn said the Malays were arrogant and colonialistic. About a year ago there occurred one episode of violence, when a senior Malay official was attacked by three Party Ra'ayat members. The Malay administrators and teachers threatened to resign and return to Malaya, and were deterred only by the personal intervention of Prime Minister Abdul Rahman. Anti-Malay sentiment, however, instead of diminishing, seemed in fact to increase, the Malays being accused of trying to exert pressure upon Brunei to join Malaysia. A little preliminary experiment in Malaysia-style co-operation, it seemed, was building up bad blood between Malays themselves. Consequently, at the time of the insurrection, fear that Federation Malays might become the first targets of a Brunei Malay uprising was one important factor which motivated the Federation government in sending more police—a move which brought forth cries of "intervention."

The Sultan had first openly announced his own position on Malaysia in an address from the throne in mid-December 1961. He then stated that he found the proposal "attractive," but that he proposed to consult the people before taking final decision. He therefore set up a commission of inquiry to determine the wishes of the public—and named Azahari as a member. He also named Azahari to the Legislative Council, a body which at that time was fully appointive. Azahari soon began leaking "information" that the people were "over-whelmingly" opposed to Malaysia. Presently other Party Ra'ayat members were challenging the government to release the commission's report, which the government refused to do. Then, in early April 1962, Azahari, who had just made a trip to Indonesia and to Egypt, made his first appearance as a member of the Legislative Council, where he introduced, among other resolutions, one calling upon the British to return North Borneo and Sarawak to Brunei. This resolution and his others, all anti-Malaysia in import, were defeated, and Azahari, describing himself as "downhearted," "despondent," and "disillusioned" about the "undemocratic" Brunei system, announced that he would "exile" himself and continue his activities abroad. He soon left on a trip to Europe, by way, possibly, of Djakarta and Cairo again, returning to Brunei shortly before the August elections.

The Sultan, meanwhile, on July 18, 1962, informed the Legislative Council that the commission of inquiry had actually heard the views of "only a small percentage of the ra'ayat," but that the people had "conveyed the impression that they agreed in principle to the concept of Malaysia." The Council, then, by a vote of 24 to 4, gave the Sultan a mandate to proceed with negotiations.

After the August 30 elections the Sultan gave no indication of having reappraised the people's attitude or of being about to call for a new mandate. Azahari, on the other hand, whom the Sultan received cordially in audience, was reported by a court official to have said that he himself and his party supported "the address made by the Sultan in the Legislative Council . . . accepting Malaysia in principle"— a rather equivocal statement which might perhaps best be interpreted as an oblique reminder to the Sultan of his promise to consult the will of the people. Azahari then once again left on a trip abroad, this time to Manila, then Malaya, then on December 3 to Manila again. The Party Ra'ayat, meanwhile, declared its intention of introducing resolutions at the scheduled December 5 meeting of the Legislative Council, calling not only for a three-state Borneo federation under the Sultan but also for the right of the Council minority to carry to the United Nations any grievances over foreign policy. While everyone was speculating what would be the next move when these resolutions were defeated—if, indeed they were defeated, for there was some talk that some of the appointive members might vote with the Party Ra'ayat and at the last moment the Council meeting was postponed until December 19—the Party Ra'ayat gave its advance answer: the December 8 insurrection.

Azahari's preinsurrection trip abroad not only distracted atten-

tion from events at home; it also added a new international dimension
to the Brunei puzzle. Azahari had gone first to Manila, then to Malaya,
and then, just five days before the insurrection broke out, back to Manila again. In Manila he had fallen in with Filipino politicians who were
seeking to establish their own claim to North Borneo, a claim which
has now become entangled with the Brunei insurrection. For the last
year the heirs of the late Sultan of Sulu (who have not, incidentally,
ironed out their own legal differences about who inherits what) have
been seeking to establish a case that North Borneo belongs to them.
They argue that their forebears merely leased the territory rather
than ceding it, as the British claim, in return for the annual payment
in perpetuity of M$5,000, payment which is now piling up in a North
Borneo bank while the heirs dispute it. The chartered company, they
argue, had no legal right to turn North Borneo over to the British Crown,
and the Crown has no right now to assign sovereignty to Malaysia. The
Filipino claimants have engaged a lawyer, Nicasio Osmeña, son of a
former President of the Philippines. Mr. Osmeña and others have built
up a press campaign which has resulted in widespread public and official support, including that of the Philippine Congress. President Macapagal has now personally interested himself in the claim on the basis
that Sulu sovereignty is in fact Philippine sovereignty. He has made
demands that the British negotiate, and has notified the United Nations
as well as Malaysia of the Philippine intention to pursue the case.

The British government dismisses the Philippine claim as
groundless, and Britishers of almost all descriptions are given to la-
beling it as nonsense. They point out repeatedly that it is somewhat
odd, to say the least, for the Philippine government at this late date
to resurrect and in fact to appropriate a forgotten private claim to sovereign power which was highly dubious in the first place. They go on
to argue, inter alia, that North Borneo was subject to at least as great
control from Brunei as from Sulu, and that they hold the actual cession
documents from both, whereas the Philippines merely raises an undocu-
mented claim; that the Philippine government in its own Constitution
defines the geographic limits of Philippine territory, and does not include North Borneo in that definition; and that a very complicated lot
of international agreements extending back over the last hundred years
give de facto recognition to British sovereignty.

The Malayan government regards the Philippine claim and the
Philippine request that Malaya refrain from the North Borneo merger
while the claim is being settled as unwarranted intervention into Malayan and Malaysian affairs. The Philippine attitude, it adds, is highly
prejudicial to the success of a new regional co-operation project, the

Association of Southeast Asia, an arrangement whereby the Philippines, Thailand, and Malaya have agreed to co-operate in economic and social affairs.

Indonesia's President Sukarno has given encouragement to the Philippine government that he will support the Philippine claim. Azahari, too, has come out in support of the Philippines against the British, inconsistent as that may be with his own claim to North Borneo on behalf of Brunei. But then, Azahari to date has elected Manila instead of Djakarta as the headquarters of his government-in-insurrection and of his campaign to inform the world press and the United Nations of the insurgent cause. His presence in Manila, apparently linking the Philippine government in sympathy with his cause and with the Indonesian support of it, has been an acute embarrassment to the government, an embarrassment which increased when left-wing Philippine labor groups offered "volunteers" to fight at once for the Philippines and for Azahari. This Philippines-Indonesia-Azahari involvement is incidental and tangential to the Indonesia-Azahari alignment, but it is one more indication, if any is necessary, that the Brunei insurrection was and is potentially far more dangerous than a small-scale local disorder.

The Brunei situation, obviously, was explosive well before the insurrection occurred; it has become more, not less explosive since. The account of the warnings which were somehow muffled, the coup which had every reason to miscarry but almost did not, and the restoration of an apparent order which may be more deceptive than before, will be the subject of subsequent chapters.

CHAPTER
XV

THE COURSE AND CONSEQUENCE OF INSURRECTION

January 10, 1963

On December 8, 1962, as soon as word had been flashed to the outside world that a mysterious little insurrection had broken out in the Sultanate of Brunei, Inche A. M. Azahari announced in Manila that he was the Prime Minister of a new revolutionary government of Northern Borneo, inclusive of the present states of Brunei, Sarawak, and North Borneo. He went on to claim that he had the full support of the Sultan, who had joined him in his move to throw off British colonialism and to achieve independence. He said that his armies, numbering 30,000 fully armed men, had captured a score of population centers, including the Brunei capital, Brunei Town, and the Seria oil center, and were about to march into Jesselton, the capital of North Borneo. He climaxed his statement by saying that he could count upon massive support from the Philippines and from Indonesia.

As detailed reports began to come through from Brunei in the course of the next few days, it became clear that Azahari's forces, first estimated at a couple of hundred, then a couple of thousand men, had indeed staged a well-co-ordinated series of successful surprise attacks. They had captured administrative centers, police stations, and other important establishments all over the state, plus a couple of towns across the North Borneo and Sarawak borders. Their most spectacular successes had been the capture of the Shell Oil installations at Seria, as well as the Seria residential area and the police station. In taking the police station, they had made use of a tactic which they also used elsewhere—they attacked under cover of a "human shield" of hostages, in the case of Seria some 45 persons, including 15 Europeans. Their most significant failure was failure to capture the Brunei Town police and administrative center, or to seize the Sultan's palace or his person. Their attack on the Brunei Town police station failed because the British Commissioner of Police quickly wakened and deployed his forces, and then demanded and received the surrender of the attackers—200 strong. Their attack on the palace failed because the authorities, acting on a last-minute tip-off which no one really believed, had posted an extra 20-man guard. The insurgent leaders, who drove up in a taxi to demand an interview with the Sultan, panicked, abandoned their taxi, and fled. They managed throughout the rebellion, however, to maintain communication by telephone with various startled officials.

The posting of an extra guard at the palace constituted the almost accidental precaution which foiled an insurrection that the authorities believed would never happen because logically it could not be successful. The Sultan, instead of falling into the hands of the insurgents and being constrained to call, presumably, for Afro-Asian support, called instead upon the British to fulfill their treaty obligations to provide "protection."

The British military command in Singapore dispatched first a couple of hundred British Commandos and Gurkha riflemen. Then, as it discovered the dimensions of the trouble, sent a few thousand more troops—Commandos, Gurkhas, and Scottish Highlanders—fully equipped and fully prepared for swift, decisive action. Supporting naval units were also dispatched. Operations were handicapped to some extent by the fact that the Brunei Town airfield was closed to large aircraft because of rebuilding; but using Labuan Island as a way point, the British were soon landing troops and equipment and patrolling the Brunei coast. Prime Minister Tengku Abdul Rahman of Malaya dispatched a unit of Malayan police to assist in restoring and maintaining order, also to assist in the evacuation or protection of Malayan citizens in Brunei. Within two weeks, the British troops, at a cost of about 30 casualties, including 7 deaths, had recaptured virtually all towns and installations which had been in insurgent hands; they had released about a hundred hostages, taken a total of about 3,000 captives (2,400 in Brunei itself), and imposed a few hundred casualties, including at least 60 deaths. Approximately 200 insurgent survivors had retreated into the jungle from which the British were attempting to flush them out again before they could reach the Indonesian border.

Azahari, still in Manila, first announced victories, then admitted setbacks, threatened blood baths, predicted the arrival of 100,000 Indonesian "volunteers," announced his intention of going into the North Borneo jungle to set up an insurgent headquarters on Mt. Kinabulu, then proposed instead to go to the United Nations to present the insurgent case there. The Sultan, meanwhile, suspended the Constitution and dis-

solved the new Legislative Council. He called upon his people to remain
quiet, as for the most part they did, doing very little openly to help the
insurgents, although they also did little to help the British troops. He
also called upon the insurgents to lay down their arms and accept am-
nesty, as more and more of them did when it became clear that not Indonesian but British troops were coming in. The Sultan appeared at a
press conference on December 14 to assure the world that he was indeed
a free agent, as Azahari kept denying. He set himself presently, as did
virtually every other participant or observer, to analyzing what had happened to date and what might happen next. Reports out of Brunei are
still fragmentary, but the following reconstruction is at least a start
toward explaining how the insurrection was possible at all.

Rumors of the formation of a secret military force in the jungle
areas adjacent to the Brunei, Sarawak, North Borneo, and Indonesian
borders began to circulate in Brunei as early as last May. The Borneo
Bulletin, a Brunei weekly, on May 26 published a front-page story that
Sarawak tribesmen had seen a hundred or more Malay youths trekking
through the jungle toward the Indonesian border. These youths, according to the jungle grapevine, were on their way to Indonesian Borneo to
be trained for a North Borneo army which would return to "liberate"
the three states.

The Sarawak police investigated the reports but could not sub-
stantiate them, the jungle folk now proving quite unwilling to talk. Similar rumors again began to circulate in September. The Sarawak police
again investigated and in late November discovered two jungle clearings
in which they found dummy rifles, jungle-green uniforms with "North
Borneo Army" shoulder patches, and certain documents indicating that
a secret armed movement had been organized. On December 4 they arrested ten persons—nine Malays and one Chinese—for complicity in the
movement. On December 7 the Sarawak police were tipped off that an
armed uprising would occur at 2:00 a.m. on December 8 in Miri, the
Sarawak oil refinery town near Seria. The Sarawak authorities took
special precautions and alerted the authorities in North Borneo, Brunei, and Singapore. In Brunei, as already noted, the police posted a
special guard at the palace of the Sultan. Nobody seems to have been
particularly worried, however, even though in July the Brunei government had felt it necessary to promulgate a new security ordinance
clearly inspired by fear of armed uprising, and in Brunei Town, at the
moment, people were speculating why Malay fishermen of the kampong
ayer had not been bringing in fish for a few days past, also why there
was a sudden run on sheath knives, flashlights, and camping equipment,
and why the tailors were unusually busy running up shirts and trousers

of forest green. The Singapore and Kuala Lumpur press on December 4 carried brief stories about the discovery of the existence of a secret army in Sarawak and on December 7 about the strange purchaser preferences in the Brunei market. That night, approximately 1,000 young Brunei Malays from Brunei Town's kampong ayer and another 2,000 or more Bruneis and Kadayans elsewhere, having uniformed, armed, and organized themselves under the very eyes and ears of the authorities, and, of course, the general populace, managed to stage a series of surprise attacks.

The great majority of the insurgents, the British now state with a mixture of candor, caution, and chagrin, were probably recruited and indoctrinated in the few weeks immediately before the insurrection. The hard core of insurgents, however, had traveled earlier to Indonesian Borneo, taken military training there, then returned to Brunei to organize and lead the insurrection. The great majority of the insurgents were Brunei Malays, mainly from Brunei Town; the minority were Kadayan tribesmen, closely akin by race to the Malays. None were Chinese, and in the course of the insurrection there occurred no anti-Chinese incidents such as might have been expected had the affair been purely local in origin. The hard core of the insurgents proved to be tough, resourceful fighters, and when they were defeated they withdrew with as many followers as they could muster, moving by boat and on foot through the jungle toward the Indonesian border. However, the majority—the late recruits—exhibited little enthusiasm for the insurrection, especially when it soon became apparent that Indonesia was not sending armed assistance. They seemed relieved to surrender, and upon being interrogated showed little comprehension of what they had been fighting for. They were more articulate about what they were rebelling against—an ineffectual and corrupt government which showed little concern for their interests.

The above summation, it should be emphasized, is based upon preliminary, fragmentary, and reluctant and highly inconclusive reports, mainly from official British sources or other interested official parties. Many of the insurgents may in fact have been fighting for a Greater Brunei in which they proposed to restore to the Sultan his ancient domain and glories. The Sultan himself had publicly repudiated this Azahari-inspired plan, but evidently not frequently enough or vigorously enough fully to convince all of his subjects. A Brunei irredenta cause would certainly exercise a very great attraction to bold and reckless young Malays, whose not-too-remote ancestors practiced a particularly ferocious combination of piracy, slave trading, intrigue, and adventure, but whose own lives had become excessively tame under a rich and paternalistic—albeit, perhaps, a slovenly—regime. Many of them may indeed

have been fighting against Malaysia or for Indonesia, although this seems
much less likely save in the case of the hard core of leaders. Many of
them may have been fighting merely for the sake of excitement, and it
is quite within the Malay tradition for hot-blooded youths to put on a
headlong, flamboyant, but otherwise almost purposeless display of violence.

Any account of the insurrection and any speculation about cause
and consequence introduces almost at once the matter of Indonesian involvement. The Indonesian Communist Party last December, at the time
of a visit to Indonesia by Azahari, stated that the Malaysia plan was a
"colonial intrigue" and that "the Indonesian people will certainly support the righteous, patriotic, and just resistance of the people of Malaya, Singapore, Sarawak, Brunei, and North Borneo against the efforts
for the establishment of this Federation of Malaysia." The PKI's position, it has been widely assumed and stated in North Borneo and Sarawak, but not by any means so openly presumed in Singapore or Malaya,
was basically the position also of the Sukarno government.

From the moment the Brunei insurrection broke out, people all
over the Malaysia area began asking: who had in fact masterminded
the whole affair? Who had supplied money, the weapons, and the training? Azahari had been in Johore Bahru during the crucial month before
the insurrection; he had then sought the safety of Manila rather than the
danger of the battlefield; he seemed from his almost hysterical Manila
press conferences to be a fanatic rather than a fighter and almost certainly not a strategist. He might perhaps have got his money from Brunei state loans. He might have got his arms from the smugglers who
abound in the waters of the Sulu Archipelago and of North Borneo, traf-
ficking not only in copra and tobacco but in World War II surpluses as
well. But where else than from Indonesia could he have acquired help
in training his cadres and planning his coup—or confidence that Indonesia was behind him and that Indonesian "volunteers" would answer
his call?

From Indonesia almost immediately came proof that if the Indonesian government had not actively backed the insurrection before it occurred, it backed it now. On December 10 President Sukarno announced,
in the course of a state dinner for the visiting Yugoslav Vice-President,
that the Brunei insurrection was one more manifestation of the "emerging forces" with which lay Indonesian sympathy and the final victory.
Ruslan Abdulgani, Indonesian Minister of Information, next day called
upon the Indonesian press and public to support the Brunei insurgents.
All Indonesian official and public spokesmen almost immediately began

to talk belligerently of "British neocolonialism" and its "puppets," the "atrocities" of Gurkha "mercenaries," the "heroism" of "Brunei freedom fighters," the "solidarity of Afro-Asian peoples" behind the "emerging forces."

In Malaya Prime Minister Tengku Abdul Rahman on December 11 stated before Parliament that the Brunei rebels had been provided with money, weapons, and training in Indonesian Borneo and that Indonesian political organizations, most specifically the Indonesian Communist Party, had long been attempting to create trouble between Indonesia and Malaya. Indonesian Foreign Minister Subandrio, whose plane happened to stop at Kuala Lumpur and Singapore on December 14 on his way home from the Colombo neutralist conference on the Sino-Indian border conflict, interpreted the Tengku's comment as an allegation of direct official Indonesian involvement. He stated publicly in Kuala Lumpur that if Malaya "accused Indonesia too much," Indonesia would "become very angry"; and in Singapore, an hour later, that "if the Tengku is determined to be hostile . . . there is no alternative other than to accept the challenge."

Charges and countercharges, protests and counterprotests gathered speed and rancor. Indonesian spokesmen of all descriptions elaborated upon the Sukarno theme and all the familiar symptoms of a new "spontaneous" mass movement began to appear. Parliament voiced full support for the Brunei rebels (December 15); General Nasution warned of the need for ceaseless "vigilance" against the "nearby" forces of "colonialism and imperialism" (December 15); government-sponsored demonstrators demonstrated, burning Macmillan and the Tengku in effigy (December 16); political parties began pledging pro-Brunei sympathies; protesters began protesting to the British and Malayan Embassies; volunteers began volunteering; the "guided press" reintensified its appeals to the government to take action; Sukarno kept making revolutionary speeches in which he reiterated Indonesian support, "both open and secret," for all revolutionaries everywhere, and accused the Tengku, inter alia, of being a "false freedom lover." More formal official statements on both sides occasionally deplored a needless rift between "blood brothers," but more frequently warned that the situation might grow worse. In Indonesia the mood was one of substituting the Brunei and Malaysia issues for Irian Barat (West New Guinea) as a national cause, an Irian Baru (New Irian), as it were. In Malaya the mood was one of apprehension that Indonesia would do exactly that.

The Tengku has now repeatedly stated to Parliament and to the public that Indonesian involvement in the Brunei insurrection constitutes a major hazard to the peace and security of the area, a hazard which must be realistically faced. The Tengku has himself been confronted with accusations by opposition politicians that by his own policies — "applying pressures" to achieve the Malaysia plan, "intervention" by sending more Malay police to Brunei, "provocative" attitudes and comments regarding Indonesia, and by "collaborating" with the British colonialists — he has himself created the problem. Many of the anti-Malaysia elements throughout Malaysia have now assumed a proinsurgent, anti-Tengku, and pro-Indonesia stand. The Tengku in turn brands many of them as "traitors" and "Communists." The Socialist Front and the Pan-Malayan Islamic Party (PMIP) are the most important of the insurgents' sympathizers in Malaya, and on December 16 the Federation police arrested nine Socialist Front leaders, some of whom are still under detention. There exists also, however, a strong pro-Indonesian Malay element within the Tengku's own United Malay National Organization.

In Singapore the PAP leaders promptly branded the insurrection as alien and Communist-inspired. They accused the Barisan Sosialis of abetting it, and said that what had happened to Brunei was a timely warning to Singapore that the same thing could happen here. The Barisan Sosialis immediately announced its sympathy for the insurgent cause. It has been both cautious and clumsy, however, about stirring up open support, a big public rally to express sympathy for the Azahari insurrectionists having almost fizzled out by comparison with the sort of excitement and enthusiasm which the party usually inspires. The Singapore Party Rakjat has announced support for the Brunei insurgents, and a few of its members have been jailed for putting up pro-Azahari posters.

Spokesmen of the various North Borneo political parties, which had managed in October to achieve coalition in a pro-Malaysia Alliance, unanimously condemned the Azahari insurrection. Just two weeks after the insurrection broke out, the North Borneo government held the state's first general elections, and the Alliance candidates, who ran virtually unopposed, won a landslide victory. The achievement of alliance and victory was greatly expedited, it may convincingly be argued, by a combination of developments unwelcome to all the Bornean parties: first, the Philippine claim; second, the intimations of Indonesian expansionism; third, the rumors of impending trouble in Brunei; and fourth, the insurrection itself. The political stability of the Alliance, however, is by no means assured. The accession of the Chinese members was at best the reluctant response to pressures applied by leading Chinese businessmen who opted rather belatedly for peace rather than politics.

The accession of one tribal party, Pasok Momogun, was the result of a
last-minute decision to go with the main political tide and to break,
therefore, with Azahari, with whom it had been flirting. North Borneo
politicians may split up again as suddenly as they united, but on the Brunei issue at least they seem to be in general agreement.

In Sarawak all five pro-Malaysia political parties, which on November 29 had also formed a pro-Malaysia Alliance, at once condemned
Azahari and the insurrection. The biggest and perhaps the most important of all the Sarawak parties, however, the anti-Malaysia Sarawak
United People's Party, experienced grave difficulty in defining its position. The leader of the right wing, Mr. Ong Kee Hui, finally on January 1
"deplored" and "condemned" the insurrection. The leader of the SUPP's
left wing, Mr. Stephen Yong, however, was reportedly Azahari's choice
to replace the British Governor of Sarawak, and not only the SUPP's left
wing but the whole party was implicated, according to official British
statements, in the Azahari insurrection, several hundred of them in the
actual fighting. Several months prior to the Brunei insurrection, the
British had arrested half a dozen left-wing SUPP members on charges
of being members of a secret Communist underground movement, desig-
nating some for deportation, others for restricted residence. As a consequence of the party's implication in the Azahari insurrection, several
hundred right-wing members have now resigned. But with the right
wing voluntarily weakening itself and the left wing involuntarily purged,
the SUPP, according to some reports, has actually gained in strength.
With less right-wing deterrent and less left-wing conspiracy, it can
now more forthrightly continue its anti-Malaysia campaign.

The Brunei insurrection, together with the regional and the international complications, seemed for a few days at least to preclude
almost any possibility that the Malaysia plan could actually be realized
by the target date, now set as August 31, 1963, if Brunei membership
were one of the requirements. Tengku Abdul Rahman, however, quickly
announced that it was his firm intent to proceed on schedule—with or
without Brunei. Other Malaysia sponsors echoed his statement. Thus,
for the first time, although there had been earlier intimations that Brunei at least might join later, the Malaysia sponsors officially acknowledged that Brunei membership was not absolutely essential to the plan
and that the original concept of three Borneo states counterbalancing
Singapore in the new Federation had been in fact gradually and greatly
altered. Then, as soon as the insurrection was brought under control,
Brunei's non-Party Ra'ayat politicians announced that they had formed
a new Brunei Alliance (December 24) to work for Brunei's entry into
Malaysia. A few days later, the Sultan announced that it was still his

intention to negotiate for merger, and dispatched a new negotiating party to Kuala Lumpur. Barring active Indonesian intervention, prospects for realization on schedule of the full five-member Federation brightened again.

Prospects brighten regarding form and schedule, but not stability. Under the present circumstances of ambiguity within Brunei and international tension over Brunei, it is highly debatable, to say the least, whether Brunei membership would serve to strengthen or to weaken either Brunei or Malaysia. The Sultan, acting on British advice, which in turn was based on irresistible international pressures, had instituted democratic processes among the backward people of Brunei. Azahari had taken advantage of those processes to build up a movement which has now reduced a large proportion of the adult male population to the role of suspect, prisoner, or fugitive, and their families to hardship such as Brunei has not known in recent years. Determination of the will of the people—including the will of the 19% Chinese population which remained inert during the election and the insurrection—now seems impossible; and if, as the Sultan has repeatedly said, the will of the people is or should be the criterion whereby Brunei will decide whether or not to join Malaysia, then the criterion itself becomes an embarrassment and a hazard. If not merely the will but the good of the people should be the criterion, then a whole new rationale is in order not only for Malaysia but for Southeast Asia in general, for it is difficult to argue that the two necessarily or even frequently correspond.

For the Malaysia area as a whole, a series of sobering new considerations has been highlighted by the Brunei insurrection. Anti-Malaysia insurrections—or disorders—can occur as readily in Singapore, for instance, as in Brunei, and Indonesia obviously will support if not in fact help to instigate them. The Malaysia sponsors are more vulnerable than before to domestic agitation about "neocolonial" philosophy and tactics—the sort of agitation which can stir up disorders. Actual achievement of Malaysia, rather than diminishing the danger, as heretofore seemed likely, may increase it, for the Sukarno regime will look with even less favor upon a consolidating than upon a coalescing Malaysia. The successful inauguration of a new Malaysia, accordingly, will require an even higher order of statesmanship than its conception.

CHAPTER
XVI

SPECULATIONS REGARDING BRUNEI

March 11, 1963

The Sultanate of Brunei, which experienced armed insurrection during the week of December 8, 1962, is now back about as close to normalcy as it is soon likely to get. It continues to be occupied by some 3,000 to 5,000 Commonwealth troops, who are quartered in the schools. A good 10% of the adult male Brunei Malay population is under detention as insurrectionists or suspects. Perhaps half a hundred armed guerrillas are still at large. The international world, meanwhile, keeps promising—or threatening—by conflicting devices to look out for Brunei's own best interests.

In other respects, Brunei is probably a lot better off than might reasonably be expected under the circumstances. The Party Ra'ayat, which swept to victory at the polls not long before it staged the insurrection, is now presumably disbanded, and a new Brunei Alliance Party is being formed to back the Sultan's reaffirmed intent to join Malaysia. The 1959 Constitution is suspended, and the Sultan rules through an Emergency Council, while the British provide both advice and protection in more massive quantities than before. The curfew has been lifted. Roads and rivers are open to normal traffic. Shops are back in business, filled with both merchandise and customers. Government offices are functioning again. The Shell Oil Company's oil installations have long since been restored to normal production and, under a new agreement which has just been negotiated, an even larger percentage of the proceeds flows into the bulging state treasury. The families of the detained insurrectionists are receiving small maintenance allowances from the government, a state of affairs which may be unique in the history of social welfare.

Nevertheless, almost everyone in Brunei who thinks about the future is very much worried, and nobody has any totally convincing answers to the basic questions: why did the insurrection break out and how can confidence now be re-established? In general, the local Malays are rather rueful and not very communicative. In general, the Chinese are garrulously uninformative about everything save their desire for British protection. The British are reappraising their reappraisals. In various quarters there have been rather more systematic attempts to explain why the insurrection occurred than to predict what is to come next, and some of the explanations, given below not necessarily in order of credibility, are worth reporting.

1) It was a case of too much money. Unused money piled up in the state treasury. People thought easy money was the answer to all problems. Schoolboys made it a voluntary arithmetic exercise to divide the latest figure on the national reserve by the latest population figure, then to budget the per-capita shares. Outsiders became envious. Many of the insurrectionists were so naïve as to think they could grab the state treasure—a shiny US$300 million, invested abroad. They intended to divide it up into equal parts, each of the 3,000 of them to pocket US$100,000. Cupidity, plus a few arms supplied on credit by smuggler-speculators: this spelled insurrection.

2) It was a case of bad government. The Sultan's government, ever since the British virtually pulled out in 1958 and 1959, has been dominated by incompetent, conspiratorial, and increasingly corrupt feudal courtiers who concerned themselves mainly with prestige and prerogative, scarcely at all with administration. While the Sultan probably continued to enjoy the loyalty traditionally bestowed by the Malays upon their legitimate ruler, he may have created the misapprehension in some quarters that he wanted to be relieved of a parasitic lot of functionaries. The evidences of bad government were mainly the evidences of bureaucratic inertia and of the immense labor required to stir a government official even to decline to act. The Sultan's "do-nothing" regime gradually become intolerable.

3) It was a case of failure to continue the national development program. Before the British pulled out, Brunei had undertaken and almost completed a five-year M$100 million program which provided the major physical facilities for a modern state. The program stopped short in 1959. The existing facilities were badly utilized thereafter, and significant new developments were stalled. New hospitals, for instance, were promised but never built. New lands were available for resettlement, but potential applicants could not even find out how to apply for homestead allotments. The only visible recent developments have been a "Guest Palace," a few rather showy residences for high officials, including one for the prime minister, and quite a lot of new

homes built by government employees on easy government loans.
Meanwhile, the Public Works Department, which had been built up for
the original construction program, was being decimated by dismissals,
unemployment was increasing, resentment was mounting even faster
than unemployment, and a showdown was inevitable. The majority of
the recent and former employees of the Public Works Department, incidentally, threw in with the insurgents.

4) It was failure to synchronize the material aspects of development with the implantation of the incentive and the initiative which
are indispensable if people are actually to profit in terms of individual
accomplishment.

5) It was a case of agitation and conspiracy. In all of Southeast Asia, nobody had it so good as the Brunei Malays, but their appe-
tite for state handouts proved to be insatiable. Their political leader,
Azahari, himself urged on and abetted by international troublemakers,
particularly the Indonesian Communists, magnified petty grievances
into major disaffections and injected important elements of adventurism, irredentism, anticolonialism, anti-Chinese racism, revolutionary
zealotry, and sheer Malay madness.

6) It was fear of Malaysia. Fear that Brunei would be sub-
merged in a big alien Federation, plus disappointment with democratic
processes—witness, specifically, the August elections which gave overwhelming victory but not political power to the anti-Malaysia Party
Ra'ayat—converted evolutionary development into violent revolution.

Singly and in combination, the above explanations are revealing
about the past but not very comforting with regard to the future—Brunei's, Malaysia's, or Southeast Asia's. Brunei's money, for instance,
is still piling up much faster than it can be spent, even though oil re-
serves are being depleted and other industries are stalemated. Brunei's few economic planners and thinkers are much more concerned
about how to maintain or increase the present fantastically high national income than with what might conceivably be the real problem:
how to get rid of a national reserve which seems in some respects
more dangerous than a national debt.

The Sultan's preinsurrection government, which virtually nobody thought was good, is still the legitimate government, and as such
it seems to warrant support as the only alternative to chaos. The Brunei government, to give it its due, has not been "bad" in the ordinary
Southeast Asian sense of oppressing and exploiting the people. Brunei

peasants, for instance, not only own the land they cultivate but sell their crops for good hard currency at free world market prices—not at artificially low government-manipulated prices, as in Indonesia, nor at artificially high prices, as in Ceylon. The ordinary family can afford a radio, an outboard motor, a sewing machine, even a record player and a refrigerator. If an administration which permits this manner and standard of living proves to be intolerable, then the prospects for much of the rest of Southeast Asia seem dim indeed.

Brunei's development program may have stalled, but the original program was probably the world's most extensive and intensive to date in terms of per-capita outlay. For all its demonstrable extravagances and imperfections, it involved a relatively efficient and productive capital investment of US$500 for each Brunei subject, as compared, for instance, with a proposed per-capita outlay of US$10 for the current Indonesian program which has placed the emphasis to date upon sports stadia and national monuments. The subsequent housing development in Brunei, although it may not be a planned state program, has resulted nevertheless in much improved living standards for at least 5% of the population, a percentage which in most other Southeast Asian nations would seem most impressive. Brunei's error, to be sure, may have been in undertaking too big a program too soon and too fast; but that is not an error which a newer, bigger program will correct. If either the implementation or the suspension of the initial Brunei program spelled more trouble than contentment and enterprise for the state, then the basic theory of development programs, not just in Brunei but elsewhere, is overdue for a hard new look. Obviously the new look must include a scrutiny of the dynamics as well as the mechanics of development, for Brunei had plenty of almost everything except psychological adjustment.

As for agitation, conspiracy, and Malaysia, all three, except possibly Malaysia, are here to stay. Brunei's adjustment to them may prove to be even more difficult in the future than in the past.

CHAPTER
XVII

TENGKU ABDUL RAHMAN, BAPA MALAYSIA

March 15, 1963

Ten years ago, Malaya's Tengku Abdul Rahman would not have been picked by very many political forecasters as the man most likely to succeed as prime minister of any existing state in Southeast Asia or as the architect of a new one. His own Malay associates had selected him, a bit dubiously, to head a political party, the United Malay National Organization (UMNO), which Dato Sir Onn bin Ja'afar, its brilliant showman founder, had almost wrecked. Tengku Abdul Rahman was not and is not brilliant or even, by choice, very industrious. His best friends smile deprecatingly, as does the Tengku himself, about his capacity for retaining facts and figures or his grasp of intellectual profundities. Nor is he a showman—his sense of theater is that of a keenly appreciative spectator, and he is quite likely to be pointing his own camera from the dais when he should be posing. As a state figure, he is a bit too plump and casual to create an impression of imposing presence. He seems more stuffed than stately when he is decked out in stiff gold and silver brocades for some official occasion. As for speechmaking, his delivery is good enough, if he keeps his eyes on the script; but his eyes, behind big horn-rimmed bifocals, tend to wander. His voice is likely to break into chuckles at some of his own witty interpolations. Self-enjoyment then prompts him to interpolate still more, and as every politician knows, wit is not always catnip to the voter. Apparently, the Tengku doesn't much care.

Retroactive prognostications notwithstanding, the Tengku is probably Southeast Asia's most successful prime minister. He is successful, that is, in the sense that he is running a good government, which is not, of course, everyone's criterion of political success. Tengku Abdul Rahman may be successful precisely because he does not care too much, not only about offending by his wit but about maintaining himself in position. He obviously likes his job and the pay is good—M$4,-

000 (US$1,333) per month, plus quite a lot of extras. But the Tengku prefers to be himself rather than public property, and he can always retire to being pensioned petty royalty. His present M$288 per month stipend as a prince of the State of Kedah can be supplemented modestly by rents from the few inherited properties that he has not sold off to pay his own debts or to help his friends. Being royalty, he is not over- whelmingly impressed with his position as prime minister, nor, being genuinely democratic royalty, is he overwhelmingly impressed with the pretensions of the politicians, especially his rivals.

The Tengku did not exactly bid for the job as UMNO leader, back in 1951, but he did make himself available. As UMNO president, he was gradually—and on the whole willingly—maneuvered into the job as head of government. He is motivated now, it is quite apparent, by a deeply felt desire to serve the state to the best of his capacity. But he is guided also by two other considerations that are rare among the world's politicians. One of them is a pretty realistic estimate of his own capacities and of what assistance he requires. The other is a con- viction that the good life embraces not mere fame and power but lei- sure, sports, friends, and family, and that he is going to enjoy these right here and now.

The Tengku frequently departs from the paths of political and diplomatic rectitude by speaking his mind and leaving to his associates the task of picking up the pieces. He refuses to get ulcers by trying to follow the urgings of some of his associates that he become prompt, precise, and perspicacious. A few months ago he seemed to be yield- ing to pressure to the extent that he suffered briefly from insomnia. His malaise was cured, less by the medication prescribed by his phy- sician perhaps than by his own reaction to such solicitous public reac- tions as an offer on the part of some elderly UMNO ladies to sing him to sleep.

To those who are satiated with great, strong, charismatic, mak- ers of new nations, the Tengku often seems too good to be true, or at least too good to last as head of a Southeast Asian government. Both his friends and his enemies think at times that they had better focus attention upon his faults. The fact is that he has so many and admits to them so disarmingly that he becomes a paragon of self-deflation. He is by nature indolent, imprudent, extravagant, self-indulgent, and frivolous. He has little truck with good books, good music, or publi- cized good works. He drinks brandy, smokes cigars, swears, and gambles, and in his youth he sowed wild oats. It should also be pointed out, however, that he observes the rigorous self-discipline of the Mus-

lim fasting month. His apprehensions at the onset of Puasa and his relief at its termination fuel Kuala Lumpur society's small talk and his
own.

The Tengku does not and cannot cast himself as the projection
of a studiously contrived image, either as the quite extraordinary, ordinary man which he is, or as the sacrosanct father of his people. A
recent careless lapse in allowing himself to be formally designated by
earnest youths as Bapa Malaysia (Father of Malaysia) seems unlikely
at the moment to lead to anything worse, for the personality cult is not
to his liking. The Tengku's unadorned personality, in fact, is no model
for earnest youth, although for many adults it seems a vindication of
their own errors.

In other words, Tengku Abdul Rahman is easy to like and hard
to dislike because he does not insist upon excelling in any other virtue
than getting people to reconcile their differences and to get on with
whatever job most immediately needs to be done. In a nation where
the center of the stage is disputed by mutually suspicious and jealous
Malays and Chinese, with Indians lurking loudly in the wings and the
British in the prompter's pit, the Tengku's genius for liking others
and making himself liked, rather than for upstaging his associates, is
something which the Japanese would probably designate as a national
treasure.

The Tengku's fairly widespread reputation for personifying in
his career not the triumphs of excellence but the compensations of mediocrity in itself invites a bit of reverse debunking. His "mediocrity"
is that of a genuine, honest, intelligent human being, the man who regards it as more important to be a good than a prominent citizen. He
manages to be both without being either pious or overbearing. His is
almost the "mediocrity" of the golden mean. While it is refreshing to
find in him a national leader who is not bedazzled by his own floodlighted image, it is well to remind oneself that, after all, quiet self-
deprecation is an art which only a truly superior public man can practice for long. The Tengku has been practicing it for over a decade,
with few symptoms as yet of becoming grandiose. He does occasionally get huffy these days about real or imagined breaches of protocol.
He is subject to quite a lot of criticism for "despotic" management of
his own party and the Alliance to which it belongs. He tolerates quite
a good deal more wheeling and dealing on the part of his cronies than
would, say, De Gaulle, if he had any. The Tengku may yet become more
of the stereotype than the maverick among the leading figures of the
emerging nations. His record to date does not give much grounds for
either the fear or the hope.

Tengku (Prince) Abdul Rahman Putra al-Haj was born on February 8, 1903, in Alor Star, the capital of the northern Malay State of Kedah, then a dependency of Siam. He was the fifth surviving son of Sultan Abdul Hamid Halim Shah (d. 1943), one of the 45 legitimate children whom the Sultan sired by his eight legal wives before he died, quite mad, at the age of seventy-nine, after a reign of 61 years. The Tengku, to continue the enumeration, was the seventh child of the Sultan's sixth wife, a circumstance which made his prospects for succession to the throne fairly remote. Even though the sixth wife was the Sultan's favorite, the Tengku was her own fourth son.

The Sultan, who was subject during most of his life to recurrent spells of insanity, at the time of Abdul Rahman's birth was climaxing a career of reckless extravagance which bankrupted the state. In celebration of the marriage of his eldest son, the heir apparent, and of four other sons who also happened to be of marriageable age, the Sultan in 1906 staged a three-month wedding party. State offices were closed for the duration; practically everyone in the state was invited and all the neighboring royalty as well; and save for activities connected with the wedding party, almost all constructive labor was suspended.

The Sultan financed the blowout with loans from Penang money-lenders. He was so lavish with his hospitality—providing, it is said, 30 cases of champagne per day and unlimited quantities of fine Egyptian cheroots, in addition to full board and lodging for his more distinguished guests—that the final reckoning came to M$3 million-M$4 million. The Kedah state treasury by then was bare, and the Siamese government, to whom the Sultan appealed for rescue, agreed to bail him out only on condition that he accept a financial adviser. This adviser, who turned out to be an Englishman, was an advance party of one who preceded the British government's extension of "protection" to Kedah in 1909.

The Tengku—fortunately, perhaps—saw little of his father except on Fridays, when the Sultan's usual schedule took him first to the mosque for prayers, then to the palace of Makche Menjelara, the Tengku's mother. Makche Menjelara (d. 1941), or Mak Chek as she was usually called, was from all accounts a most extraordinary member of the harem. She was not a Malay but a Siamese, the daughter of a provincial governor of Burmese descent, who, having plenty of daughters, had sent her as a young girl to Kedah where she lived as a foster child of one of the sisters of the previous Sultan. She grew up to be both beautiful and intelligent. By her beauty she attracted the Sultan, and by her shrewdness—the business acumen more characteristic of the Burmese and

Thai women than of their men—she made herself rich. She acquired properties not only in Alor Star but in Bangkok as well, and she wisely kept her own finances quite separate from those of her husband.

As a mother, Mak Chek seems to have combined strict discipline with affection, and to have maintained at the same time an agreeable tolerance toward the leisure-time occupations of her children. The Tengku lived in her "palace"—a curious three-story Chinese pagodalike structure, long since vanished—but he wandered about Alor Star almost like a barefoot, barebottomed kampong child. He was in and out of the trees, the river, the stalls of the wayside food vendors, and the homes of the neighbors, like one more member of the pack of boys who constituted one of the liveliest elements of a sleepy town.

The Tengku's education was spotty from the first, and what his teachers remember best is his capacity for inattention and for enjoyment. He started out at the age of four in a sort of kindergarten where Malay was the language of the morning, English that of the afternoon. He progressed to the government-sponsored English school in Alor Star, but when he was ten he was sent to study in a Siamese school in Bangkok. There he lived with his brother, Tengku Yusoff, who had been brought up as a ward of King Chulalongkorn, and had studied at Rugby and at the Royal Military Academy at Woolwich. Tengku Yusoff had returned from England with an English wife, and upon encountering both British and Malay resentment in Kedah, had settled in Thailand as a captain in the Siamese Army. Abdul Rahman remained with him in Bangkok for about a year. When Tengku Yusoff died suddenly of pneumonia in 1915, the younger brother returned to Malaya. There he entered first a Malay-language school in Alor Star, then in 1916 transferred to the English-language Penang Free School.

The Penang Free School, the oldest and by common repute the best secondary school in Malaya, was then attended mainly by sons of well-to-do or rich Chinese families and by sons of British families who had not yet been sent back to school in England. As a Malay, the Tengku was in a small minority, and as a royal prince, whose mother rather unwisely equipped him with gold-embroidered bed pillows and other similar tokens of affection and rank, he was soon obliged to establish the fact that he was good with his fists. So far as his no-nonsense British masters were concerned, he had also to establish the fact that he could pass examinations, which he did, although without much margin.

In early 1920, as soon as passage could be engaged after the end of World War I, Tengku Abdul Rahman sailed for England to continue his studies as the recipient of a newly established Kedah state scholarship. It was his intention to enter Cambridge, but the Kedah state government had prudently arranged for some preliminary private tutoring. On arrival in England, therefore, Tengku Abdul Rahman proceeded to the village of Little Stukeley, near Huntington, where the rector took in foreign students for special coaching. The Tengku found country life and sport more agreeable than study and quickly acquired a favorable local reputation as the athletic prince "Bobby." He made little academic progress until he was moved to Cambridge and there enrolled with a private tutor who managed, in the course of about six months, to cram in enough learning that he qualified for matriculation.

Once enrolled in St. Catherine's, one of the smallest of the Cambridge colleges, the Tengku's first really memorable encounters were not with intellectual stimuli but with race prejudice. When he applied for residential quarters in the College, he was informed that none were available, and when he persisted, he was advised that the College was "built for English students." He was keen to play football for the university, but although he was clearly an outstanding player and his name was proposed, he was never called for the freshman trials. The Tengku's reaction in each case was characteristic. First he got angry, then he shrugged his shoulders and made the best of it. He found completely satisfactory "digs," where he enjoyed more independence than he would have had inside the College. He played football for St. Catherine's, if not for the university, and found plenty of time to travel about attending country matches.

The Tengku managed to travel about quite a lot, for his £800 (US$4,000) per year allowance enabled him to live in style and to drive a £525 Riley car, a racy red and aluminum open sports model. Addiction to football, horse racing, dog racing, dancing, and miscellaneous other diversions left him little time for study and almost none for lectures. He propelled his Riley with such speed and verve from one non-academic engagement to another that he began collecting convictions for traffic offenses in Cambridge, London, and elsewhere. He scored a grand total of 23, not all of them in this early period but over the 16 years which he spent at various times in England more vigorously in pursuit of pleasure than of a degree. Just as he forgot to watch his speedometer, he also forgot to watch his calendar, and his leisurely academic progress was the result not only of failing his exams but of failing on at least one occasion to appear on the right day to take them. Nevertheless he managed in 1925 to become the first Kedah prince to take a B.A. degree from an English university, although the academic basis of the distinction does not invite close scrutiny. He then started what was to be a marathon pursuit of a law degree, ending at last in 1949, after repeated failures and prolonged interruptions. Then, at the age of forty-five, almost as much to his own surprise as that of the friends who had managed to fix his attention on law by reading it aloud to him, he just barely made the pass list. The Tengku promptly staged a gala celebration of what he called the "silver jubilee" of his matriculation.

The Tengku's true distinction consists perhaps in not taking himself very seriously, and one of the results has been that until the last few years almost no one else took him very seriously either, especially in politics. His first real experience in politics, as an undergraduate, came when he played chauffeur to a young British Liberal who chose to campaign for his party's candidate, Lloyd George, in a workingmen's district and provoked such outrage that they had to decamp as swiftly as the Riley could gather speed. This episode, his friends thought, taught him little except the social value of a political anecdote. One of his later experiences, after he had already passed a prolonged apprenticeship, came when he decided in 1946 that it was time for the Malay students in London really to organize for political action as did the other foreign students. He himself, in reviving the Malay Society of Great Britain which he had helped to found back in 1927, ran into near insubordination on the part of his associates, who claimed—with considerable justification—that he wanted them to do all the work. As a politician, his friends in London thought, the Tengku was a wonderful cook. The evenings when the Malay student population huddled in out of the London cold to eat highly seasoned Malay food and to talk of home in the flat of one or another of the set, turned out generally, with the Tengku in charge, to be as much culinary or social as political, the Tengku having a deft hand with both the skillet and the bottle.

Reports of the Tengku as a playboy prince, however, do not take into account quite a good deal of evidence that, unlike all too many of the other Malay princelings, he was quite earnestly if unmethodically attempting to be a useful citizen. During the long interval between periods of study in England, he entered the Kedah Civil Service. Beginning in 1931, he was assigned to a series of posts, soon achieving the rank of that all-purpose administrator, the District Officer, as legal, police, sanitation, agricultural, education, and tax officer all combined.

As a District Officer, the Tengku earned about M$300 per month, a figure which contrasted rather sharply with the £800 annual allowance (M$1,000 per month) he had enjoyed in England. He began to achieve a reputation as a champion of the rights of the poor and became immensely popular with the people of his administrative districts but not with the senior British and Malay officials back in Alor Star. On one memorable occasion, he sided against the government and with the Sungei Patani taxi drivers, who were being arbitrarily forced to form a company. For this, he was transferred on 24-hour notice to another post. The following day he was escorted to his new post of Kulim by a convoy of Sungei Patani taxi drivers. He was District Officer at Kulim when the Pacific War broke out.

One of the Tengku's exploits at the very beginning of the Japanese invasion of Malaya has now become a part of Kedah state folklore. The British and the Kedah court decided, when the Japanese advance began, to transfer the Sultan from Alor Star to the presumed safety of Penang Island. They packed him into the royal Rolls-Royce and pointed it southward, trailing him at some little distance to make sure that he was not surprised from the rear. Tengku Abdul Rahman, alerted to the maneuver and determined that the Sultan should remain in Kedah with his people, waited at a road fork not far from Butterworth and the Penang Straits ferry. He intercepted the royal yellow Rolls, kidnapped his father, Rolls, driver and all, and carried them off to Kulim and from there to a quiet kampong, one which has just recently been rechristened Kampong Raya to memorialize the event. When the British and Malay officials caught up with the Tengku by telephone he admitted to the crime, defied orders to return the Sultan to Penang, although threatened with arrest—and was promptly vindicated when the Japanese staged heavy air raids on Butterworth airfield and Penang.

The Tengku remained in Kedah state government service throughout the Japanese Occupation, on more than one occasion, according to the report of those who should know, boldly confronting the Japanese authorities on behalf of his people. At the time of the Japanese collapse, when Kedah, to an even greater extent than the rest of Malaya, was seething with the intrigues of Communists, nationalists, feudalists, and others, many of whom were armed, the Tengku was largely responsible for the fact that British troops reoccupied the state without any incidents of violence. Nevertheless, the taint of collaboration with the Japanese attached to many royal names in 1945, and accusations were made also against Tengku Abdul Rahman. It was not for some time that his name was completely cleared. Meanwhile, both Kedah and Malayan politics had become vastly complicated as small nationalist organizations mushroomed all over the country, most of them with but vaguely defined programs and bitterly jealous of one another. The Tengku, despite the geniality which characterized him in most of his dealings with individuals and groups,

tangled both with left-wing extremists—especially the Communists—
and with right-wing feudalists—especially his brother, the new Sultan.
In January 1946 he left for England again, motivated more by desire to
absent himself from Kedah than to present himself before the British
bar examiners whom he decided to face yet again—as he did, successfully, three years later.

In early 1949 Tengku Abdul Rahman returned once again to Malaya and joined the Legal Department of the Kedah state government. It
soon became obvious to everyone, himself included, that he had no future
in Kedah, since his personal and political relations with his brother, Sultan Badlishah (d. 1958), an arrogant feudalist who had come to the throne
in 1943, were bordering on the explosive. Tengku Abdul Rahman welcomed the opportunity, therefore, to go to Kuala Lumpur as Deputy Public Prosecutor. He did not resist very vigorously, if he did not actively
encourage, the pressures which a few of his friends began putting upon
him to devote himself more and more to politics. Finally, in 1951 circumstances conspired at last to unleash the Tengku's special talents,
which obviously were not for jurisprudence but for public life, and a career which had been to date unillustrious at last began to brighten.

The United Malay National Organization at that time was experiencing a major crisis. Under Dato Sir Onn bin Ja'afar, the UMNO had
been largely responsible for persuading the British to modify their immediate postwar proposal regarding the future status of Malaya. The
British had worked to create a Malayan Union, in which the Sultans would
have been relegated to the background, a new central government would
have gained sweeping authority, and the British themselves would have
remained in the ascendant. The Malays balked, and the British then con-
sented to form a less highly centralized Federation in which they would
allow an increasing degree of democratic self-government.

The UMNO, having achieved its first major objective, then split
wide open. In particular, it repudiated a proposal by Dato Onn that it
achieve interracial co-operation in building the new nation by accepting
Chinese members into the organization. It also repudiated Dato Onn
himself, so that the UMNO, Malaya's one big and important political
party, was without program or leader. At this point the Tengku's friends,
who knew his skill at maintaining amity and suspected that he might have
appeal as a popular leader, maneuvered him into the presidency. The
Tengku, with the help of those same friends—most of them fellow students from his London days—put UMNO back on the rails. By display
of his usual patience and affability, as well as a willingness to accept
other people's ideas and to capitalize on their efforts, the Tengku man-

aged soon to work out an Alliance with the leading Chinese and presently
with leading Indian factions. With the Tengku at its head, the Alliance
won a landslide victory in the July 1955 elections, then formed a new
government for the transition to independence. The Tengku managed to
negotiate so successfully with the British that, despite a series of crises over precise terms, the new Federation of Malaya achieved its independence on August 31, 1957, with the Tengku, naturally, as prime minister.

Between 1951 and 1957 the Tengku maintained a working schedule
which belied his earlier reputation for indolence and piled up a record
of achievement. He engaged in endless consultations and maneuvers,
first to keep the UMNO and the Alliance from falling apart, then to build
them into really strong organizations. He engaged with the British in a
contest of political pressures which resulted, far more quickly than the
British expected, in increased autonomy and in agreement about independence. After the 1955 elections, as chief minister, he headed the
new Malayan government, which managed far more smoothly than even
he expected to assume broad responsibilities for the administration.
The period of transition from colonialism to independence overlapped
that of the Communist Emergency, when guerrilla jungle fighters were
attempting to sabotage the nation. The Tengku, by gaining Malayan co-
operation with the British in military action against the Communists —
and by achieving a good record of administration — reassured the British that the gamble on Malayan independence was a good one. Growing
British reassurance, combined with growing Malayan sense of confidence and competence, made the transition remarkably painless and
postindependence prospects, consequently, remarkably good.

The Tengku himself, during this period, became a seasoned political leader, wise in the actuality if not always the philosophy of national development. He still exhibited a disinclination to burden his
mind with position papers; he proved capable of political indiscretions
which set the British intelligence service to shuddering and his own
followers to wagging both their tongues and their heads; he still liked
to consult the racing calendar before committing himself to conference
appointments and even then might turn up late, unbriefed, and unruffled.
But he did adopt an absolutely unequivocal position on the really critical issue, i.e., the necessity for negotiating, not fighting with the British for achievement of Malayan independence under conditions which
would give the nation the best possible start, such conditions to include
respect for the rights of all racial components of the new nation and continuing British co-operation. The measure of the success of the Tengku
and his associates is that the Federation of Malaya, alone among the new

Southeast Asian nations, passed from dependent to independent status without serious disruption of government services, another outbreak of violence, or deterioration in standards of official and public integrity.

The Tengku's life since 1957 has been full of the responsibilities of public life in an independent nation—election campaigns, parliamentary sessions, state visits, diplomatic receptions, and public appearances on all sorts of occasions. It has been full also of big and small domestic crises ranging from a threatened Alliance crack-up in 1959 to recent protests from teetotaling Muslims about his presiding at the opening of a new brewery. Fortunately, it has been less full of international crises. There have been minor ones, such as the problem of Communist guerrillas finding sanctuary across the Thai border; and at present there is a major crisis with Indonesia over Brunei and Malaysia.

For the most part, the Tengku seems actually to enjoy his formidable public schedule, not so much because it turns the spotlight on him as because he really likes the crowds, the bustle, and for that matter, the confusion. He has particularly enjoyed his campaign for Malaysia, although he has had some acute misgivings about having involved himself in the project. He was especially disturbed when he discovered that all non-Chinese Borneans were not necessarily Malay by blood or outlook, again when many Borneans began accusing him of being himself a colonialist, and yet again when Indonesians began to denounce him as a "neocolonialist." But the Tengku, although he has frequently reached explosion point of late over Indonesian accusations that he is a "puppet" and a "neocolonialist," has a most enviable ability quickly to shrug off his worries and to keep his public life from blotting out his private one. On the Malaysia matter, as on others, he works conscientiously, but usually he refuses to let it interfere seriously with his recreation or his sleep.

The Tengku lives a good part of his private life today in a hilltop mansion overlooking downtown Kuala Lumpur. It is a spacious old British colonial "bungalow," now refurbished and air conditioned. He prefers it to the modern villa the government built for him, then assigned to the deputy prime minister. He lives with his third wife and their two adopted children, both of them Chinese by race, and a large household of relatives and retainers. His first wife, a Siamese Chinese, who died of malaria in 1935, bore him a son and a daughter. The son is now an officer in the Malayan Army. The Tengku's second wife, an Englishwoman, returned to England before the war. Technically, at least, he has practiced polygamy in that he married his present wife before he and the Englishwoman were divorced in 1946. He was the subject of a mild sensation in 1953 when he was named as correspondent in a London divorce case, and again in 1954 when, on returning to England to negotiate his country's independence, he finally paid the £700 damages.

The Tengku makes the opportunity several times a week to play golf, a game at which he might excel if he kept his eye on the ball and his mind off the conversation. His handicap is 24. He has set the fashion for Malay officials, many of whom have tended to be rather aloof from Kuala Lumpur society, to turn up at the golf club and, by extension, at other clubs as well. The Tengku also finds time to patronize football and almost all other sports, being in fact President of the Malayan Football Association. He never misses a Kuala Lumpur race meet if he can help it, and his tips on the horses are highly regarded in racing circles, even in Australia, where he startled the nation during his state visit by picking the winners. Without neglecting sport, the Tengku manages also to patronize education. He has lately accepted the honorary post of Chancellor of the University of Malaya, an institution whose swift growth and progress he has greatly encouraged. He is a devout Muslim, turning up regularly on Friday at the mosque and performing the orthodox schedule of private prayer. He is a serious, if not altogether a discriminating student of Malayan history and culture. His own ventures into cultural creativeness consist mainly of writing. He has to his credit two rather thin Malay novels, one a romantic thriller, the other a vampire chiller. He also likes to dance and quite disregards criticism—much of it originating in Indonesia, where Sukarno is an avid dancer—that this is an evidence of frivolity. What he prefers is the Malay ronggeng, a dance of sinuous, sometimes rather sophisticated steps in which the partners do not touch but skillfully follow each other's lead through a succession of figures. Under the Tengku's patronage, the ronggeng is enjoying a revival in Kuala Lumpur's upper social circles, not only in the taxi dance halls or at the stag parties to which ronggeng girls are invited. The wives of important Malay officials, including the Tengku's own, have been taking lessons in order that they may emerge from the near social eclipse to which Malay tradition consigns them.

Tengku Abdul Rahman, despite his years and bulk, displays quite a degree of youthful agility and gaiety at ronggeng, as he does also in politics. Not only his admirers but a great many of his detractors as well hope that he will continue to do so for a long time to come. In Malaya, as is frequently the case elsewhere, the critical question may be: "Who next?" The Tengku's qualities are not easily matched, and they seem, on the basis of the record of the last ten years, to be almost exactly the qualities which Malaya needs—as will the new Malaysia.

CHAPTER
XVIII

FROM COLONY TO STATE IN SARAWAK

March 22, 1963

As it moves toward membership in the Federation of Malaysia, the British Crown Colony of Sarawak is confronted with an assortment of problems typical of the Malaysia area, some of them in particularly acute form. Sarawak faces Malaya's and Malaysia's general task of blending diverse racial elements into a single nationality. The difficulty is intensified by the fact that 50% of its population of about 750,000 is made up of tribal peoples, mainly Dayaks (Sea Dayaks 31.5%, Land Dayaks 7.8%) and Melanaus (5.9%), plus numerous small tribal minorities. These highly individualistic people are not easily integrated with the economically more advanced Chinese (31%) or the politically more experienced Malays (18%). Sarawak shares Singapore's hazard of an extreme left-wing Chinese element which has deeply infiltrated the labor unions, the schools, the press, and the political parties. These Chinese are suspected, with considerable justification, of actively plotting subversion. Sarawak, with an area of 50,000 square miles, approximates the Federation of Malaya in size. Like North Borneo, it has vast tracts of unpopulated jungle that can be opened up only by well-planned and well-financed development programs. Unlike North Borneo, it has not yet ascertained whether its timber stands are commercially attractive or whether the soils of the undeveloped areas are reasonably good. Along its northeastern border, Sarawak shares Brunei's problem of an actively insurgent Brunei Malay and Kadayan tribal population, which recently took up arms against the government and will not soon put aside the obscure grievances which led to the uprising in the first place and have not been healed in its repression. It lacks Brunei's money, which, as a matter of fact, many people in Sarawak regard as a curse—a curse to Brunei by reason of the cupidity it arouses, a curse also to Sarawak by reason of the contrast between what they regard as rich but futile Brunei and poor but gallant Sarawak. Like the rest of Malaysia, Sarawak has Indonesia to worry about. Its busy capital, Kuching, lying within 30 miles of the Indonesian border, is alert to the fact that Malaysia, being relatively rich, stable, and pro-Western, is an affront to Indonesian ultranationalism.

For all of its problems, however, the mood in Sarawak is one in which hopefulness prevails over apprehension. Hopefulness has long been a characteristic of Sarawak. A century ago, when the corrupt, piratical Brunei Sultanate was losing its grip on northern Borneo, Sarawak emerged under the benevolent rule of Rajah Brooke as a relatively happy little state. To be sure, Sarawak has had its troubles in the past, including protest, near insurrection, and the assassination of a newly appointed governor—all within three years after the last Rajah Brooke ceded the state to the British Crown in 1946. Its troubles, however, have been relatively brief and mild, and its steady progress has been impressive. Most important of all, tolerance at least, if not active good will, has prevailed within a community so complex in its racial make-up and so marked in its racial differences that racial friction could swiftly become explosive.

Today, as Sarawak prepares to join Malaysia, the long-suppressed conflicts are both modified and intensified. Dayaks, Chinese, Malays, and others have now developed a taste for nationalist politics and for its rewards. They are taking active satisfaction in competing for the attention of a public that is itself just awakening to the excitements of political self-assertiveness. Somebody—no one can be sure exactly who—is soon to inherit the prerogatives of the British colonial administrators. For all their own errors and all the built-in errors of the colonial system, including the failure to train their successors, the British have put on a good show. The really critical question in Sarawak tomorrow may boil down to this: whether the next show will be one of endless political maneuverings or one of relatively good, steady administration. The developments of the last year or so, since they indicate some of the specifics the new administration must deal with, should provide some clues to the answer.

Sarawak has been much preoccupied of late with the CCO, the SUPP, the MSC, the TNKU, and the Five-Year Plan. These, being interpreted, are the Clandestine Communist Organization, and anti-Malaysia Sarawak United People's Party, the Malaysia Solidarity Committee, the Tentara Nasional Kalimantan Utara (Azahari's Northern Borneo Liberation Army), and a M$150 million (US$495,000) scheme for providing more roads, schools, rubber, and other essentials for accelerating progress and prosperity. As of late 1962 and early 1963, Sarawak was particularly concerned with the TNKU and with a newly emerging element, an Alliance Party, as a counterforce to the pro-TNKU CCO and the SUPP.

The CCO used to be known to the British colonial administration as the Secret Communist Organization but has now been more ominously rechristened. The government has staged a series of arrests, trials, exposés, and countermeasures which some observers, including many knowledgeable local residents, judge disproportionate to the real danger. The British were so vigilant in their counter-Communist precautions, some of the British themselves admit, that they virtually ignored the signs of impending trouble elsewhere. Specifically, they overlooked the trouble that was brewing among the Brunei Malays and the Kadayan tribesmen on the Brunei border. So far as any available evidence shows, there was no direct tie-in between the Sarawak CCO, which is almost exclusively Chinese, and the Brunei insurgents, who were almost exclusively non-Chinese. The CCO, in fact, was apparently just as surprised by the outbreak as the British. It lost the ready-made opportunity to stage the disorders which the British had been anticipating. The CCO, it seems, may not have been as pervasive—and certainly it was not as alert—as the British administration believed.

For the last several years the British administration has been openly accusing the SUPP of allowing itself to be used as a Communist front organization. The government has prepared and published a series of white papers, the most recent and the most alarming of them just now released. By use of captured documents it has exposed a Peking-inspired Communist strategy to infiltrate and capture Sarawak labor unions, agricultural organizations, sports clubs, singing clubs, schools, newspapers, and political parties, especially the SUPP. Two of the one-time top leaders of the SUPP have been identified as CCO members. They have been arrested, tried, and deported, along with half a dozen other CCO members or agents. Leading Chinese-language newspapers—one each in Kuching, Sibu, and Miri—have been suspended. Their editors and publishers have been implicated in the subversion trials indicated above. A series of alarming episodes in Chinese secondary schools—efforts by Communist-affiliated teachers and students to disrupt all ordinary and orderly study and to convert the classes into political cells—has demonstrated that the CCO scare is no figment of official imagination.

The government case against the CCO and the SUPP is a sobering one, particularly, of course, for those who take the trouble to read white papers. It is weakened to some degree, however, by official admission that CCO members and sympathizers are few in number. It is even more seriously weakened perhaps by countercharges that the administration, by its reiterated and vehement accusations against the CCO and the SUPP and their Chinese supporters, has unjustly implicated major segments of the Chinese community, whose basic loyalty to the state would remain unshaken were it not for the government's pervasive suspicion.

The actual position and potential of the SUPP, particularly with reference to the CCO, is difficult to analyze unless one takes either the government's anti-SUPP fulminations or the SUPP's outraged rebuttals at face value. The SUPP was originally planned and organized with official encouragement, the expectation being that it would be a multiracial, progovernment party. The sponsors included types as diverse as Kuomintang Chinese capitalists and Communist-influenced labor leaders, and the party stood a good chance of attracting strong Malay and Dayak adherents. The government, on taking a second look at the SUPP backers, thought better of its encouragement. It actively discouraged Malay and Dayak membership, and as actively encouraged a split which promptly developed between the more rightist and the more leftist of the party members, whereupon both wings of the SUPP turned antigovernment. When the critical Malaysia issue arose, they adopted the position that Sarawak's independence should come before merger, that negotiation for membership in a North Borneo-Sarawak-Brunei union should follow, and that consideration of Malaysia was premature until Sarawak's people were freed from British colonial influence and pressure. The right-left split within the SUPP has widened, with the wealthy Kuching banker Ong Kee Hui heading the right wing and a brilliant young British-educated lawyer, Mr. Stephen Yong, heading the left. But the party holds together nevertheless, and there is considerable traffic between and among party and extraparty factions, including—government evidence seems to show conclusively—contact with the CCO.

The SUPP remains the strongest and best organized of the Sarawak parties, and its branches extend throughout the state. It enjoys a particularly powerful hold upon the laborers, not only in Kuching but in the towns of Sibu and Miri, and among Chinese farmers as well. The SUPP position is seriously challenged today, however, by an emerging but incessantly bickering Alliance Party. In this new coalition of various small parties of recent origin, the anti-SUPP, pro-Malaysia Chinese, Malays, and tribal peoples are seeking to resolve their differences and to form a dominant political group on the model of the original Alliance in Malaya and the new one in North Borneo. The Sarawak Alliance relies heavily upon appeal to the Dayaks and other tribesmen. One of the most potent bases of its appeal is the conspicuous role it assigns to tribal leaders. Two of the most important, themselves friendly political rivals, are Temenggong Jugah, Paramount Chieftain of the Ibans, or Sea Dayaks, and Temenggong Oyang Lawai Jau, Paramount Chief of the Kenyahs. Both have featured prominently and colorfully in recent years as appointive representatives of the tribal peoples in the British colonial councils. In a new state where tribesmen predominate and the minority Chinese and Malays are extremely jealous of their prerogatives, the two chiefs seem destined to occupy key positions.

Temenggong Jugah anak Barieng, O.B.E., chairman of the Alliance Party, now sixty, leader of 31.5% of the population of Sarawak, grew up in the Balleh River area where he lived the traditional life of the Sea Dayak tribesman, becoming skilled in hunting and fishing and in the rice and rubber agriculture of the Dayak community. By his ability and courage he rose fast to the top of the tribal hierarchy. He distinguished himself particularly during World War II when he waged guerrilla war against the Japanese, as an ally of the British. Since the war he has been a prominent member of Sarawak and Kuching official society. A handsome, spirited, totally outgoing individual, picturesque in his soup-bowl bangs and tribal dress, he is a warm friend of the British, and a member of practically every important state body, including the Supreme Council. Although Temenggong Jugah has never learned to read and write, he has acquired proficiency in spoken Malay and has picked up considerable English, so that he misses very little of the complicated political maneuvering in Kuching. In recent years Temenggong Jugah has adopted a modernized way of life. He now lives not in a long house but in his own bungalow; he fancies orchids and owns rather a showy collection. He has one wife and four children. His second son, who has just graduated from high school, is about to proceed to England for advanced education. Temenggong Jugah himself has traveled to England—for the Queen's coronation—to Australia as a state guest, and also to Japan, Hong Kong, and Malaya.

Temenggong Jugah is one of the Borneo tribespeople who have converted to Borneophiles such Britishers as Sir Malcolm MacDonald. Another is Temenggong Oyang Lawai Jau. Bigger and even jollier than Temenggong Jugah, and literate besides, he always appears in a beautifully woven straw hat ornamented with feathers, and his ear lobes have been stretched to extended loops by leopard-tooth earrings. He has a nephew who has already completed two years of study at Cambridge University. A Roman Catholic convert, he presides over what is perhaps the biggest and most elaborate long house in Borneo. His wartime guerrilla career was as distinguished as Temenggong Jugah's. He has played a cautious political role, and in the flurry of political activity in Borneo in recent years had neither formed nor joined any party until he became a member of the Alliance. He was originally lukewarm to the Malaysia proposal but is now a strong supporter.

Sarawak's tribal politics are as intricate in their way as are national politics and as unpredictable. The impact of tribal development upon national political affairs is a phenomenon which can only be watched, not controlled. Among those who are watching are not only the other tribal leaders, including the chiefs of the Land Dayaks together with the Chinese and the British, but also the Malays. Most prominent among the Malays is the fifty-six-year-old Datu Bandar, Abang Haji Mustapha, C.B.E., chairman of the Party Negara. The Datu Bandar is the grandson of the Datu Hakim who was a close friend of the first Rajah Brooke. He was educated in English in Catholic missionary primary and secondary schools in Kuching. A retired civil servant, he has traveled to the United Kingdom, Indonesia, and Australia. Datu Bandar is notably convivial, but, by reason of failing health, possibly not one of the most vigorous contenders for top position in the new government.

All of the Sarawak politicians and all of the parties have been engrossed during the last two years in the Malaysia proposal, which started off by eliciting almost nobody's open support, then, as the SUPP defined its opposition, attracted the increasing support of almost everybody except the SUPP and, of course, the CCO. The leading politicians, both pro- and anti-Malaysia, have played an important role in clarifying Borneo points of view in the Malaysia Solidarity Committee, which worked out the basic formula for merger. They played an important role also in presenting the Borneo case for and against merger to the Cobbold Commission, a joint British-Malayan investigative group which visited North Borneo and Sarawak in 1962. The commission turned in a report that two thirds of the population of Malaysia approved the plan. It also formulated a set of recommendations providing safeguards to Borneo interests. On the basis of its findings, final negotiations were undertaken for transfer of Borneo sovereignty from the British Crown to the proposed Federation.

The British colonial government in Sarawak is now scheduling general elections for mid-May, and Malaysia, naturally, will be the key issue. It plans to broaden the electorate to include the total adult population and to follow, with some modifications, the rather elaborate procedure of the first general elections of 1959. The voters then elected by direct ballot the members of District Councils, who elected the members of the Divisional Councils, who in turn elected 24 members of the 43-member Council Negri (State Council), the administration exercising the power to "nominate," i.e., appoint others, some of whom, of course, may also be Divisional Council members.

The British administration now is giving attention to another urgent problem—when and how to phase out the British colonial officials and to phase in their replacements. The orderly transition to a new form of government might seem almost prohibitively difficult were it not for the precedent of the nearby Federation of Malaya. There the government offered generous "compensation for loss of career" to all British administrators, retained some on special contract basis, promoted local persons to more responsible positions as rapidly as was compatible with the good of the civil service, and in the first general elections after independence made the transition to fully elective legislative bodies.

The administration in Sarawak is about to face another problem of peculiar delicacy—the preparation for a local chief of state who, according to present plan, will be appointed jointly by the British Crown and the Chief of State of the Federation. In all probability, no Malay or Chinese would prove acceptable to the majority of the people. On the other hand, the nomination of a Dayak or another tribesman would have to be handled with particular skill to win for him the support of tribal communities other than his own.

The new government, whoever heads and conducts it, is going to have to deal with a major problem of national development. The Sarawak government got off to a much slower start than did the government of North Borneo, but it is now spending about M$125 million per year on administration and development, at least M$40 million of it on special projects relating to a comprehensive new plan. Sarawak's towns, in consequence, are rapidly being rebuilt and expanded; the Sarawak hinterland is being opened up as new roads are built through swamp and jungle; education, public health, agriculture, and other services are being swiftly improved. Nevertheless, the major part of Sarawak remains accessible only by jungle river. Of the population, ten years of age and above, only 25% are literate; of the children of primary-school age, only 40% of the indigenous, as contrasted to 80% of the Chinese, are enrolled in school. The major part of the state's rubber acreage remains to be replanted, Chinese, Malay, and Dayak planters alike—virtually all of them small holders—having as yet to be impressed with the simple economic fact that newly developed stock yields four times as much latex as the old. The Sarawak timber industry lags far behind North Borneo's. The pepper industry is subject to blight, glut, and to manipulation by Singapore middlemen.

One area of Sarawak highlights the state's problem in its most extreme form. It is the Limbang district in the Fifth Division, where

there occurred the most serious Sarawak phase of the Azahari insurrection. The Limbang area, the last segment of Brunei real estate to
be acquired by Rajah Brooke, is a wedge-shaped river valley which
separates the two little enclaves of Brunei. To the southeast is the
Indonesian border. Limbang is difficult of access from Kuching; it
has little apparent development potential; it is an area of small-scale
rice, rubber, and copra production; and in Southeast Asian terms it is
only moderately prosperous.

Limbang is inhabited mostly by Brunei Malays and Kadayan
tribesmen, both Muslim and both racially akin to the Indonesians. A
century ago these Brunei Malays and Kadayans welcomed release from
the tyranny of the Sultan of Brunei, but in recent years they have looked
longingly toward their suddenly prosperous ancestral land. They have
only to travel a few miles down river to see the elaborate new schools
of Brunei Town, the completely equipped hospital, the totally and handsomely rebuilt urban area with its huge mosque and community center.
In order to appreciate the economic difference between tax-free Brunei
and tax-financed Sarawak, they have only to pay M$0.70 instead of M$1.40
per gallon for gasoline to propel their outboard motorboats home again.
Those of them who get to distant Kuching quickly grasp the fact that few
of the Limbang Malays and none of the Limbang Kadayans enjoy any official position or privilege. In Brunei they observe that the Brunei Malays
are predominant. They have only to listen to traders' reports from Indonesia to know that in Indonesian Borneo the fires of localism and of
nationalism burn very high indeed.

The Limbang district, consequently, has been one in which dis-
content has proved easy to mobilize. Large numbers of Limbang citizens last year supported a Revert to Brunei movement which received
sympathetic support in Brunei itself. A high percentage of adult Limbang males joined Azahari's army. It is one of the illogical inversions
of the insurrection that whatever the Brunei insurrectionists were rebelling against, the Limbang contingent seems in effect to have been rebelling for. They captured the police station and seized control of Limbang town, killing four constables in the engagement, then held the District Officer, his wife, and various others—including an American Peace
Corps member—as hostages. When the British attempted to reoccupy
the town, they precipitated the bitterest battle of the insurrection. In
the course of the engagement 21 rebels and eight British Green Jackets
were killed and the main town area was heavily fought over.

Limbang today represents a very serious problem of rehabilitation and readjustment. The loss of life and property in the course of

the insurrection was a severe blow in itself; then, immediately after the insurrection, Limbang was hit by the worst flood in its history. The short-range problem in Limbang is to repair the physical damage and then to get a meaningful development program started. The long-range problem is to repair the psychological damage and to get the Limbang people really integrated into Sarawak—or into Brunei, should decision now be taken to restore at least this one piece of former Brunei territory. But the problem of Limbang is also something of the problem of the State of Sarawak as it faces integration into the new Malaysia, and of Malaysia itself as it faces integration into Southeast Asia. The differences and suspicions which have now been aroused are going to be extremely difficult to dispel.

CHAPTER
XIX

MALAYSIA'S CAPITAL COMPLEX

May 20, 1963

Malaya's national capital of Kuala Lumpur, popularly known as "K.L.," its satellite town of Petaling Jaya, or "P.J.," and the nearby harbor town of Port Swettenham, abbreviated to "P. S'ham," constitute, together with the Selangor state capital, which bears the apparently irreducible name of Klang, an urban, suburban, and rural complex representative of the new Malaya. Kuala Lumpur signifies government and business; Petaling Jaya, the new bourgeoisie; Klang, the rural and feudal Malaya, now being modernized; and Port Swettenham, labor. All are dependent upon rubber, tin, and tolerance, of which the rubber supply is rapidly increasing while prices drop, tin is a wasting asset, and tolerance is a highly speculative intangible.

K.L., P.J., P. S'ham, and Klang have achieved remarkable growth and prosperity to date because Malays, Chinese, Indians, and various minorities, including the British, have been able to reconcile their many differences in search for a good living, which here rather more readily than in most other places in Southeast Asia becomes an excellent one. Port Swettenham 100 years ago was a mangrove swamp. Klang was a river town where Malay princeling pirates preyed upon everyone within range. Petaling Jaya was swamp and jungle. Kuala Lumpur was a shantytown of Chinese tin miners who expected to be decimated by ruffians, malaria, tigers, and cobras, and overestimated the menace only of the tigers and the cobras.

The two-hour drive today from Ampang Village, the original Chinese mining area, through Kuala Lumpur, Petaling Jaya, and Klang to Port Swettenham takes one through the richest, handsomest, best-run national capital area in Southeast Asia. Save to devotees of progress, it does not generally seem an exciting journey. But it was exciting in 1950, when Communist guerrillas made it dangerous to travel outside of convoy by day or to venture out onto the road at all by night. It could quickly become so again, if the Muslim Malays were to let themselves become really fanatical about the Chinese affinity for pork and profit, or if the Chinese were to become really outraged over the Malay's special privileges, or if the Indians and other minority members were to become as revolutionary as some of their more impassioned leaders sound, or if any one of a dozen other unhappy contingencies were to develop—a labor union appeal to Indonesia, say, for the area to be "liberated" from "neocolonial exploiters."

In Kuala Lumpur even the most loyal citizen is likely to admit that as a capital the city is extraordinarily lacking in any very distinctively national character. One cannot say that it is nondescript, for it is highly varied in architecture and its population is colorful, what with Chinese gangsters, Indian fire walkers, Malay magicians, and Nepalese peddlers, to mention some of the more or less arcane types to be found in the tenements, the kampongs, and the holy places that intersperse the modern city. Certainly it is not sleepy and placid, as it used to be, for its traffic is now worse than that of its more cosmopolitan neighbor, Singapore; its cocktail circuit is more animated; its gossip is more intimate; and its air of urgency is increasingly pervasive. All the same, Kuala Lumpur is a city which has never yet managed to achieve any striking personality or to look or feel as though it belongs where it is. Its most distinctive physical feature is also its most deceptive—a complex of administrative buildings, railroad station, and mosque built in what is officially described as "Modern Saracenic" but is in fact "Victorian Rajput." It is an architectural pastiche which lends an air of Arabian Nights levity to a town which is at once bureaucratic British, bourgeois Chinese, and burgeoning Malay. It seems a bit accidental, as though designed for some decadent Indian ruler who rejected the plans but sold them to a carefree Malay Sultan.

The appearance of not quite fitting in, while nevertheless making out very well, extends to virtually all aspects of the city and its population. The British, for instance, are still very much in evidence. Some of them still live in rambling old colonial mansions set in spacious gardens shaded by tremendous rain trees. Almost all of them seem to patronize the Selangor Club, play cricket, drive sports cars, wear suede shoes, and choose very seriously between fish-and-chips and sausage-and-mashed. One of them is the Chief Justice, another the Army Chief of Staff. Most of them, of course, are private citizens. The very fact that they are still here signifies Kuala Lumpur's stability. Stability in itself seems a bit exotic in Southeast Asia today, and the presence of masses of Britishers being very, very British in the tropics seems somehow to belong to the era of Somerset Maugham, not of Sukarno.

The Chinese, on the other hand, fit in almost as naturally as they do ubiquitously. This Federal capital of the new Malaya, and soon perhaps of the new Malaysia, is to most practical intents and purposes an Overseas Chinese city. The Kuala Lumpur Chinese run the Overseas Chinese gamut, from those who are almost completely Anglicized to those who are almost completely immersed in the Chinese ghettos.

The Chinese millionaires live in bigger mansions than do the British, some of them in ultramodern cliff-hanging residences in the Kenny Hills district, where shrewd investors, like shrewd investors in other Kuala Lumpur real estate, have seen their properties double in value every few years. The rich to well-to-do Chinese businessmen share with the big Western concerns the greater part of Kuala Lumpur's commercial enterprise. The Chinese get the dragon's share. They are interested not only in rubber, tin, banking, industry, and import-export, but also in the nearly identical little shophouses which line many miles of Kuala Lumpur's streets, the small stands which obstruct pedestrian traffic on the "five-foot ways" in front of the shops, and the pushcarts which carry even a full meal to the ultimate consumer.

The soon-to-be well-to-do Chinese work at all the trades and services. Some Chinese, whose prosperity has eluded them or been unduly delayed, man the city's few remaining trishaws—many of these trishawmen are opium addicts. Some drive the trucks and taxis, careers which they share with the Indians and the Malays. Some of the women of the most vigorously struggling lower class carry earth, brick, and cement for the construction industry, an occupation by no means incompatible with feminine vanity, it would seem, for on the job young and middle-aged alike wear coal scuttle bonnets and fingertip-length sleeves to protect their complexions and hands against sun tan. Practically all of the Chinese send their children to school, through secondary school and even into the university if the children can pass the stiff competitive examinations which weed them out, year by year, according to the British system, and condemn the rejects to the poorer jobs. The boundless industry and ability of the Chinese is at once exhilarating and sobering to the observer. The Overseas Chinese, one often feels, if they have not already in effect taken over Kuala Lumpur and the area will soon do so, and who is to stop them or why?

Even today, in Kuala Lumpur, save in a government office or a special residential area, one usually has to look twice for the Malay who is not the messenger, the driver, the casual passer-by, or the school child. In the government offices, however, now that most of the British are out, the Malays are in, especially in the top positions, although the Chinese and the Indians still supply most of the clerks. But the Kuala Lumpur Malay is often a recent comer, at least to high position, not yet truly at home in the capital, more disposed to be completely at ease in Johore Bahru or Alor Star or even Kota Bahru on the more backward East Coast.

The Malay official is just beginning to patronize the Selangor Club, the cricket club built on the padang, or green, facing the main government buildings. Following the lead of the Prime Minister, Tengku Abdul Rahman, he is also beginning to favor Kuala Lumpur's splendid golf course, where, in fact, the diplomatic corps lies in wait to intercept him. Even yet, however, the Malay official generally leads a life apart, most particularly the orthodox Malay Muslim, who fears the taint of pork or alcohol. His wife, who probably does not speak English, seems especially remote to the Chinese or the Westerner, who is just beginning seriously to study Malay.

Traditional Malay life in Kuala Lumpur still centers largely upon certain restricted areas. One of them is Kampong Bahru, a Malay preserve in downtown Kuala Lumpur where only Malays can own property or operate businesses. Here Malays of Sumatran Minangkabau origin predominate, small Malay houses outnumber Western-style bungalows, and community life revolves around the mosque and the adjacent market. Many of the younger generation stray much farther afield, to Bukit Bintang Park, for instance, Kuala Lumpur's amusement center, where the young men perform the ronggeng with taxi dance partners. In Kampong Bahru, however, although young couples now yearn to stroll hand in hand, the community elders are alert for scandal. Some—whether the more vigilant or the more salacious-minded is open to dispute—are alert to detect cases of khalwat, euphemistically translated as "close proximity." It is any occasion of an unmarried couple being together under even slightly questionable circumstances, an offense actionable in the Muslim religious courts which have had a rash of prosecutions in recent months.

The Malays of Kuala Lumpur are in fact less conspicuous than the less numerous Indians. Indian provision and textile shops dot the city. Indian laborers perform the hardest, dirtiest, worst-paid services, such as refuse collection and street repair. Indian clerks make up a large part of the staffs of Western business offices. Indian dress, Indian temples, Indian cows are commonplace. Pakistanis and Ceylonese make themselves relatively inconspicuous. All three manage, for the most part, to reconcile the political differences of their homelands to present not a united but also not a fragmented minority front on the Malayan scene.

"Communalism"—British usage for "racism"—is the almost inevitable and, from the government's point of view, the deplorable point of emphasis in describing Kuala Lumpur. Quite clearly, anything which serves to strengthen racial separatism and hence suspicion serves to increase the hazard to the stability of the city and the nation. Just as clearly, the welding together of all these racial communities into one coherent city or nation is going to be a long, hard task. It is one in which progress, as a result of deliberate effort, is just beginning to make itself felt. The government is attempting to achieve this objective by "Malayanization." The process entails creation of a national educational system allowing for education in all the prevailing languages but requiring competence in Malay. It involves also a tremendous national development program in which special attention is paid to improving the economic and social condition of the Malays so that they can compete on more equal terms with the Chinese. It ties in with the even more difficult and tendentious system of guaranteeing certain special Malay privileges—a high quota of civil service jobs, licenses for such enterprises as transport services, and preferential treatment in the awarding of scholarships. Whether this policy implies avoidable "discrimination" and "favoritism," or even the suppression of a "superior" culture (the Chinese) and the elevation of an "inferior" one (the Malay), as some argue, is one of the major issues of the new nation. So far, the program has worked out without any major outbreaks, mainly perhaps because everyone is alert to the danger and when an incident threatens, sober counsels quickly prevail.

Downtown Kuala Lumpur today still seems less a blended composite than a collage by a whimsical city planner. Much of the old Chinatown still congests one bank of the narrow Klang River. Two-, three-, and four-story shophouses stretch repetitiously along its tangled, traffic-clogged streets. The upper story or stories constitute a tenement, the ground floor a narrow shop open to the arcaded "five-foot way" onto which it overflows its contents and activities. More and more shophouses are now being razed to make way for modern air-conditioned office buildings faced with louvers against the sun. One of the newest of the buildings features an extremely popular Escalator.

Across the muddy river is the administrative center, and beyond it a hilly area, the original residential district in which the British developed a botanical garden and built their bungalows. On the fringes of the Lake Garden are now being erected a M$10.6 million, 15-story Parliament building, a M$1.5 million national museum, and a new national mosque. In all directions about Kuala Lumpur stretch old and new suburban areas, the new ones distinguished by expensive modern villas, the old by great pillared bungalows with almost as much space devoted to sheltered verandas as to interior rooms. Scattered about the town and its outskirts are densely packed Chinese, Indian, and Malay working-class settlements into which intrude, as they do not commonly elsewhere in the city, the fly, the mosquito, the rat, and other evidences that life is not as well arranged as it might at first seem.

Kuala Lumpur began about ten years ago to develop a program to resettle squatters who had moved into the city during the Emergency as refugees. The result is Petaling Jaya, which has long since ceased to be merely a small experiment in low-cost housing for the near-indigent. Petaling Jaya spreads out today over 4,000 acres of land which ten years ago was worked-out tin mine or superannuated rubber plantings. The government laid out building lots, laid on all city services in abundance, and then waited—not very long—for private enterprise to move in. P.J. now has some 8,000 homes, ranging from rather rudimentary row houses to semiluxury villas. It includes an adjacent "industrial estate" where about 200 new factories are turning out such miscellaneous products as matches, biscuits, cigarettes, pharmaceuticals, paint, soap, tires, air conditioners, beer, and soft drinks.

In Petaling Jaya today, one can buy a brick-concrete-tile house for US$5,000 to US$15,000, most of it readily available as a bank loan to any responsible party. In addition to the usual living-dining area it will have two to four bedrooms, each commonly with bath, a modern kitchen, a carport, a terrace, and a garden in which hibiscus, oleander, and ground orchids grow fast. This may not be exactly what you want if you demand spaciousness, shade, quiet, and an unobstructed view, but it is almost exactly what a great many Chinese, Indians, Malays, and Britishers feel meets their needs and their budgets. There is growing up in P.J., consequently, the genuinely intermixed, interracial community which Kuala Lumpur has never achieved. For better or for worse, it is predominantly a community of bourgeois salary-earning property owners. They are becoming increasingly interested in insurance-pension schemes, savings accounts, and other manifestations of the private enterprise system, including new Malayan mutual funds, the first of which sold at M$1.00 per share a couple of years ago and is quoted at M$1.88 today.

Beyond the outskirts of Petaling Jaya lie some of the enterprises which have made Kuala Lumpur and Malaya rich: tin mines and rubber estates. At the big mines, £1 million dredges float in artificial ponds, digging and washing the tin ore which, as the years go by and the known lodes are worked out, is declining sharply in quality and quantity. Beyond the tin mines are the rubber lands, the big estates owned by the British and the Chinese, and the small holdings by the Chinese and the Malays. Recently planted high-yield rubber trees are now coming into production. Since they produce four times as much latex per tree as did the old stock, they demonstrate to the optimists that natural rubber can continue almost indefinitely to compete on favorable terms with synthetics. The pessimists these days are shifting to oil palm, the market for palm oil at present seeming almost insatiable. Those who are pessimistic about tin are prospecting for iron.

In Kuala Lumpur, practically everybody of any property knows the day's quotation on tin and rubber and feels poorer whenever he thinks of the vast American stockpiles and of Washington's stockpile disposal policies. Nobody likes to be reminded, naturally, that if prices drop because the United States unloads, prices rose originally because the United States overbought.

Declining profits on rubber and tin do not yet spell loss to the producer and will not do so soon. One has only to look into the settlements of the tin miners (mainly Chinese) and of the rubber tappers (Chinese, Indian, and Malay) to see that the benefits have been reaching down to the laborers. A miner or tapper can earn M$4-M$5 per day, and generally more than one member of the family holds a job. This income does not mean opulent living, to be sure, but more and more commonly it can mean a new home with light and water, a radio, a sewing machine, a motor scooter, adequate food and clothing, and at least primary schooling for the children.

Eastward from P.J., in the middle of the rolling rubber country, lies the town of Klang, one of the problem towns of Malaya. Klang has more near-slums, more street litter, fewer new shops and homes, and less civic spirit than almost any other community of its size in all of Malaya. It has earned the distinction of repeated citation by civic-minded organizations for looking unkempt. Whether this is because of or in spite of the fact that it is the seat of the Selangor Sultanate and of the state government, it is hard to say. Klang has expected for years that the whole of the state government might migrate to Kuala Lumpur, as a great deal of it has done, but on the other hand it has had almost as much reason to expect that state offices already in Kuala Lumpur might start backtracking from the congestion of the nation's capital. Meanwhile, Klang has been the site of some big development projects. One of these is a new double-level highway and railroad bridge across the Klang River, a multimillion-dollar structure which seems to have benefited Kuala Lumpur and Port Swettenham much more than Klang. Another is a splendid new royal palace, which quite possibly, as Klang's non-Malay population is likely to say, the town did not really need. The Sultan much prefers yet another new palace which he maintains in Kuala Lumpur.

The Sultan, a young man of thirty-seven, who came to the throne in 1961, typifies the dilemma of the traditional ruler in Malaya today. He is English educated, and his schooling included a year of private tutoring in London. He has given inconclusive indications of being interested variously in business, agriculture, modern administration, and the ceremonial functions of the traditional ruler. But he has not really devoted himself to any of these, and indeed his constitutional powers being strictly limited to customary and religious matters, it would require great exertion on his part to chart out for himself a career in the modern manner. Meanwhile, he draws a state stipend of M$135,000 per year, the Sultana draws M$12,000, and the maintenance of the court costs another M$380,000. This expenditure the government can easily afford, provided, of course, that subsidy for the Sultanate continues to express the loyalty of the traditional-minded Malay to the state government without giving affront to the younger generation, or, for that matter, to the Chinese. The problem is one which is not much discussed in public in Malaya today, but it weighs on people's minds.

The adjacent town of Port Swettenham on first sight seems no more prepossessing than Klang, but then no one expects much of a small port town. Off the main road one can still find pleasant, shaded streets and agreeable homes, also a seaman's club which offers visiting ships' crews rather an unexpected degree of comfort and even a swimming pool. Until very recently, when a big new port development program began to take effect, P. S'ham's facilities have been inadequate, antiquated, and badly managed. Labor troubles were inevitable. Union tactics in the past concentrated on "work to rule" campaigns which at various times virtually stalled the movement of cargo through the port. During the past two years, P. S'ham's harbor facilities have been greatly expanded and improved; port procedures, including the handling of labor, have improved also; a whole new port area with three deep-water berths—built with a US$10 million grant—is about to open. Then, just when it seemed that P. S'ham might at last begin to fulfill its purpose of easing Kuala Lumpur's excessive dependency upon Singapore, came a railway strike in December 1962 which stopped rail traffic throughout Malaya and closed the port. In the course of negotiations, first in the endeavor to prevent and then to settle the strike, certain facts became quite clear. The nation's labor leaders, who in the past have been willing generally to negotiate on the basis of quick mutual compromise, have suddenly become much more aggressive. The employer—in this case the national government—is so unaccustomed to handling serious labor problems that it proved maladroit. Serious labor trouble, such as Singapore has been long plagued with but which Malaya has been spared, can spread as swiftly in Malaya as anywhere else and bring quick and adverse consequences. Some of the effects of the railway strike were immediately apparent in the town of P. S'ham, where labor earnings suddenly dried up, shopkeepers began raising prices, and others than the laboring classes felt the pinch. The railway strike was finally settled after 25 days, but new strikes were clearly in prospect. Nevertheless, in a P. S'ham by-election held while the strike was still on, Tengku Abdul Rahman's United Malay National Organization (UMNO) candidate won by almost as big a majority as the party's candidate had in 1959, and new labor difficulties did not, at the outset at least, signify political upset.

From P. S'ham to K.L., along a new 27-mile "dual carriageway" (superhighway) which is now partly completed, it may be seen on every side that this is a prosperous and progressive rural-urban complex. It does not require any very deep penetration, however, to turn up the evidence that here, as almost anywhere else, the tensions are potentially serious. Upon once sleepy little K.L. are now converging some of the national and international conflicts which, save for the critical period of the Communist Emergency, it has generally been able to avoid. The city is regarded by many of its citizens as a model Southeast Asian capital, one which its neighbors would do well to visit, as more and more are beginning to do. However, it has moved so fast and so far in such a different direction from most of Southeast Asia that nobody can be certain whether the visitors will be moved to emulate it, expunge it, or engulf it.

CHAPTER
XX

FOUR CITIZENS OF KUALA LUMPUR

May 22, 1963

Mahmud bin Ahmad, twenty-one, is the eldest son of a Malay father and a Sumatran mother. He was graduated two years ago from an English-language secondary school and is now a teacher in a Malay-language primary school, earning a salary of M$160 per month. He lives with his parents and his three young sisters in Kuala Lumpur's Kampong Bahru, where the family occupies a small house built of wood in modified Malay style, raised on brick piers, and provided with piped water and electricity. Mahmud contributes M$50 of his salary to the family budget, his contribution being just about enough to meet the living expenses of his three young sisters, who are enrolled in the Malay-language primary school. Although Mahmud suggests that they might continue into secondary school, his parents think that for girls primary education is enough. Mahmud has a seventeen-year-old brother, who is studying on a full government scholarship in the Boys Wing of the Federation Military College near Kuala Lumpur. He hopes next year to be accepted for officer's training in the Cadet Wing of the college.

Mahmud himself is rather uncertain at the moment what he wants to do as a permanent career. He may continue to teach, in which case he wants to attend one of the new Malayan teacher-training colleges to which it would be rather easy for him to get a two-year assignment, all expenses paid and a M$75-per-month allowance as well. He is also thinking of entering the University of Malaya, where he could probably get a scholarship sufficient to cover most of his expenses. He would prefer, however, to study in the United Kingdom and take up law or history or both. Competition for foreign study grants is stiff, and he would probably have some difficulty in qualifying, his secondary-school record having been satisfactory but not brilliant. He has heard that young Malays with secondary education in English are now much in demand in Western business offices in Kuala Lumpur, where they are given training for executive jobs. He is not investigating these possibilities because he is not at all sure he would really like to go into business. He might try to enter the civil service, but to advance in a government career he thinks he should have a degree from a foreign university. He could enter a government office now and hope for a study assignment abroad later, but for the next year or two he will continue to teach. Meanwhile, he will make applications for foreign study and continue to improve his English, which, as a matter of fact, is already quite fluent.

Mahmud's chances of getting what he wants, when and if he decides what it is, would seem far better than reasonably good. Despite the fact that his academic record is not outstanding, in comparison with that of many of his Chinese classmates, he has other qualifications which perhaps more than compensate. He is a personable young man, with even more than the average Malay good looks and a bearing of quiet self-assurance which is exceptional in one of his youth and inexperience. He is obviously bright, healthy, and energetic. His handicap, to put it bluntly, is his family background. His father is merely a "peon," a M$150-per-month orderly in a British Army hospital in Kuala Lumpur. His father had the discernment, as a result of long association with the British, to recognize the value of an English-language education for his son and to arrange for him to get it. Owing to his own limited background, he has not been able to give him much guidance. Several of his British schoolmasters took an interest in the boy, but they returned to England before he was far enough along for them to be of really great help. Had Mahmud come from a higher class family, he would certainly have been pushed ahead fast and would already be enrolled in the University of Malaya or a school abroad.

Mahmud's present life as a schoolteacher is fairly strenuous. He has a class of about 40 boys, and he carries a good deal of extra responsibility at times. On the occasion, for instance, of state visits to Kuala Lumpur of foreign heads of government, it is his job to get the pupils turned out in good order to help line the roadsides and to wave flags. He has more than enough personal interests to fill all of his free time. He wakens each morning at 5:00 and spends an hour at prayer, reading the Koran or other religious writings, and another half hour at English-language study before bicycling to school at 7:00. School closes at 1:00 p.m., and generally he spends his afternoon hours at sports. He is a member of a soccer club in which there are Chinese and Indian as well as Malay players. He enjoys tennis almost as much as soccer. Frequently he goes to the mosque to perform his evening prayers, and he regularly attends the Friday services of the Muslim Sabbath. Most nights, he is in bed by 8:30 or 9:00.

On Saturday evening Mahmud always goes to the Kampong Bahru weekly night market where practically the whole community assembles. With his friends, he strolls up and down the market area, back and forth across the bridge, stopping now and then for a bottle of orange pop, some satay (small Malay shish kebabs), or some fried bananas. Like the other boys, he keeps his eyes on the girls who are also promenading. Unlike some of the other boys who are beginning to stroll about with particularly bold young girls, he keeps his distance. The fact is, he does not want to get involved with a girl just yet. He is resisting his parents' suggestions that it is time that he think of marriage, and he refuses to have anything to do with the matchmakers. He does not want pressures upon him to mount, as they will if the community elders get it into their heads that he is in danger of an entanglement— as some of his friends certainly are. Consequently, he very seldom goes along with his friends to Bukit Bintang Park to dance the rong-geng with the Malay hostesses, the joget girls. Instead, he goes to a movie, generally an American musical or a "spectacular" of the "Hercules" variety. He likes to dance, however, and he is thinking of joining a cultural group which rehearses traditional Malay dances for state occasions. Indeed, belonging to such a group might also give him a chance to travel abroad.

During school holidays Mahmud has several times taken the chance to travel. Once he bicycled northward to the Thailand border, once south to Singapore. He took his time, stopping off in out-of-the-way kampongs and small towns for several days at a stretch, eating at the streetside food stalls and sleeping in the mosque. He enjoys listening to village tales of hantus and pontianaks (ghosts and vampires), and confesses that at times he gets rather frightened. He takes every opportunity also to go hunting. Once he accompanied some aborigines into the mountains to shoot and trap mouse deer, and when the hunt was over he enjoyed his share of the sweet tender meat. He once hunted hornbills, too, but since he was trying to use an aborigine's blowpipe, he did not actually get any. Killing mouse deer and hornbills is illegal, of course, but no one really interferes with aborigine hunters.

During his next vacation, Mahmud would like to go to Indonesia. An acquaintance of his went on a student tour two years ago and brought back reports of a nation bigger and culturally much richer than Malaya, one which was claiming a place among the world's really great nations.

Prompted by his friend's accounts, Mahmud began to listen to Radio Indonesia and to go occasionally to an Indonesian movie. After listening to Radio Indonesia for a while, he began to adopt some modern Indonesian idioms in his own written and spoken Malay, especially some of the racy Djakarta slang. He has been rather puzzled, however, in trying to reconcile what he hears over Radio Indonesia about the splendid new nation and what he hears in Kuala Lumpur about poverty, hardship, and general deterioration in Indonesia. He questions the Minangkabau shopkeepers in Kampong Bahru about conditions in Sumatra, and they tell him that although it is a marvelously beautiful and rich island, they do not want to go back right now because conditions are "bad." Anyhow, they add, they can't go back, for it is too hard to get all the Indonesian government permits. They all agree, however, that in Sumatra everything is bigger and could be better than in Malaya. His mother, who vaguely remembers a visit she made to Sumatra as a child, says so too.

Mahmud is just beginning really to take an interest in politics. It was not until the Malaysia debate came along that he began to read the newspapers attentively. Now he reads two each day, one in English, one in Malay. He has also begun to listen to youth recruiters who are at work in Kampong Bahru. One of them urges him to join the United Malay National Organization's youth group, if he would like to attend the conferences and join in the parades and even one day meet Tengku Abdul Rahman. Another, a brisk young man who made the pilgrimage to Mecca last year and now proudly introduces himself as a Haji, has been suggesting that he join the Pan-Malayan Islamic Party. Only the PMIP, he says, can make sure that bright young Malays, rather than the Chinese, will run the businesses and the government of the country, and that Malaysia will join the Indonesian rather than the British bloc.

As yet, he has not made up his mind to join anything, except, perhaps, another sports club, this time a motorcycle club. He has now saved up M$500 and is shopping for a good secondhand motorcycle on which to make a down payment. He is thinking that if he goes to England, he can sell it, and that if he goes to Indonesia, he can perhaps take it along. In any event, possibly during the next long holiday, he can ride it as far as Bangkok.

*   *   *   *   *

Inche Mustapha bin Dato Abdul Gani, forty-one, was born on the East Coast of Malaya, the son of an official of the court of the Sultan of Pahang. He holds a high-level civil service post at a monthly salary of M$1,200. He began training for the civil service when he entered the Malay College in Kuala Kangsar, a secondary school patronized primarily by the sons of the Malay feudal families and others likely to hold government jobs. After the war he was sent to England on a government grant supplemented by an allowance from his family. He spent five years at the University of London and took a degree in history. Upon his return to Malaya in 1951 he joined the Malayan civil service as an Assistant District Officer and since then has risen steadily. His present post is one which he took over from the previous British incumbent in 1958, the year after Malaya achieved its independence.

Inche Mustapha lives in Petaling Jaya, about five miles from his office in Kuala Lumpur. He drives to work in a 1961 Morris Minor sedan on which he is soon to pay the final installment. His house is in one of the better areas of Petaling Jaya and the property is spacious enough that he does not notice his neighbors' radios. The house has three bedrooms and three baths, and two of the bedrooms are air conditioned. He paid the builder M$10,000 down, and is paying off the balance at the rate of M$150 per month over a 15-year period. He likes the house and has budgeted carefully to furnish it in teak and plastic, but now he is beginning to wonder whether it is really big enough. Relatives drop in frequently from Pahang, and they expect to be put up. His son, seventeen, now studying in a Kuala Lumpur secondary school, needs a room of his own and he wants it air conditioned. His two daughters, eight and ten, who attend a Malay primary school in Petaling Jaya, do not like sleeping on mats on the floor, Malay style, while visitors take over their beds. His wife, the daughter of one of the lesser princes of Trengganu, thinks they should convert the carport into an extra bedroom, and he is thinking it over.

One of Inche Mustapha's next door neighbors is a young Englishman, an employee of a British firm in Kuala Lumpur which oversees the management of rubber estates. He earns M$1,500 per month, plus free housing. He likes Malaya and talks of getting himself a job as an estate manager and staying on permanently. Inche Mustapha's other neighbor is a middle-aged Indian who earns M$800 per month as chief clerk in a British insurance office, owns his own house and car, and has some money in rubber shares. He likes Malaya, too, but he talks occasionally of retiring to India, where, he says, the British no longer throw their weight about as they do in Malaya, but where, he concedes, politically and economically, things are not too good. Inche Mustapha gets on very well with both of his neighbors, and they occasionally drop in on one another in the early evening to drink beer and

talk over the day's news. On such occasions, Inche Mustapha's wife
quietly disappears. When the neighbors' wives try to enter into conversation with her while she is out in the garden, she smiles, says a
few words, and drifts away with a polite excuse. The neighbors, who
are now taking language lessons, try to speak Malay with her, but they
do not get much further in Malay than in English.

Inche Mustapha has always gotten on well with the British, perhaps all too well, for some of his colleagues mutter that he is much
too Anglicized. He knows that they occasionally gossip about an episode which, as a matter of fact, he himself thinks of quite often. During his stay in London, he formed a liaison with a young English girl,
also a university student. They lived together quite openly in his flat
in Bloomsbury and were popular hosts to the other young Malay students in London, several of them young princes engaged in desultory
study, most of them serious students of the sort who were the main-
stay of the politically conscious Malayan Students Union. The affair
lasted for two years. When they were graduated from the university, they
made a tour of the continent, finishing it off with three months on the
Costa Brava. Inche Mustapha tried to persuade the girl to marry
him. He already had a wife in Malaya, whom he had married on his
parents' insistence before leaving for England. The British girl would
consent neither to become a second wife nor to allow him to divorce
his first, by whom he had had a son. The dilemma was resolved only
when his family cut off his allowance, thus forcing him to return home.

He feels fairly well satisfied these days with both his family
and his job. He is running his office, he is sure, as competently as
did his British predecessor, any decline in standards being the result
of a shortage of competent personnel at the lower levels. He has a bit
of difficulty keeping some of the minor Malay employees on their toes,
and some of the Chinese seem disgruntled about promotion policies,
but this is only to be expected during a period of transition. At any
rate, there have been no cases of malfeasance or corruption. As for
corruption, the opportunity is there, and in some offices, he has reason to suspect, the resistance to temptation is not as high as in his
own. He himself remembers a visit from a Chinese businessman who
hinted at an offer of 500 shares in a proposed new industrial concern,
in return for his official concurrence in the issuing of a license. He
neither rejected nor encouraged the tentative proposition, the license
was never actually applied for, and he sometimes wonders what would
have happened if he had adopted either one course or the other.

Unless he goes into politics, Inche Mustapha cannot advance

much further in government, for he is already very close to the top of
the civil service ratings. He is not at all sure that he wants to enter
politics. He has been paying the expected 5% of his salary into the
UMNO treasury, which is a great deal more than a lot of his UMNO
colleagues are doing, but he has not been attending party meetings and
has argued, in fact, that civil servants should stay clear of political en-
tanglements. He heard during the 1959 campaign that his name was being mentioned for a ministerial post, but nothing came of it. He also
heard that as soon as his name was proposed, some of the East Coast
UMNO conservatives started at once to whisper about his liking for
brandy and joget girls. As a matter of fact, Inche Mustapha does like
brandy and joget girls, but he thinks this is strictly his own business.
He learned to like brandy in England, and he sees no reason why he
should not drink it in Malaya for the Koran's prohibition against alcohol is not categorical. As for joget girls, he goes quite openly to
stag parties for which they are engaged to dance the ronggeng with the
guests. Better such parties, he thinks, than the furtive sorts of affairs
which many of his ostentatiously orthodox Muslim acquaintances of the
PMIP indulge in, in addition to their multiple marriages. His wife does
not object to the parties, and she herself prefers to stay quietly at home.
Her tastes in entertainment run to the moving pictures or an occasional
court function in Trengganu. Occasionally, he tries to persuade her to
go with him to the Selangor Club, where one can sit and have a drink
and dance a bit and see everybody in Kuala Lumpur. She usually refuses to go, so he goes alone. Sometimes he falls in with friends who
take him on to one of the private night clubs, which generally turns out
to be rather dull.

If politics does not particularly attract Inche Mustapha, diplomacy does. He speculates about the number of new diplomatic posts
which Malaya, or the new Malaysia, may have to fill in the next five
years. He has also counted up the likely Malay candidates for diplomatic assignments and it seems quite obvious that he could manage,
if he really tried, to get his name placed quite high on the list. A
Latin American post, when any are established, might do very nicely,
and it would not involve a lot of political competition. He has consulted
his kris, an heirloom weapon which came generations ago from Sumatra. The kris signaled an emphatic "yes" to the leading questions he
put to it. Strictly on specualtion, for of course he does not rely upon
the kris, although it does no harm to refer to it, he has begun to re-
view his Spanish, which was not at all bad 12 years ago.

*   *   *   *   *

Lim Yew Siew is the eldest son of a minor branch of a Chinese family which has lived for many generations in Malacca and more recently in Penang and Kuala Lumpur. Some of the older members of the clan declare that on the tombstone inscriptions in the Chinese graveyard in Malacca they can trace the family history back to the Malacca Sultanate. In any event, in the clan temple in Malacca there are records that purport to go back through the British and the Dutch eras into the Portuguese period. Members of Lim's immediate branch of the family, however, are not much interested. They never visit the Heeren Street mansion in Malacca. The once-elegant mansion, which stretches back the depth of a city block to the seashore through a series of courtyards, is now rather a shabby establishment. Its ornately carved and gilded doors and window shutters are chipped and peeling, and the next door neighbors have converted their front rooms into workshops. The Lims have been Methodists for the last two generations, they have adopted English as their first language, and until recently they referred to themselves as "Queen's Chinese." The original Malacca line of the family, rather than setting the pace for the rest of the clan, has dropped behind the cadet branches.

Mr. Lim was brought up in Penang, where his parents still live in a big old mansion. His marriage to a Malacca girl was arranged by his parents, who thought even the Penang girls too forward. They found for him a convent-educated daughter of a good Malacca family, a parental choice which Mr. Lim has never regretted. With his wife and three children, he now lives in Kenny Hills in suburban Kuala Lumpur. Their new split-level home is built into a steep hillside. The living room opens onto a broad terrace commanding a splendid view of the mountains to the east. In the garden is a particularly fine collection of orchids, which Lim's wife, supervising a Tamil gardener, keeps in prime condition. She supplements the collection from time to time with new plants for which she refuses to pay more than M$100, although some of her rival orchid fanciers rarely pay less. In the garage are a Mercedes-Benz 220 SE and an Austin-Healey sports car.

Mr. Lim describes himself as the proprietor of an electrical appliance store in Kuala Lumpur. In fact, however, he has put the store under the management of a young nephew, while he devotes his own time to rubber plantings, tin mines, and stock market operations. He has taken responsibility, on behalf of his father, the legal owner, for about 1,000 acres of rubber holdings, scattered between Kuala Lumpur and Penang, and for two small tin mines near Kuala Lumpur. He has put his own share of the proceeds into rubber and tin stocks on the London and Singapore markets, shifting his shares as market conditions indicate.

He is not altogether happy these days about his rubber and tin enterprises. He is clearing perhaps 10% on the value of the properties, as against 20%-30% a few years ago. He made a serious mistake in 1953 by not cutting down all of the old rubber trees and replanting at once—on a generous government subsidy—with new high-yield stock. He preferred to replant by degrees. The result was that much of his rubber land was out of production when prices were high three years ago. It has not yet come into full production today, when prices have dropped and quantity counts more than ever. He made a mistake also, he feels, in not "fragmenting" the holdings and selling off high to individual small holders. Had he done so, he might have used the money to buy one big estate and thus simplified his management problems. Formerly, he had managers he could trust—mainly close relations—but the best of them have now enough money to go into business on their own. He is forced on some of his holdings to contract the tapping to entrepreneurs he does not really know or trust, men who have no vested interest in keeping the trees in prime condition but a very real interest in making side deals with illicit tappers.

The tin mines are also a perplexing problem. These are not big mines, worked by efficient but expensive dredges. They are pits in which the workmen wash out the gravel with high-pressure hoses, then pump the liquid sludge to the top of a bamboo scaffolding from which it flows down through a series of shallow basins into which the heavy tin ore settles out. The tin lodes are thinning out, operations are expensive, labor troubles are increasing, and the price of tin has dropped. He is not sure, under the circumstances, that he would risk very much on opening new mines on half-prospected property nearby which, in any event, the government will not now alienate to Chinese for mining purposes.

His rubber and tin shares are another matter. Not that they have been doing well, but he did anticipate the precipitate drop in rubber two years ago and the drop in tin last year. He sold off high and bought again low. He is not sure he wants to put more money right now into either rubber or tin shares. He is thinking of applying for "pioneer" status to set up a new textile mill in Petaling Jaya. Businessmen from Hong Kong are ready to supply him with technical help; he himself and his friends can easily raise the capital; and the government will probably grant him a tax holiday and other benefits that make "pioneer" enterprise attractive. The question is, even considering the 20% protective tariff and the advantages of "pioneer" status, whether he can really compete with products from Hong Kong and Japan. Local labor is untrained and expensive. If Singapore is any criterion, the recent upsurge of union demands spells trouble. The labor unions actually put a new textile mill out of business in Singapore some months ago, and even though labor in Malaya is more tractable than that in Singapore, the far-leftist Singapore unions are deploying to export unrest northward across the causeway.

Mr. Lim would prefer to have nothing whatsoever to do with politics. Back in 1957 he would have preferred that the British stay in control, although he now concedes it would have been impossible. Sheer pragmatism makes him a supporter of the Malayan Chinese Association, a minor partner, along with the still more minor Malayan Indian Congress, in the Alliance Party which the United Malay National Organization dominates. Mr. Lim does not care much for the MCA. He fears it represents mainly the well-to-do, educated Chinese and that it does not interest or attract the bulk of the lower-class Chinese population which few members of the MCA seem to know or even to care much about. Nor does he care much for the MCA leaders. He thinks they are too acquiescent in their political relationship with the Malays, although, he admits, they do not have much choice. He likes the Socialist Front even less than the MCA. He is disturbed by its apparent acceptance of much of the Communist line and its apparent policy of looking to Indonesia for guidance and protection. He does not see any alternative, then, but to support the MCA. It may not have managed to assert Chinese rights or even to maintain Chinese prestige, having yielded, for instance, on the issue of Chinese language and culture in the Chinese educational system, an issue more important by far to his friends than to himself. It has managed, all the same, to maintain the political peace which has made prosperity possible. For that reason he makes a generous contribution each year to the MCA, although he declines to take any active part in the organization.

When asked what he wants from a government, Mr. Lim says that he wants only to be left alone to make a good living, to enjoy it, and to ensure it to his children. He is confident that he is a good citizen and he means to see that his children are, too. He does not engage in the fancy financial manipulations of which many of the Chinese businessmen are accused. He has no mistress and he does not intend to have one, although he is often urged by his business friends to experiment with extramarital joys they say he can so easily afford. His two older children are enrolled in Methodist secondary schools in Kuala Lumpur and are both near the top of their classes. He intends to send them to England for advanced study. He and his wife and children, incidentally, have learned to read, write, and speak fluent Malay in the last several years. None of them has ever bothered to learn much Chinese, and none of them is at all attracted either to Nationalist or Com-

munist China. They regard themselves as Malayans, but they all feel
more than a little doubtful whether the Malays do too.

                    *   *   *   *   *

     Ong Teck Kiam is a twenty-one-year-old teacher of English in
a Chinese-language primary school in Ampang Village on the outskirts
of Kuala Lumpur. Teck Kiam is learning to like his job and he may
make teaching his career, but until about two years ago he and his family had high hopes that he was headed toward some much better paid
occupation. Now they feel thankful that he has any job at all, and they
are rearranging their ideas about the future.

     Teck Kiam's "parents" are in fact his maternal aunt and her
husband, an elderly couple, both of whom were born in Ampang Village,
the children of immigrant Chinese tin miners who failed to strike it
rich. Shortly after they were married they went to work as a cook-
amah team in a British household. They have since worked for a succession of British families, one of them for 12 years. Having no children of their own, they adopted the wife's nephew, whose mother is the
grass widow of another Ampang Village tin miner. Although illiterate
themselves, they were determined to give Teck Kiam the best possible
education, and with the help of their British employers got the promising boy admitted to the Victoria Institution, Kuala Lumpur's English-
language prestige school for boys. Teck Kiam maintained a highly
creditable record, particularly in his science courses, up until the time
of his Senior Cambridge examinations.

     Several weeks before the examinations, Teck Kiam began to suf-
fer abdominal pains. He consulted the Ampang Village folk doctors who
first prescribed external applications of Tiger Balm, then opiates. One
night the pain became unbearable. He was brought to the Kuala Lumpur
General Hospital, but by the time he reached the operating table his ap-
pendix had already ruptured. Because he was young and sturdy his re-
cuperation was fairly fast, but he was barely on his feet again when the
Senior Cambridge examinations were held. Although he did not fail, he
did not pass with high enough grades to qualify for more than a class
two certificate. By this time, both Teck Kiam and his frugal hard-
working parents knew that he would soon be needed as the family wage
earner. At the age of eighteen he abandoned his hopes to continue his
studies through the two senior years, as well as his dreams of an engineering course, and his student life came to an abrupt halt.

     Teck Kiam began at once to look for a job, and very soon made

some unhappy discoveries about the Kuala Lumpur employment market
for young men of his race and academic qualifications. His Senior
Cambridge certificate was not enough to qualify him for any reasonably good white-collar job—indeed, holders of class one certificates
were job hunting as assiduously as himself. The certificate in effect
disqualified him from quite a number of jobs, those in which competence in the Chinese language, rather than English, would be a prime
consideration. His schooling had not prejudiced him against manual
labor and, actually, he would have enjoyed work which kept him out of
doors. However, there was no use in applying for a workman's job
for there was already an excess of qualified laborers.

For some months Teck Kiam circulated among government offices, business firms, factories, and employment agencies, following
every lead, filling out dozens of application forms and getting few answers, none of them satisfactory. It was no comfort to him to learn
that had he been a Malay, even with a class two certificate he would
have been much in demand. With the reluctant consent of his parents he
tried to volunteer for the Army officers' candidate school which formerly had had difficulty filling its Chinese quota. Now the Army, too,
had plenty of candidates and he failed narrowly to pass the extraordinarily stiff physical examination. Finally, almost in panic, he gladly
settled for a low-paid job as an electrician's apprentice at a remote
tin dredge, at a starting wage of M$100 per month and meager long-
range prospects.

After a year at the mine, Teck Kiam had saved a little money,
learned all that he felt the job could ever offer him in technical training, and decided to start job hunting again. Six disheartening months
later he was offered a job as a probationary teacher of English in the
Chinese primary school at Ampang Village, at M$120 per month.
There is a chance that he may be accepted for training in one of the
new teacher-training colleges, but even then he will be faced with a
major difficulty. His parents, whose most recent employers have left
Malaya, are too old to find or to hold new jobs much longer, in competition with younger people. Their support is an obligation which
Teck Kiam faces matter of factly. The M$75-per-month cash allow-
ance he would receive at a teacher-training college would hardly stretch
to meet his own basic needs as well as the support of his parents.

The family's current financial and domestic arrangements are
a bit complicated. Teck Kiam is now living, together with his adoptive
parents, in the home of his natural mother. She rents a modest property in Ampang Village for about M$100 per month, and takes in vari-

ous members of the family to help pay the household expenses. She
herself works as a tin washer, that is, she goes off each day to the
muddy stream which carries the overflow from the mine, pans the
stream for ore, and sells her take to a local collection agent. On a
good day she may earn M$3.00. When the mine is shut down, as it
frequently is, she is out of work. Teck Kiam's M$120 per month is
now a major source of income for the whole household, which includes
Teck Kiam's jobless younger sister, and three school-age boys.

Teck Kiam's adoptive parents are able to contribute toward
the household expenses even though they are without work. During the
12 years they worked steadily for one British family, they accumulated
some savings, and when the family left Malaya it made them a substantial termination gift of cash with which to buy a small house in Petaling
Jaya. They paid M$3,000 down and M$50 per month over the next five
years, and now they own it outright. They rent it out for M$75 per
month, and that M$75 is now their sole income.

Teck Kiam's setbacks may prove purely temporary, and his
new job may in fact be the beginning of the secure career his parents
have sacrificed and hoped for. In any event, he is making the most of
it. In his free time after school he plays soccer, and since failing the
Army physical examination, he has taken up weight lifting and become
a dedicated muscle builder. He reads everything he can lay hands on,
particularly anything related to the natural sciences. Sometimes on
weekends he gathers specimens for his fish tank, but he has given up
his butterfly collection, once a fairly good one, after a long and losing
battle with the mice. He goes to the village community center, where
there are occasional lectures—mainly about rubber planting—and
stray magazines and newspapers to read. He has managed throughout
his periods of adversity to keep the portable typewriter he bought in a
rare fit of extravagance some years ago, and he has trained himself to
be a good typist, an accomplishment which should now enhance his prospects somewhat on the job market.

Teck Kiam has not yet developed any keen interest in politics,
nor has he, in spite of a cautious approach or two, taken any interest
in Chinese secret societies. Serious beyond his years, he has avoided
the Teddy Boy set and has not been tempted to fit himself out in tight,
low-waisted trousers or to oil and comb his hair into sculptured whorls.
His chronic lack of pocket money, his English-language education, and
his filial piety toward his adoptive parents, toward whom he is consis-
tently considerate and obedient, have been something of an insulation
against the society of the young drifters, many of whom have flunked

out of the Chinese-language schools. His new status as a schoolteacher is an even more effective insulation. As a matter of fact,
he got the job as schoolteacher precisely because he was not a potential Teddy Boy.

Teck Kiam cannot yet even think of getting married. Until
his prospects improve, he is not likely to be sought out by the matchmakers as a promising candidate. Nor is he likely on his own to
persuade any English-educated young Chinese girl, the kind he has
in mind as an eventual prospect, that marriage to him is a good risk.

[Note: Each of the foregoing is a composite of several individuals.]

CHAPTER
XXI

MAJULLAH SINGAPURA

May 24, 1963

        The island city-state of Singapore seems destined ideally, if
that is the word, to become Malaysia's New York City, the great shipping center and melting pot of a thriving new nation. It may, of course,
end up more like a Chinese Israeli enclave on the border of a new Malay Muslim League, the rich infidel whose professions of devotion to
Malaysianism are suspect. What many people fear and some hope is
that it may become either Malaysia's Cuba or Indonesia's Irian Baru
(New Irian). In the midst of a nationalist and anticolonialist revolution, it still bills itself as the Lion City. The Lion—the "Singa" of
Sanskrit Singapura—was originally, perhaps, no lion but a local tiger
glimpsed by Indian trader-explorers many centuries ago, a beast ulti-
mately transformed into Queen Victoria's royal emblem. Stripped of
his whiskers and mane, he might today prove to be a wonk; not the
mangy street cur of the old-time Chinese markets, but the sleek, tough
mongrel who outthinks and outfights his pedigreed cousin. All muddled predictions and images aside, Singapore may remain just what it
is today: the busiest, liveliest, brashest element of a rather garishly
prosperous system, resembling New York's old lower East Side rather
than uptown Manhattan.

        Singapore, with its 1.6 million residents, 75% of them Chinese,
and more than half of them China born, has the appearance of being
Southeast Asia's most extensively and successfully Westernized state.
It constitutes, however, even by Southeast Asian standards, an explosive mix of incompatibles. As yet, it is a quasi-colony of the British,
but its Chinese-dominated government seeks merger with the Malay-
dominated Federation of Malaysia rather than separate independent
status. It is a major British Commonwealth military base for Southeast Asian defense, but it relies for its internal security against easily provoked street rioters upon troops from nearby Malaya. It is a
stronghold of British and other Western business firms and of Chinese

multimillionaires, some of whom are among.the strongest backers of
its left-wing Socialist government. It is a bustling entrepôt dependent
for its prosperity upon Malaya, which seeks to duplicate its facilities,
and upon Indonesia, which views with outraged suspicion its colonial,
capitalist, and alien relics, all still very much in evidence.

Singapore's ordinary citizens, an unassimilated assortment of
Chinese, Indians, and Malays, share the Southeast Asian craving for nationalist revolution but do not agree on what kind of nation it is they are
rebelling—peacefully, as yet—for or against. They have been busily ed-
ucating themselves in two or more languages (English, Chinese, Malay,
and Tamil) for more and better jobs than now exist. They have been un-
ionizing at least as energetically, under bitterly inimical left-wing leaders. While the government has been trying to attract industry and capital, the workers have been going on strike on such whimsical pretexts
as "impolite" reprimands to notorious goldbricks, then striking again
over "insincere" apologies from the management. They already enjoy
Southeast Asia's highest standard of living, with still more improvements in sight, and yet their slums are still some of Southeast Asia's
most squalid, and the contrasts between rich and poor some of the region's most dramatic. Above all, they are self-consciously on the move.

Majullah Singapura (Onward, Singapore) is a phrase one hears
more and more frequently these days from the lips of the politicians
and of the people. It is the new state motto and the title of the new
state anthem, and to the zealous new Ministry of Culture it signifies
a splendid national future. To the Chinese, the Indians, and for that
matter the British, the phrase means in fact what modern Singapore
has always stood for: Business as before, only better. Or, as the Prime
Minister put it even to the Malays during the recent referendum on Malaysia, "Keep what you have and get more."

Majullah Singapura, then, means today specifically "Onward
into Malaysia," and Malaysia, translated into Singaporese, means more
and better business, trade, industry, opportunity, prosperity, and security, but above all else, business and trade. Singapore's major trade
preoccupation is natural rubber, some 600,000-700,000 tons of it annually, or one third of the world's supply, worth at least US$350 million.
This means much of Malaya's rubber, much also of Indonesia's, which
Singapore buys, sells, and ships, taking a profit on every transaction.
Singapore's ogre, therefore, like Kuala Lumpur's, is synthetic. Every
time synthetic rubber drives down the price of natural rubber another
US cent per pound, Singapore calculates that it loses US$12 million per
year and that it is that much nearer the Communist scavenger heap.

The price of natural rubber dropped from a high of about M$1.50 (US$0.-50) to about M$0.75 per pound between mid-1960 and mid-1963. The People's Action Party (PAP) government's Legislative Assembly representation fell from a 43-8 majority to a 24-26 minority (one seat unfilled). The correlation may, of course, be quite irrelevant.

Singapore has other ogres, too, and one of them is the American tin stockpile, which threatens Singapore's profit in buying and selling newly mined Malayan tin. The United States's tin surplus sales this past year or so have been largely responsible, Singapore believes, for lowering world tin prices from a high of £990 per ton in November 1961 to about £900 today. Many a Singapore Chinese businessman, whether or not he deals directly in tin, feels that he personally lost the £90, multiplied by whatever factor his imagination dictates. Another ogre is Indonesia, which is by far Singapore's best customer for such entrepôt goods as textiles and small manufactures. Indonesia, however, keeps threatening to buy direct from the manufacturer unless Singapore, as seems unlikely, stops taking profits, accepting smuggled goods, and flirting with capitalism.

Singapore has a remarkable way of adjusting realistically to its ogres when it cannot exorcise them. The British military installation, for instance, is an affront to Singaporean nationalism. It is also a welcome source of employment (40,000 jobs employing 9% of the total working population), of profit (M$260 million per year from payrolls and local expenditures), and of cost-free defense. So Singapore, in anticipation of more and better business under Malaysia, allows 10% of its restricted land area still to be used for military base purposes and thus lets the British pick up the check—and the blame—for deterring possible alien encroachments. Singapore withdraws more and more of its remaining rubber, copra, and fruit lands from agriculture in order to build up new industrial and housing areas in anticipation of big factories serving a new Malaysian common market. It stockpiles bigger and bigger inventories of entrepôt goods in anticipation that newer and bigger Indonesian crises will mean emergency purchase orders. In spite of recurrent flurries of political excitement, Singapore has always reverted in the past and seems to be reverting today to an attitude of: let who will have the politics, so long as Singapore has the profits.

Singapore's guiding philosophy is that government is government and business is business, that the two should complement but not infiltrate each other. This concept was laid down by modern Singapore's founder, Sir Stamford Raffles, who had had his fill of bureaucracy stifling commerce in the Dutch East Indies and had resolved that Singapore would be different. Raffles founded Singapore in 1819, and five years later, when he himself left Southeast Asia for good, it was already a thriving seaport of 10,700 inhabitants, a triumphant vindication of his policy of free trade, good government, and welcome to enterprise and to enterprising immigrants. Singapore ever since, taking free trade as its cause, has battled bureaucracy's attempts to encroach upon man's inalienable right to make a profit and to enjoy it.

Singapore has demanded that government earn its keep by providing essential services but be cautious in arrogating to itself special privileges. The essential services, naturally, have multiplied with the passing years and Singapore has Southeast Asia's best. It also has a left-wing Socialist government which proposes in principle to make them all-inclusive. In order to improve them it now proposes not only to maintain the import duties on automobiles, tobacco, petroleum products, and liquor, which long since proved irresistibly taxable, but possibly to extend the duties to other yet unspecified items as well. While Singapore braces itself further to restrict free trade, it still forswears for the most part the all too familiar features of welfare statism elsewhere: the endless queue, the unanswered inquiry, the reduplicative form, the inaccessible official, the unimplemented plan succeeding unimplemented plan. It avoids also the system of official squeeze and payoff. For the last few years, however, since the advent of the people's politician, it has taken to the slogan, the rally, the demonstration, the people's cultural show, and the other manifestations of an artificially stimulated mass-awakening with unforeseeable consequences.

Like the British colonial government before it, the Singapore state and city government today devotes itself to a great extent not only to the provision of services but also to the preservation of law and order. It has plenty to keep it busy, for behind Singapore's flashy façade live the typical industrious Chinese, bent upon rising in two generations from rags to near-riches, as he often does, the typical Indian, moving from the ranks of the day laborer, who feels and is downtrodden, to that of the clerk, who feels persecuted, and the Malay, with his flair for either looking or being gracefully at leisure. Here also live more than the usual assortment of unsavory urban types. The Chinese secret societies, long the scourge of the Singapore underworld, resort to all the techniques of modern gangsterism, and there are plenty of hoodlums, goons, and Teddy Boys to assist and to rival them.

The Singapore towkay—the rich businessman—seldom feels completely at ease these days without his bodyguard to protect himself and his family from kidnapping. Even the smallest street hawker is subject to extortion. The 50 cents which the leeches exact from his day's earnings of M\$5 add up, when multiplied by 10,000 hawkers, to as much as the M\$100-M\$500 per month protection money they get from a professional man, or the occasional M\$100,000 ransom for a towkay.

The unions can be relied upon regularly to contribute their share to the excitement. Every day in downtown Singapore strikers are picketing some business establishment or another, generally with posters which border on the scurrilous and the subversive. Memories are still fresh of the 1955 and 1956 strikes which climaxed in riots that terrorized the city. Quite a lot of Singapore's Chinese secondary-school students, instigated by superannuated student leaders who deliberately fail just enough examinations to avoid either graduation or expulsion, participated formerly in bloody riots. They keep in practice these days by striking or demonstrating occasionally against such affronts as changes in curriculum. From the unions, from the students, from somebody—Singapore is constantly expecting some outbreak of violence. Speculation in late 1962 centered on whether the extreme left-wing leaders, whom almost everyone has suspected of planning violence, would be jailed before or after the next attempt, whether the attempt would come before or after the inauguration of Malaysia, and whether the Singapore, the British, or the Kuala Lumpur government would then have to accept the responsibility—and the odium—for dealing with the situation. The joint Internal Security Council, composed of three British representatives, three Singaporeans, and one Malayan, took the decision. In early February over a hundred extremists were jailed, including Lim Chin Siong, Secretary-General of the Barisan Sosialis party. The city still speculates whether their followers will long remain passive.

Singapore's governing People's Action Party, which now just barely controls the Legislative Assembly by lining up a right-wing opposition vote or two, in the mid-1950's started out, just as its name indicates, by stirring up "people's action." It then had the enthusiastic support of many labor and student unions and other far-left groups which have now deserted it. Since assuming responsibility for government in 1959, it has had sober second thoughts about the true efficacy or expediency of people's action. It hesitates to appeal to the little man's resentment of the big man's privileges, or, since almost everyone in Singapore is a foreigner, including the majority of the Malays who are Indonesian by origin, to appeal to the nationalist's animosity toward the alien. The PAP has in large part forfeited leadership in these potent causes to its own extremist splinter elements, which have now defected and formed the Communist-line Barisan Sosialis party.

The PAP may have forfeited many of the causes, but it has not forgotten the tactics. Many of its own leaders are thoroughly familiar with the theory and practice of communism and Communist agitation by reason of former personal involvement in the movement. The PAP, therefore, has proved quite capable of whistling up a furor over an alleged "deal" between the British High Commissioner and the Barisan Sosialis whereby the two "agreed" to jettison the PAP, the British to reward the Barisan by recognizing its claim to government, the Barisan to reward the British by allowing them to retain the Singapore military bases. The PAP has its cadres, purges, confessions, and dogmas; it plants informers, instigates defections, engages in machinations and manipulations which lead many of its critics to denounce endless PAP-Barisan intrigue and counterintrigue, such as all right-thinking citizens must abhor.

In recent months the PAP has made tentative preliminary moves itself to achieve greater rapport with the moderates, who now think that just as absolute power would have corrupted absolutely, so severely limited power has reformed the party. The PAP leaders have also begun of late, after long shunning the Singapore cocktail circuit, admittedly one of the world's dullest, to exhibit an interest in international society. They are still skittish about Westerners, but have begun vigorously to court the Afro-Asians. Politicians of all brands, including the farthest left of the opposition, are now beginning to get worked up over state visits, international congresses, and communiqués asserting identity of interest. All this, of course, means to live and to govern dangerously, as has just been brought home to the PAP leaders, who may now become as sophisticated in international politics as in international economics. They recently rejoiced publicly over Indonesia's acquisition of Irian Barat, but now, viewing subsequent Indonesian involvement in Brunei, they quote the Chinese—not Afro-Asian—proverb: "Big fish eat little fish; little fish catch shrimp." Singapore, they say, is the shrimp, and the rest is left to conjecture.

Whether or not it disguises itself as an Afro-Asian neutral, Singapore will probably continue for some time to come to look like a sprawling Overseas Chinese ghetto. It is a ghetto shadowed by skyscrapers, interspersed with British colonial and Anglo-Chinese garden villas, scarred by arid Hollywood-style real-estate developments, pocketed with "industrial estates" and vast blocks of low-cost housing, some of them 20 stories high and containing 1,000 units. This conglomerate Singapore stretches along a busy waterfront of dock areas, business blocks, residential suburbs, esplanade, and small boat harbors. It extends inland to scatter itself in rolling wooded countryside where

fruit orchards and florists' gardens crowd in on Chinese graveyards.
It is quite the handsomest, cleanest, and best-administered of the major cities of Southeast Asia. Within Singapore City itself or its outskirts are many features which should have made it famous as a tourist center as well as a seaport, market, and military base. There are
Malay fishing villages built on piles over the tidal flats; Chinese farms
featuring in close juxtaposition the pig, the cockle, and the orchid; Indian settlements whose wandering cows exasperate the motorist. There
are mangrove swamps inhabited by mosquitoes and pythons; idyllic off-
shore islands inhabited by tropical birds; and a 581-foot "mountain," a
nature preserve of primary jungle, now endangered by gravel miners.
To almost everybody, however, Singapore still means not scenery but
Raffles Place, Change Alley, Chinatown, Canning Rise, the Tanglin
Club, and their equivalents of all levels and degrees.

Raffles Place and its immediate environs typify Singapore; How
and Why It Grew. When Raffles arrived in 1819, he disembarked a few
yards up the Singapore River at the point where it begins to widen to
form a small boat basin, now the center for Singapore's lighter-borne
freight traffic. In his day, the left bank was a mangrove swamp sur-
rounding a low rise. On the right bank, where he landed, was a small
Malay kampong. Swamp, hill, and kampong had disappeared within a
few years, and Singapore ever since has been leveling hills, filling
swamps, and overflowing its boundaries to accommodate the people and
goods which come and go with every ship (now 20,000 per year) and 20
plane flights per day.

By 1823, utilizing the Chinese, Indian, and Malay labor which
was pouring into the island, the British had established Raffles Place
(then called Commercial Square) on the site of the filled swamp and
had offered the land about it at public auction. Raffles' biographer,
his Malaccan secretary, Abdullah, a few years later bitterly regretted
not having taken his employer's advice to buy. For about M$1,200 he
could have purchased a plot which was already worth ten times that
amount by 1833 and is valued in the hundreds of thousands today. The
old business firms which still surround Raffles Place, itself at one period a tree-shaded horse market and now a crowded parking lot, displaced and expanded over the sites of still older establishments back-
ing on the seafront. The Raffles Place properties are themselves overshadowed today by massive Victorian and post-Victorian commercial
buildings and postwar skyscrapers. The latest and finest of these are
built along Collyer Quay and Raffles Quay, where fill land now allows
for a six-lane sea-front roadway. Between Raffles Place and Collyer
Quay stretches Change Alley, one of Southeast Asia's narrowest, busi-

est, and most variegated bazaars. Change Alley amalgamates Wool-
worth's, Sears Roebuck, and Walgreen's, all crammed into small shops
and tiny cubbyholes. To the congestion it adds money changers, pick-
pockets, barkers, and touts, overflowing at both ends onto the "five-
foot ways" (sidewalks). Change Alley reproduces itself in modified
form and scale all over town; such is the pressure of Singapore's population and salesmanship that whenever the police relax their vigilance,
the hawkers stake out their pitches and presently acquire tenure.

Inland from Collyer Quay and Raffles Place, to the north and
northeast, stretches the old Chinatown, now as crowded, shabby, busy,
noisy, and almost as colorful as Hong Kong. Here the modern bank is
neighbor to the dried fish-shark's fin-bird's-nest wholesaler. The
guildhall and the temple adjoin the labor union and the recreation club.
Fruit, fish, and vegetable hawkers help to congest the streets by day;
outdoor eating stalls operate late into the night, dispensing Singaporean
specialities which the restaurants cannot rival. Politicians, hawkers,
and Chinese opera troupes compete for attention in a "people's park,"
on the fringes of which the new proletariat lives in low-cost government-sponsored flats. Some blocks from the park are institutions
which Singapore no longer cares to talk about or to show to the visitor. These are the Chinese "death houses," where the aged and in-
firm of the poor retire voluntarily or are sent by their families to
await the end. They divert themselves in the interim by watching the
funeral preparations that are always under way, listening to the re-
hearsals of the funeral bands, and feeling themselves part of the endless bustle of activity in a tightly packed business-tenement district.

On the eastern bank of the Singapore River, the British soon
displaced the Malay kampong which migrated down the shore. Along
the ever-busier riverbank the British built not only their godowns but
their baronial merchant houses. Of two surviving mansions, one is the
nucleus of the present Legislative Assembly building, the other a tenement. After a sharp contest between devotees of profit and of prophecy,
one large sea-front area was bequeathed to the future. It is now the padang, the city green, bordered by splendid flame trees. It is bounded
on the north by government (the administrative center), on the south by
seascape, on the east and west by sport (the British and the Eurasian
cricket clubs). On its periphery are represented religion, education,
science, and history. The Anglican and the Catholic cathedrals and the
Raffles Institution stand on little padangs of their own; three blocks inland are the Armenian Church, the new National Library, and the National—formerly the Raffles—Museum. Atop nearby Mt. Sophia, named
for Lady Raffles, rise the cupolas of a Chinese millionaire's mansion,

a monument to Overseas Chinese prosperity and taste. Overshadowing it rises Singapore's oldest skyscraper, the Chinese-owned Cathay theater-hotel-apartment building which served the British as an observation point during the Japanese invasion in 1942, then as headquarters for rehabilitation of the city in 1945.

West of Mt. Sophia and behind the National Museum is Canning Rise where Raffles built the first Government House, planted a botanical garden, and enjoyed the panorama of a swiftly growing city and port. Today's Government House, which stands a mile farther inland, is a huge colonial mansion surrounded by fine lawns and parks. The house itself is open only on state occasions since it was vacated by the last British Governor-General, for the Malay Yang di-Pertuan Negara, the titular Chief of State, prefers a more modest bungalow within the grounds, while the Chinese Prime Minister lives in his own expensive modern villa in one of the city's residential areas.

Canning Rise today is a conspicuous reminder to downtown Singapore that British Crown property has included quite a lot of the island's most valuable and strategic real estate. It was until recent weeks the site of headquarters, barracks, and other installations of the British Base Command, which have just been handed over to Singapore's own military forces. Canning Rise is also the site of a "royal" grave, the only relic of a semiauthenticated 13th-14th-century sultanate linked with Sumatra. It is a reminder that for all their inconspicuousness in modern Singapore, the Malays, who appear mostly as drivers, messengers, elevator operators, and rural fishermen, were the original proprietors of the island. What is more, they are as much Indonesian as Malay and one day may be disposed to assert that fact.

The city of Singapore is growing today as it did in the past, not only by extending itself seaward and skyward but inland as well. British residents very early on started to turn gentleman farmer. They bought up land in the hilly interior of the island, cleared it of jungle and tigers, planted nutmeg, gambier, and cloves. They built themselves hilltop mansions, and when the spice trees succumbed to blight, sold off land at a vast profit. The Chinese and the other Europeans decided —as they have done again and again since then—that no one could lose money by speculating on Singapore's strictly limited real estate.

The British also built clubs, for they brought into Singapore as into the rest of the empire that characteristically British colonial taste for the gentleman's private pub and playing field, where verandas were spacious and shaded, drinks long and cool (but not iced), cricket was leisurely and healthful, and acquaintances as enduring as they were slow to form. The Tanglin Club, one of the last preserves of pillars of empire, still flourishes today in Singapore's best residential area, open at last to Asians, but to no one, Asian or European, in the evening and in its formal rooms unless he is wearing jacket and tie. Sir Malcolm MacDonald, the postwar Governor-General, battled and almost beat the British no-Asians restrictions, battled but lost the dress-for-the-tropics cause. Almost all of Singapore, in fact, including the small and noncompetitive American Club next door to the Tanglin, feels very strongly about jackets and ties for the tropical evenings. The postwar boom in air conditioning apparently refroze the British just as they were showing signs, after all these decades, of melting. Even the PAP, which started off not merely as a shirt-sleeves party but as a tie-less, rolled shirt-sleeves party at that, has buttoned its cuffs, put on its tie, reached for its jacket, and resigned to the Barisan Sosialis much of the comfort of social protest.

Social protest preoccupies Singapore today, but protest of rather more significance than that over conventions of dress which, along with British standards of cookery, sportsmanship, and spoken English, many of the Chinese, Indians, and Malays have enthusiastically adopted. Social protest preoccupies all of Southeast Asia, to be sure, but Singapore differs from most other cities—the exceptions are found in Malaya and British Borneo—and is perhaps more dangerous in that it is a place where opportunity has long been open. In Singapore the little man, i.e., the ordinary Chinese, here not a member of a minority but of the majority, has been able by his own enterprise and ability not only to rise to the top quickly but to stay there. In Singapore today there are more and more of these little men, and more and more of them are educated. They are more eager than ever before to get ahead, and are growing more resentful of obstacles. The range of opportunity, however, seems suddenly circumscribed to overcrowded Singapore Island; Malaya and Borneo jealously guard the interests of their indigenous peoples, or at best their local Chinese, while Indonesia holds any Chinese in abhorrence unless he is in distant Peking. The Singapore population, by Southeast Asian standards, is already overprivileged, overdeveloped, and overly ambitious; it is also the world's youngest and fastest growing. The PAP has taken on the difficult and dangerous mission of counseling patience, tolerance, and hard work, at just the time that the Barisan Sosialis opposition is advocating the "genuine Socialist revolution" as contrasted with the "spurious" PAP model.

Paradoxically, the very gravity of Singapore's dilemma becomes the best insurance of its sanity. Most of its people seem now to know that it cannot afford the luxury of violent revolution. Even among the most active social protesters, there are many who admit that as Overseas Chinese—or as Overseas Indians, for many of the most vigorous and some of the most zealous are Indian—they are peculiarly vulnerable to any revolutionary force which they themselves unleash. One of the best deterrents to recklessness may be the feeling that one is almost surrounded by those who are even more reckless, and in Singapore that feeling already exists. Singapore's citizens have given reassuring evidence, by their vote in the referendum on Malaysia, that when the choice lies between what is feasible but imperfect and what is theoretically perfect but unfeasible, revolutionary ardor may still be restrained by the Chinese shopkeeper's comprehension of profit and loss.

CHAPTER
XXII

FOUR CITIZENS OF SINGAPORE

May 26, 1963

    Amat, an Indonesian by origin, earns M$200 (US$66) per month
as personal driver to a Singapore British businessman. In 1935 he emigrated from the small island of Bawean, north of Madura, to join the
community of Boyanese in Singapore, which by tradition provides a
large share of the city's professional drivers, stableboys, and horse
trainers. His brother was already working in Singapore as a driver,
and with his help Amat learned enough English to get by, qualified for
his driver's license, and found a job. In 1940 he married a Malay girl
from Johore Bahru, the marriage having been arranged by his sister-
in-law whose family was of Javanese origin, as was the family of Amat's
bride.

    Amat now lives together with his wife and six children in two
adjoining rooms of the servants' quarters behind the colonial mansion
occupied by his employer in the Tanglin district of Singapore. The
rest of the quarters are occupied by the Chinese cook and the Indian
gardener and their families. The Chinese wash amah prefers to live
out with relatives. Life in the servants' wing is on the whole harmonious. Amat has now resigned himself to the fact that the Chinese are
going to cook and eat pork. The Chinese and the Malays have resigned
themselves to the fact that if the communal toilet is to be kept reasonably clean, they will have to attend to it. The Indians have resigned
themselves to the fact that no one else is going to tolerate a cow, even
a calf, on the premises.

    For the most part, Amat's family and the others go their sepa-
rate ways. The adults have little in common save their employer and
their conversation is generally about his affairs. The children attend
different schools—Malay, Chinese, and Tamil languages, respectively
—where they all study some English. The children frequently play together and manage to do so without any undue quarrelsomeness. They

have adopted a mixture of Malay and English as their common language, and they all know the words of the most popular new songs, Malay or English, heard over Radio Singapore. The three young children of the British family sometimes join them. The grounds are large enough that even the noisier games cause no particular disturbance in the open upstairs drawing room and verandas of the main house. Any quarrel among the adults in the servants' quarters, however, brings prompt orders to desist.

Amat has now become a citizen of Singapore, and his wife assumes that she is a citizen of Malaya, although she has not bothered to check her registration. Amat is keenly conscious that he comes from Indonesia. A few years ago it did not much matter to him, but he has heard much of late about Indonesia being big, powerful, and progressive, and much more important than Malaya. While he makes it very clear that he is a citizen of Malaya and takes good care of his registration papers, he makes it equally clear that he is not a local Malay but an Indonesian Malay, and people seem to accept the distinction as meaningful. The Chinese taxi drivers, he thinks, are particularly impressed. He spends quite a lot of time waiting in public places for his employer, and he has come to resent the taxi drivers, particularly the Chinese, who try to jockey him out of the line. He has trouble with them in traffic, too, for they cut in and out around him, blaring their horns, slamming on their brakes, knowing that he will not risk a scratch on his employer's beautiful Jaguar, but knowing also that when the law is clearly with him he cannot easily be bluffed into yielding right of way. It takes a great deal to disturb Amat's normally placid disposition, but when the Chinese push him too far, Amat tells them that in Indonesia people know how to handle the Chinese and perhaps some day Indonesia will show Singapore how, too.

Amat reads the newspapers while he waits for his employers. He does so rather ostentatiously, for many of the other drivers—Chinese, Indian, and Malay—cannot read; so whether or not he is genuinely interested in the news, he never misses the papers. At the religious school of his village mosque in Indonesia, Amat had learned to read the Arabic script in which most of the Malay—but none of the Indonesian—newspapers are published. While learning some spoken English in Singapore, he had also learned the English alphabet, and now he can read not only the jawi but the new Romanized Malay papers as well. The differences between Malay and the Indonesian language used to puzzle him, but he has long since passed that stage and is inclined to feel a bit superior when he explains such differences to some of his friends.

In recent years Amat has begun to take an interest in politics. He has some rather clear-cut opinions. Malaysia is a good thing, because with its advent Singapore Malays, including those of Indonesian origin, will get more pay, more education, better homes, and better jobs. Indonesia is a good thing, because Indonesia is the leader in a struggle to help people like Indonesians and Malays get ahead. The Singapore Party Rakjat is a good thing, because it supports Malaysia, and Indonesia, and the struggle of Malayan and Indonesian peoples. The British are not as bad as the Dutch, and some British employers, including his own, are quite a good thing because they like the Malays. The People's Action Party (PAP) and the Chinese are another matter. You can't believe a word they say, and you know that they are rich and you are poor. Tengku Abdul Rahman is a good man, but not as great as Sukarno.

Amat depends not only upon the newspapers and his fellow drivers for his views. He depends, in fact, far more upon his kampong friends. He has a day off each week, and he is generally free in the evenings because his employer then prefers to drive himself, unless, of course, there is a big reception and he must be delivered and collected in style at the door. On his day off and sometimes in the late afternoon, Amat gets on his bicycle and goes off to a kampong about two miles away where some of his wife's Malay Javanese relatives live, also some of the Boyanese. There he talks about things in general or listens for hours on end. When he gets bored with things in general, he goes to the house of a particular friend, a retired policeman, who came originally from Malacca, and whose family came from Sumatra three generations back.

Amat's friend, the ex-policeman, is now a practicing bomoh. As a combined fortuneteller and magician, he enjoys a growing reputation. People come not only from Singapore Island but from Johore Bahru to consult him and leave gifts which range from a catty or two of rice to—on one occasion—a check for M$100. His visitors suffer from all sorts of troubles: physical illness, mental disturbances, unrequited love, jealousy, or perhaps mere loss of property. The bomoh, putting himself into a trance by staring into a bowl of water on which floats a piece of benzoin, becomes possessed by a genie which, speaking in a falsetto voice, gives advice that in a remarkable number of cases turns out to be helpful.

Amat thinks that he himself may have a gift as a bomoh, and there exists between him and his friend the tacit understanding that he, Amat, is understudying, and that some day all of the secrets of the profession may be imparted to him. Most of Amat's family take his stories about the accomplishments of the <u>bomoh</u> seriously, but his eldest son, who has just entered secondary school, scoffs at them as so much superstition. The boy himself, not long ago, however, was severely shaken at seeing, when accompanied by a schoolmate of his, a malicious looking genie gesticulating from a rambutan tree which, in point of fact, they had just been stoning to bring down ripe fruit.

For years now Amat has been trying to put aside a little money to buy himself a house in the kampong, but so far his efforts have not come to much. He has invested much more in bets at the race track than in his postal savings account. He has a sympathetic accomplice in his employer, who never misses a Singapore race meet, and several times Amat has driven him to the meets in Kuala Lumpur. The two of them discuss the racing form with avid interest, but his employer, from a box, and Amat, from the car park outside or occasionally from the enclosure, seem rarely to pick the winners. Amat invests also in the Singapore lottery. He has never won more than M$50, but he hopes one day to win at least the M$1,500 prize which would enable him to buy one of the more modest houses in the kampong. Although it would be a mere shack of wood, bamboo, and thatch, even for houses such as these the price is rising. The rumor in the kampong is that the city government is going to buy up the houses at a good price, then replace them with new multiple-story low-cost flats, into which it will move the kampong people. Amat hopes the report is not true, for even if he could make a profit on the sale of a house, he has no desire to live in a flat.

All this, to be sure, is conjectural. Still, the day will come when Amat will want to retire. He knows that his employer, who gives him a two-week bonus each year, is good for at least a three-month bonus on retirement, perhaps even six. There is also a provision, which he does not quite understand, about a city provident fund to which his employer has been contributing on his behalf. All that, however, does not add up to a house and an income. Unless he really does become a <u>bomoh</u>, he will be dependent on someone, presumably his children.

*   *   *   *   *

Ah Ying is employed as an amah in a small Singapore apartment occupied by an Australian family. For 25 years she has worked in Singapore for a succession of Westerners, and just once, during the Japanese Occupation, for Chinese. She is quick and efficient, managing the basic housework, laundry, and cooking for a family of three—

the husband, who works in an airline office, the wife, who teaches in a
British secondary school, and the eight-year-old daughter, who attends
a British Army primary school.

Ah Ying has her own room and bath adjoining the kitchen. She
starts work each day at 6:30 a.m., has one day off each week, and generally she is free from shortly after lunch until teatime, and again, of
course, after doing the dinner dishes. She earns M$150 per month, and
it is understood that the proceeds from the sale of newspapers and bot-
tles to the itinerant junkmen are hers. She rarely spends more than
M$50 per month on herself for food and clothing, the balance of her earn-
ings goes into her savings account, upon which she draws from time to
time for special purposes.

Ah Ying was born in Kwangtung Province, near Canton, one of
half a dozen children of a fairly prosperous peasant family. At sixteen
she was married to the third son of a neighbor's family and as a new
bride entered the home of a tyrannical mother-in-law. Her young husband died of pneumonia within the year, and her situation in her mother-
in-law's house became intolerable. She had heard of girls from the village who had emigrated overseas. With her own mother's consent, she
packed up and went to Hong Kong where she found work as a laundress.
As soon as she had saved the money, she bought a deck-passage ticket
to Singapore. Upon arrival, she immediately got in touch with a group
of older women from her home district. She was allowed to move into
their kongsi, a sort of guildhouse which 35 amahs maintained in two
rented rooms in the most densely populated section of Singapore's Chinatown, using the rooms as a combined meeting place, storage locker,
and transient dormitory for unemployed or ailing members. Within a
couple of weeks her friends managed to get Ah Ying a job as wash amah
to a British family. Presently she was graduated to baby amah, and
two years later, having picked up a little English and Malay and a working knowledge of the routine of a foreign household, she found a job with
a couple of British bachelor girls. With them she improved her job
qualifications further by learning the rather simple rudiments of British cookery.

After five years in Singapore, she was ready to move up to the
status of fully experienced amah, capable of earning as good an income
as the average Singapore Chinese head of family. She had only herself
to support in Singapore, and she subscribed readily to the philosophy of
her amah friends that their relatively independent and prosperous life
was much to be preferred to marriage. Mothers-in-law aside, as a
housewife she would have to bring up a family of children and to retain

the affections of a male who would in all probability be given to smoking, drinking, and gambling, if not worse.

Ah Ying today is a strong-minded female of forty-five, one who takes no nonsense from her employers because she knows she can easily get as good a job somewhere else. She has a strong sense of responsibility toward her employers all the same, even a degree of affection for them, and is thoroughly honest in handling household funds. She is punctilious in her duties toward the kongsi where she generally spends her days off. Occasionally she stays the night there, but she does so reluctantly for she is no longer accustomed to the noise from the narrow street below. In return for her monthly dues of M$3, she is assured of a place to live between jobs, storage space for her extra belongings, membership in something approximating a small social club, and insurance against being without help in serious emergencies. If a member of the guild falls ill, the others contribute to her support; if a member dies, the guild covers her funeral expenses and sees to it not only that burial is conducted with proper ceremony and decorum but that subsequent memorial rites are observed and fully attended. This insurance system is based upon a complicated scale of payments and repayments, but it adds up, if the member maintains her contributions over at least a ten-year period, to fairly complete social security, including even provision for retirement. Furthermore, the Singapore government a few years ago put into effect a compulsory pension plan system, and Ah Ying has now a tidy little provident fund account to which her employer contributes 5% of her monthly salary, the total amount, plus interest, to be paid to her in a lump sum after she reaches the age of fifty-five.

Relatively speaking—as compared, say, with the ordinary Singapore working woman whose wages go into a family kitty—Ah Ying is already well off. She would be considerably better off if it were not for the fact that over the years she has sent help to her own family in China. These remittances currently take the form of miscellaneous goods which cannot be purchased in China. By the time she has gathered together a parcel of food, clothing, medicines, and household items, and committed it to the keeping of someone traveling to Canton—who charges a stiff fee for the service—the shipment represents an investment of some hundreds of dollars.

Pooling their information gathered from letters from home and from travelers, the sisters of the kongsi operate what amounts to an economic intelligence service regarding conditions in rural Kwangtung. They have a very good idea at any given time exactly what will be most welcome to their families. They know also what the Chinese customs authorities are most likely to pass without confiscation or prohibitive duties. During the last famine in South China regulations relaxed. When local food supplies became normal they were tightened up drastically again. With the reraising of bureaucratic hurdles, safe-handling charges have risen commensurately. For the moment, Ah Ying is stockpiling against the day when she can resume her shipments.

Ah Ying has made two visits to China since her arrival in Singapore 25 years ago, one before the war and one in 1957. The second trip cost her M$1,000, and she went in company with a group of other amahs who patronized a small travel service specializing in such trips. In 1957 she found her family in good health and spirits, but letters she has received from them since leave her in no doubt that they have been through difficult times. It is the economic, not the political problems of China which strike her most vividly—the periodic shortages of food, medicinal herbs, and clothing—and she worries about her mother to whom she is devoted. Perhaps because she never knew good government in China in her girlhood, she shows no particular feeling that the present Communist regime is worse than any other. Her home district has not been affected by the commune system, but she has no desire to return there to live. She would like to see her mother again, but travel costs are high, she dreads the "cold," and she hates the certain prospect of missing her daily bath.

Two years ago, when the opportunity presented itself, Ah Ying registered for Singapore citizenship. Singapore politics, however, leave her so unconcerned that she votes only to avoid the fine for not doing so. Her interests are focused upon her guild, on sewing clothes and quilts for her family from bargain remnants—she owns a sewing machine—and gossiping with other servants in the apartment building about the doings of their employers.

*   *   *   *   *

Lee Liang Seng is a forty-year-old Singapore towkay, but by no means the stereotype towkay. By consensus, if not by definition, a towkay (a Cantonese term roughly equivalent to "big shot") is a rich Overseas Chinese businessman, often one whose dealings will not withstand very close scrutiny by the Rotary Club, the Better Business Bureau, or the tax office. The towkay need not be but very frequently is China born, also Chinese educated—if at all—and not only unreconstructably a mainlander Chinese but fairly low class by instinct and habit. Nevertheless, he is someone who has struck it rich and lives it up. The popular image of the towkay is that of a crafty and ruthless business operator who squeezes out the last penny of profit and the last gasp of his

employees' labor.   He practices every known trick of short weight,
short change, and misrepresented quality.   He is quite capable of burning down his own warehouse to claim insurance on goods he has already
sold twice over for cash and shipped C.O.D. to yet a third party.   He is
equally capable of letting a menial employee, even a relative, take the
rap if the law catches up with him.   He is likely to have at least two
wives and a cabaret girl or two whom he is keeping on the side.   He
usually has on his payroll at least a couple of goons who seldom let
him out of their sight, for towkays not only need strong-arm men for
their own nefarious business but are themselves fair game to Singapore
kidnapping gangs.

In actual fact, the towkay is often a rigidly honest businessman
—honest, that is, within the Overseas Chinese business tradition.   It is
not a tradition for the novice to emulate, but only for those with the organization to retaliate if anyone breaks his pledged word.   The towkay
may also be a practicing philanthropist, building temples and schools
and bequeathing large tracts of lands to endow them.   He may, for that
matter, be so Westernized in his way of life and business methods that
his employees, his family, and the press no longer refer to him as a
"towkay" but simply as a "millionaire."   The social columns reporting
the marriage of a son or daughter are very explicit about where the
millions lie, whether with the one family or with both.

Mr. Lee is a highly Westernized towkay far removed from the
classical stereotype, into which, it should be repeated, few living towkays quite fit.   He is in fact a third-generation international towkay.
He was born in Surabaja in the then Netherlands East Indies, the grandson of a sugar millionaire whose own father had come as an indentured
coolie from Canton.   Mr. Lee's mother was the daughter of a Hong Kong
Chinese businessman-philanthropist whom Queen Victoria had knighted.
Mr. Lee was sent to Europe after the war for his advanced education,
first to Holland, where he was graduated in economics from the University of Leiden, then to England, where he spent a year at the University
of London.   From London he traveled to Malaya, and worked in Kuala
Lumpur for a time in a firm owned by a branch of his mother's family.
In Kuala Lumpur he married an English-educated daughter of a rich
Malayan Chinese family, and with her returned to Indonesia to work in
his own family firm in Djakarta.

Not long after Mr. Lee's return to Indonesia there was an outbreak of particularly virulent anti-Dutch and anti-Chinese sentiment.
Since he himself held a Dutch passport, and since his family was identified with the Kuomintang, he felt it expedient to leave Indonesia again

in 1958. Other members of the family left at almost the same time, virtually abandoning some extremely valuable family properties. They managed, nonetheless, through the black market, to transfer abroad enough of their holdings so that Mr. Lee himself had at his disposal a capital of one million Malay dollars with which to set himself up in Singapore.

Mr. Lee now heads a new import-export firm doing business with Indonesia, doing on the whole such remarkably good business that other Singapore towkays are willing to put up additional capital if he should need it. Singapore Chinese businessmen look upon the vast Indonesian market potential as their really great opportunity. It is a market which now makes the difference between a prosperous and a depressed Singapore. Next to the Federation of Malaya, it is the largest single factor in Singapore's entrepôt trade, and until Singapore can industrialize, which may not be soon, that entrepôt trade is vital.

Doing business with Indonesia is not easy. Indonesian trade regulations are incredibly complex, and no matter how many papers and permits and agreements are forthcoming, there is absolutely no assurance that any particular business deal will actually come off. Nobody can be certain that the quantity or quality of goods shipped out of Indonesia will correspond to contractual specifications, or that shipments will not be interminably delayed, or that after corrupt key officials have been paid huge bribes, they will not demand still more and even then obstruct shipment. Singapore Chinese dealers, however, are willing to take the gamble, as Western dealers, whether in Europe or in Singapore, generally are not. If the gamble pays off at all, it may pay off very well indeed. The very complexity of Indonesian import-export and foreign exchange controls, for instance, makes it possible for those who know the ropes to pay a lot of the expenses in virtually worthless rupiahs and to take a lot of the profits in good hard Singapore dollars. Indonesia's total export volume is dropping off alarmingly, but Indonesian rubber, copra, and other commodities continue to flow to Singapore and to the Singapore Chinese.

Mr. Lee is in a particularly advantageous position to do business with Indonesia. He has strategically placed contacts in Djakarta, and he is able to judge reasonably well when and how and with whom a deal is likely to go through. His associates in Singapore are willing to share the risks. He does not like to remember a recent M$100,000 cash payment in Djakarta which he helped to finance in expectation of rubber shipments which were never made. Enough shipments actually have been made that he cleared at least M$50,000 last year—not as much as his opposite numbers in Djakarta think he made, but enough to set them to wondering whether he did not in fact outsmart them and whether this year they may not reverse the situation.

Mr. Lee finds life in Singapore congenial on the whole, but in the last few months he has had reason to worry about his own physical safety and that of his family. He has had a series of anonymous letters and phone calls, suggesting that he "contribute" to a "welfare society." The figure M$25,000 has been mentioned; the "delicate health" of his children has been alluded to as a reason he should take special interest in this particular form of welfare. Mr. Lee has stalled, but the telephone calls are becoming more insistent and more threatening. He has decided against going to the police, for the telephone callers have mentioned that if he feels M$25,000 is too much, they will be happy to go over his income tax returns with him. He has decided to have barbed wire put along the top of his garden wall, buy another police dog, and hire a guard as well as a watchman.

Mr. Lee's wife assures him that every wealthy Chinese is subject to the same sorts of threats and that they are in no greater danger than a thousand other families. Nevertheless, she sees to it that the family driver—they prefer a Malay to a Chinese—always delivers and calls for the three children at their schools. She makes a point of not curtailing her own schedule. She plays golf twice a week at the Royal Island Club; she is active in the Singapore Anti-Tuberculosis Association; and she belongs to an amateur dramatics society which periodically puts on a Gilbert and Sullivan operetta.

The Lees now regard Singapore as their permanent home. He plans to apply for Malaysian citizenship as soon as he can qualify under the new conditions yet to be announced; his wife is already a Malayan citizen, so there should be no real problem about the children.

Since he is not yet a local citizen, Mr. Lee tries to stay aloof from politics. His major interests, aside from business, are stereophonic hi-fi and automobiles. He follows the Singapore and Malayan motor rallies enthusiastically. He keeps himself well informed on local politics, of course, and he is anxious that the Malaysia plan should succeed. As he sees it, unless Singapore can merge with Malaysia, it will certainly turn Communist, and it will then be no place for him—nor will Malaya. To be sure, he has interests in Hong Kong and a bank account in Switzerland, but he would prefer not to have to fall back upon either.

*   *   *   *   *

Ng Kim Huat is the proprietor of a small shop located on a narrow street off North Bridge Road. He deals in a miscellaneous assortment of commodities, of which the most important are shark's fin, bird's nest, trepang, turtle shell, and many varieties of dried fish. He rents a three-story shophouse for M$500 per month, using the ground floor as his shop, the second floor as the family home, and renting the top floor to a group of Chinese laborers who occupy it as a dormitory. He is doing enough business now to clear about M$1,000 per month. He is planning to serve notice on the laborers and rent the top floor to some relatives. He will get less rent, to be sure, but the present tenants are something of a nuisance, coming and going at all hours.

Kim Huat is Singapore born, the only son of a Chinese immigrant who saved every possible cent of his wages, sent back to China for a bride, then himself died of pneumonia just three months after the wedding, still in debt to the moneylender for the wedding feast. Kim Huat's mother supported herself and her son for a few years by working as a servant in the moneylender's home. As soon as she was free of the debt, she married again, this time to a sailor who deserted her two years and one son later. At this point Kim Huat's mother "gave" him to a Chinese shopkeeper, whose shop and home he entered as a small servant, graduating presently to apprentice status. The shopkeeper treated him reasonably well, providing him with sufficient food and clothing and a place to sleep in the loft above the shop area. He also trained him in the business of buying, cleaning, grading, and selling dried sea products. His hours of work were 6:00 a.m. to 8:00 p.m. seven days a week, but the drudgery was not as great as the hours might indicate. In actuality, he had a good deal of leisure time when business was dull and on the whole he was treated as a member of the family. He shared, for instance, in the family excursions to clean, redecorate, and then picnic at the graves of the ancestors, and in all of the ceremonies and festivities of the Chinese New Year. By the age of fifteen he was already a sharp little businessman, and at nineteen he notified the shopkeeper that he was leaving and did so. On his departure tokens of esteem were exchanged, he himself receiving M$50 in cash.

Kim Huat found a job on a 500-ton vessel which operated between Singapore and the Riau Archipelago, a tramp trading craft which carried cargoes of opportunity each way and went to whatever ports offered business. He stayed with the ship for five years, meanwhile using his small earnings to do occasional buy-sell business on his own. In the Riaus he got acquainted with some Buginese boatmen who regularly made the voyage from the Moluccas to Java, along the Java coast to Sumatra and across to the Riau Archipelago from which they slipped into

Singapore. They carried cargoes of sea products from the east, and traded variously as they went. He began to buy up some of their cargo in the Riaus, thus saving them a trip to Singapore and getting the goods at slightly reduced prices. He carried it to Singapore and sold it to his former master, splitting the profits with the ship's captain.

When Kim Huat decided to go into business on his own, he managed to borrow a little capital from a friend of his former master. His contacts among the Buginese boatmen were good, and it was not long before he had built up his sources of supply. The Buginese checked in with him as soon as their boats arrived in port; he made them fair offers for their cargoes; if they needed extra money to purchase the trade goods they wanted for their return voyages, he advanced it to them; if he himself was momentarily short of cash, they waited. The relationship became one of mutual trust and mutual advantage.

In recent years, however, business has become increasingly difficult. The Buginese have been following their trade routes for many centuries, without paying much attention to controls which ancient and modern bureaucrats have attempted from time to time to impose upon them. So great is their reputation as fighters that the authorities and everyone else have been chary of them, even when their activities seemed less like commerce than smuggling or piracy. Of late, Indonesian patrol craft have taken to chasing them, inspecting them, and sometimes confiscating all or part of their cargoes, particularly on the return voyage when they are loaded with textiles and foodstuffs from Singapore. The Singapore harbor police give them little trouble, for their papers are in order, but Singapore immigration officers are becoming more and more sticky about temporary residence permits. The Buginese live aboard their vessels while in port but would like to be free to wander about Singapore at will for weeks at a time while awaiting favorable winds for the return voyage. Frequently they ask Kim Huat to vouch for them, and he is glad to do so. He worries about how long the notoriously short Buginese tempers will bear with modern bureaucracy, whether in Singapore or in Indonesia. Since his business depends largely upon them, he hopes it will be a good deal longer than seems likely.

Kim Huat has other reasons for uneasiness these days. He has attempted to follow the example of the shopkeeper with whom he himself lived for 13 years. He has taken on three young apprentices, whom he provides with food, clothing, and a place to sleep. He trains them to clean and grade the produce, and in the rudiments of wholesale buying and selling. He gives them one or two dollars a week in pocket money and extra cash at New Year and other special festivals. But he is running up against Singapore's new labor regulations, which have provisions covering hours and pay and child labor, as government inspectors have recently been pointing out to him. He did not think that any of this applied to him, and as a matter of fact he thought he had been particularly generous in allowing the boys to attend nearby schools for at least a few hours a week. Two of the boys are now fifteen years old, and their world has expanded beyond the shop, the street, and the school. They now want money for the moving pictures, and somehow, he does not know quite how, they have acquired a cheap transistor radio. In the shop these days he hears popular music, newscasts, and announcements of all sorts of events which, it seems, the boys take an increasing interest. During the course of last year's referendum campaign, most of the boys attended the big public rallies in Hong Lim Park, near his shop. Kim Huat himself had listened to the Chinese Chamber of Commerce and had decided to vote for the government-endorsed merger proposals. To his intense surprise, he heard the boys asserting that anyone who was interested in Chinese rights should follow the advice of the United People's Party and cast a blank ballot.

Kim Huat's own family has also occasioned him some surprises of late. His wife is a woman of no education but of basic good sense. She helps in the shop when necessary and is a frugal manager in running a home for him and their five children. For the most part, she buys their food already cooked from the street vendors, thus saving on kitchen expense and gaining perhaps in food flavor. She knows exactly where and when to buy bargain textiles and household goods, and always manages to stock up on new clothing for the family well before prices start going up for the Chinese New Year. Of late, however, she has begun to point out to him that he could afford a motorcar, that other families of their position already have cars. In fact, she argues, it would actually mean a saving, for he frequently has to hire a taxi for business, and he contracts by the month for a "pirate taxi" which takes his own and the neighbors' children to school.

Kim Huat's children are all in Chinese-language schools, the oldest two in secondary classes. He was startled a few months ago to learn that the older boy and girl were planning to take part in a demonstration against a new examination system. He promptly called a halt by threatening to stop their tuition payments. He has since then overheard them discussing a youth society which is not connected with the school, the government, or a neighborhood organization, and he does not quite know what to make of it.

Kim Huat has a second wife, not a legal wife, to be sure, but a woman with whom he went through a "tea drinking ceremony" which passes for a wedding. She is neither young nor pretty, for he is much too sensible for that; she is, in fact, the widowed mother of three children and supports herself and her family by operating a fruit stall near his shop. She lives in a two-room flat for which he pays the monthly rent of M$35. For a couple of months now she has been urging him to go to the temple with her, cut off the head of a white cockerel, and swear that if anything should happen to her he will take care of her children. If he does not, she says, then there are new laws in Singapore about polygamy and she can cause him trouble.

When he finds himself worrying too much, he goes to the Happy World amusement park for relaxation. He buys a ticket to the Chinese opera and sits there for four or five hours, enjoying as much the coming and going in the audience as the stage performance itself. He has thought several times of late about going to a taxi dance hall, just to see what it is like. He might even venture into a night club. If he does, he will first get a new outfit of clothes and have his front teeth capped in gold. All of that would add up, but after all, he does have the money.

[Note: Each of the foregoing is a composite of several individuals.]

CHAPTER
XXIII

TOWARD M-DAY

August 16, 1963

Malaysia Day is now scheduled for September 15, 1963, not August 31, as previously proposed; the Malaysia boundaries are now redefined to allow the Sultanate of Brunei, so long as it chooses, to remain aloof. Barring the unexpected—which, in view of Sukarno's known disaffection, should constantly be expected—the new Federation of Malaysia, inclusive of Malaya, Singapore, North Borneo, and Sarawak, will emerge almost in accordance with its original schedule and blueprint. In surmounting the last, presumably, and the most formidable of its prenatal crises, the as yet unborn Federation of Malaysia has already demonstrated high survival value. The most recent crises, into which were sandwiched incidental smaller troubles, have consisted of two prolonged sequences of Indonesian konfrontasi (confrontation, i.e., caveat), and a series of complicated maneuvers over final terms regarding the entry of Singapore and Brunei.

Indonesian konfrontasi, President Sukarno being its architect, proved complex and combustible both in motivation and manifestation. From the time of the Brunei insurrection on December 8, 1962, Sukarno branded Malaysia a "neocolonialistic plot" and pledged total Indonesian support to the anti-Malaysia "freedom fighters." He failed, however, either to intimidate Tengku Abdul Rahman or to gain widespread Afro-Asian approval. He was himself confronted with the choice of forgoing either further foreign adventures or further American aid. Sukarno then staged a "brotherly" reconciliation (May 31) with the Tengku, in the course of which he gave "heart to heart" advice about the desirability of consulting Indonesia in all matters of significance and reminded him yet once again that the Philippines, which claims North Borneo, joined Indonesia in calling for negotiations. The Indonesian, the Malayan, and the Philippine negotiators then met in Manila (June 7-11), where they agreed to propose to their respective heads of government that a United Nations representative should be asked to "ascertain" the views of the Borneo people. The Tengku went ahead, meanwhile, with his Malaysia plans and on July 9 signed a final agreement with the British regarding transfer of sovereignty over Singapore, North Borneo, and Sarawak. Sukarno thereupon (July 10) accused the Tengku of "breaking his promise" and suddenly cranked up konfrontasi into high gear again by threatening full-scale military action.

President Sukarno, Prime Minister Abdul Rahman, and President Macapagal met in summit conference in Manila (July 31-August 5) to discuss their differences. Sukarno made a series of demands, the acceptance of which would have thrown Malaysia completely off schedule and quite probably outside the range of possibility. The Tengku stood pat—or almost. Macapagal intermediated. The conference climaxed, after many times threatening to break down, with a request to the United Nations Secretary-General to make a quick "assessment," basically to determine whether Malaysia had indeed been the issue, as the Tengku said it was, in the recent North Borneo and Sarawak elections and whether the electorate had indeed exercised free choice. Shortly afterward, in view of the time needed for the "assessment," the Tengku set the Malaysia date back two weeks. A team of nine assessors, appointed by U Thant, arrived in Singapore on August 15 to begin their work—with two Indonesian, two Philippine, and two Malayan observers invited to look on. Now, unless the "assessment" somehow miscarries, as it may, with Indonesia attempting behind the scenes manipulation, or unless Sukarno quickly and more effectively revives konfrontasi or devises some new tactic, as he is quite capable of doing, the Tengku seems merely to have conceded two weeks' delay in return for certification that the Malaysia plan conforms to the principle of self-determination of nations.

In addition to konfrontasi, in the process of formation Malaysia has encountered four major domestic crises. The first, one which continues to the present time, has centered on Bornean opposition to the Malaysia proposal. Many of the Borneo leaders feared originally that they were being pressured by the British and the Malayans into an arrangement more advantageous to everybody else than to themselves. From the Malayan sponsors, as time went on, they gained major concessions of states' rights which added up to special Bornean privilege, and in North Borneo, at least, the opposition not only subsided but almost died out.

The North Borneo colonial government in late December 1962 ran off the first elections in the state's history, and the pro-Malaysia

North Borneo Alliance, a coalition of a half-dozen heretofore feuding parties, won a landslide victory—90% of the total vote. In mid-May the Alliance designated its two leaders, Datu Mustapha and Mr. Donald Stephens, for posts as Yang di-Pertuan Negara (Chief of State) and Chief Minister, respectively, and preparations for the installation of a new state government and entry into Malaysia went smoothly forward.

In Sarawak the political contest was more prolonged, more heated, and far less conclusive. In late June, when the government ran off elections for members of District Councils (the second in the state's history), pro-Malaysia candidates won in a majority of the constituencies, and accounted for 73% of the total vote. The over-all pattern was confused, however, by subsequent inter- and intra-party shiftings about when District Councils elected Divisional Councils, and when Divisional Councils elected members to the State Council, which also included government appointees. In the original District elections, the pro-Malaysia Alliance, under the leadership of Temenggong Jugah, won 138 of the 429 constituencies; Independents, mostly pro-Malaysia, won 116; the pro-Malaysia Party Negara won 59; and the anti-Malaysia Sarawak United People's Party (SUPP) won 116. The Party Negara, however, had split off from the Alliance just before the elections as a result of quarrels between its Malay leaders and the Dayak and Chinese leaders of the Alliance; and it further clouded the picture by collaborating with the SUPP in the subsequent Divisional and State Council elections. Many of the Independents, meanwhile, threw in with the Alliance. By the time all the indirect elections were run off, the Alliance was clearly in control of the government, but the SUPP-Negara coalition offered strong opposition. The Alliance in late July announced its Secretary-General, Mr. Stephen Kalong Ningkan, to be Chief Minister-Designate of the new state. Merdeka (Independence) preparations, including installation of the new councils and ministers, made satisfactory progress, notwithstanding serious distraction of official and public attention to a series of border raids staged from Indonesia, and to border crossings into Indonesia of small bands of SUPP- and Clandestine Communist Organization-aligned young Chinese students—"refugees" from government persecution, said Indonesian spokesmen, who gladly offered them military training.

The Borneo political situation remained changeable, but not so obscure as to leave the UN assessors any reasonable basis for doubt that Malaysia was in fact the issue in the elections and that the electorate had freely given its mandate. Had the UN assessors been called upon to extend their inquiry into Brunei, they would have faced a really delicate problem. There, the August 1962 elections had gone over-

whelmingly against the pro-Malaysia candidates. In mid-1963 many of
the insurrectionists remained under confinement, apparently repentant,
but what might be the current will of the people in general, nobody could
even guess.

The second domestic crisis over Malaysia, now half-forgotten,
revolved about the Singapore referendum of September 1, 1962. The
Singapore electorate then showed that it could think its way through
miasmas of contradiction created by Malaysia opponents and proponents alike. Given their choice of three complicated formulas for
merger, but denied the simple alternative of voting "no," the electorate neither destroyed nor defaced the ballots, as the opposition rec-
ommended, nor boycotted the polls, nor staged riots, as many feared,
but voted a resounding 71% endorsement of the one really feasible
plan.

The biggest 1962 domestic crisis, however, was the December
Brunei insurrection. Some 3,500 Brunei Malay and Kadayan adherents
of A. M. Azahari, and his anti-Malaysia, pro-Indonesia Party Ra'ayat, attempted by resort to arms to seize control of the state. Within two
weeks British troops had put down the insurrection. By mid-1963, a
few insurrectionists, either original or later recruits, remained at
large, mainly in Kalimantan (Indonesian Borneo), where they enjoyed
Indonesian military support and may have joined in a series of border
raids into Sarawak. Azahari remained under wraps, presumably in
Djakarta, although his voice was beamed regularly over mysterious
radio broadcasts, purportedly from a Kalimantan station. The Sultanate of Brunei, meanwhile, remained virtually a British-occupied
territory, a state of affairs which seemed to suit the Sultan, the local Chinese, and even a great many of the local Malays.

The fourth and most recent domestic crisis, which developed
in early April and lasted into early July, was a prolonged and sometimes vehement dispute over final terms of merger. Negotiations began in Kuala Lumpur, deadlocked, and then continued to successful
conclusion in London. The most tendentious of the problems, at least
as publicly reported—personalities being perhaps even more significant—involved money. This subject is always close to the heart in
Singapore and in Brunei, and it has become increasingly serious of
late in Malaya, where revenues to the government from rubber and tin
exports are sharply off, and expenditures on defense and development
are sharply up.

The trouble began in early April, when Singapore protested both the procedure and the amount of the proposed assessment against state revenue for Federal expenses. Singapore's Prime Minister Lee Kuan Yew thereupon announced, "Anything can happen," and he seemed to mean it. Things worsened when Singapore rejected Kuala Lumpur's decision that it should make an outright grant of M$50 million toward a M$500 million development fund for North Borneo and Sarawak; and the dispute reached crisis proportions when Kuala Lumpur held that discussion of detailed conditions for the establishment of a Malaysia common market could and should be postponed until after August 31. Singapore's negotiators protested that the common market was too vital to Singapore's interests to be a matter of mere reassurance. They complained that the M$50 million grant constituted a Federation "entrance fee," one arbitrarily calculated after Kuala Lumpur had pried into the sums cached away under their "carpets and mattresses" (the reference is to Singapore's big state reserves, which, until quite recently, had been billed as annual deficits). Singapore was quite prepared, its representatives said, to consider an interest-bearing loan of up to M$150 million, but not an outright grant—after all, they added, as though this were no new idea, aid funds should be repaid. The Singapore politicians then took their case to the public via press, radio, and Singapore's new government-operated television station, much to the indignation of the cabinet in Kuala Lumpur. Prime Minister Lee Kuan Yew, head of the People's Action Party (PAP), and Malaya's Finance Minister, Tan Siew Sin, head of the Malayan Chinese Association (MCA), engaged in a series of vitriolic exchanges which made prospects for smooth PAP-MCA or PAP-Alliance relations in the future Federation look fairly unpromising. Dispute over the Borneo development fund almost obscured the fact that original differences over method and amount of Federal assessment against Singapore revenues were rather quickly reduced to a mere 1% factor, and that Kuala Lumpur was in fact willing to come to an explicit if not a fully detailed understanding on the common market prior to Malaysia Day.

Brunei, meanwhile, after a couple of months of quiet maneuvering to get itself reinstated in the Malaysia negotiations, rejected Kuala Lumpur's terms about oil revenues. Kuala Lumpur was willing to concede to Brunei full control over its M$900 million state reserves and over its oil revenues for the first ten years of Malaysia. The Sultan seemed determined, however, to reserve the oil revenues to Brunei in perpetuity. He proposed that Brunei merely contribute M$40 million annually to the Federal treasury. The Brunei case was further complicated by the fact that the Sultan wanted to enter the Federation

Council of Rulers as the fourth-ranking rather than the lowest-ranking member—order of precedence to be calculated on the basis of date of accession to the throne, not date of membership in the Council. The Tengku rejected the Sultan's financial offer. He referred his protocol problem to the Council of Rulers, which was not sympathetic even when the Sultan intimated that he was willing to waive his right to stand for election as Paramount Ruler.

Prolonged discussions in Kuala Lumpur proving fruitless, the various parties to the disagreement agreed informally to transfer the locale of negotiations to London. Tengku Abdul Rahman had already scheduled a trip to London to complete arrangements for transfer to Malaysia of sovereignty over the Borneo states. He now dispatched his deputy, Tun Abdul Razak, to work out the details and to discuss the special Singapore and Brunei problems as well. When Singapore's Lee Kuan Yew and the Sultan of Brunei also showed up in London, the British, working through the Commonwealth Relations Office, used their good offices to arrange for renewal of the discussions which had deadlocked in Kuala Lumpur. To good offices, the British added both inducement and pressure. They held out, for instance, for decision about Singapore and Brunei before committing themselves to transfer of sovereignty over North Borneo and Sarawak. Withdrawal of British troops from Brunei, they intimated to the Sultan, might occur whether or not Malaysia took over Brunei's defense arrangements. New British contributions to Malaysia's defenses, they intimated to Tun Razak, would be contingent upon Singapore's participation in merger. British support for the common market, they intimated to Lee Kuan Yew, would be contingent upon further Singapore concessions to the Federation.

First out of Kuala Lumpur, then out of London, came so many reports of ultimatum, deadlock, and failure that veteran observers, who had earlier regarded the difficulties as minor, began to think this might indeed be a grade A crisis. Speculative reports about wheels within wheels added engrossing embellishments. Some of the British, according to persistent rumor, were simultaneously urging Kuala Lumpur to stand firm and encouraging Singapore and Brunei recalcitrance, in the hope, presumably, that the negotiations would fail. The oil interests, naturally, were suspected of preferring a separate rather than a merged Brunei with which to do business. The military interests, similarly, were suspected of wanting a separate and defenseless Singapore in order to ensure a continued need for British bases. Then, too, there were those who conjectured that the Tengku was no longer very keen about Brunei membership in Malaysia, especially in view of the possible renewal of <u>konfrontasi</u> and embarrassing demands for a referendum. There were others who speculated that Lee Kuan Yew was proving himself more arrogant than any of the other Malaysia sponsors could stomach. It was also possible to argue, and some did, that the whole crisis was synthetic, a demonstration to skeptics that Malaysia was no "neocolonialist" plot but a genuine example of self-determination in action. In the multilateral London maneuvers, everyone in fact shrewdly bargained for the very best deal that he could get, and everyone, except perhaps the Sultan of Brunei, compromised.

The London crisis had at least one important side effect which was not calculated. It distracted attention from a special problem which a great many politicians were just as glad to defer—that of political detainees. On December 16, 1962, the Federation government had picked up nine persons suspected of complicity in the Brunei insurrection. On February 13, 1963, after laboriously accumulating masses of evidence, it had also picked up Ahmad Bustamam, Party Rakjat Member of Parliament and Indonesian-affiliated organizer of the anti-Malaysian Socialist Front, a coconspirator, said the authorities, with Azahari. In the course of "Operation Cold Storage," conducted during the early morning hours of February 2, Singapore had jailed some 113 suspected subversives, including the Barisan Sosialis' Secretary-General, Lim Chin Siong, whom Lee Kuan Yew offered to deport rather than hold in jail (Lim ignored the offer). Among the others were both men and women prominent in labor, youth, and press activities. Members of the opposition soon began to protest that the Singapore detainees were being subjected to "harsh treatment." There were allegations of bad quarters, bad food, solitary confinement, and third-degree methods. The government admitted that the prisoners were not being allowed to shout party slogans or sing party songs. The Barisan on April 22 organized a protest march of some 100 persons, who staged an "illegal procession" through downtown Singapore to City Hall and ended up by rioting on the great staircase leading to the Prime Minister's office. Eight persons, including five Barisan Assembly members, one of them Barisan President Dr. Lee Siew Choh, were arrested. All but one of the eight spent a few days in jail—the exception was a Barisan Assemblywoman, embarrassingly pregnant, who was hustled straight home from the riot. The problem of detainees became increasingly serious as the Malaysia date approached. The question was whether to yield to pressure and let some of them out, as Singapore began to do, or to jail a few more as a precaution against anti-Malaysia disorders.

July 5, 1963, turned out to be a date to feature in Malaysia's history along with May 27, 1961 (the original proposal), September 1, 1962 (the Singapore referendum), December 8, 1962 (the Brunei insurrection), and also, as it later developed, July 10, 1963 (the renewal of konfrontasi). On July 5, the Kuala Lumpur and Singapore negotiators resolved most of their outstanding differences and flashed the signal to the Tengku to proceed to London. There, on July 9, he signed an "Agreement Relating to Malaysia," which triggered Sukarno's July 10 renewal and reintensification of konfrontasi.

The terms of the London settlement included predictable compromises but also some surprise arrangements which showed that Lee Kuan Yew, once again, had been busily outthinking almost everyone else. Lee Kuan Yew agreed to make a M$150 million Borneo loan on which Singapore would waive interest on the first M$100 million for the first five years (in effect, a M$20 million grant) and possibly even waive interest thereafter, the ultimate decision to be left to the World Bank. He yielded to Kuala Lumpur's demand for a 40% rather than a 39% factor in remission to Kuala Lumpur of Singapore revenues, but he added a clarifying political clincher—this was 40% of the Federal taxes to be collected in Singapore, but only 28% of Singapore's total tax collections of about M$120 million per year at current rates. As compensation for these concessions, Singapore, it turned out, was to inherit some 1,300 acres of British Crown property, inclusive of three big parcels of tremendous financial and symbolic value: Fort Canning, a 19-acre military establishment on a downtown Singapore hilltop (an area which, in point of fact, had already been transferred to Singapore control); the 685-acre island of Belakang Mati in Singapore Harbor (to be cleared of British military installations within five years and converted thereafter into a "Free Trade Zone"); and the 220-acre grounds about Tanglin Barracks in Singapore's best residential area. Singapore billed Great Britain, besides, for M$15 million in back rent on military-occupied lands to which the Crown had failed to clarify the title; it settled, however, for a mere M$10 million, Lee Kuan Yew graciously making the gesture at the Tengku's personal request. The Tengku himself, it turned out, was to get £30 million (M$255 million) over a three-year period as a British contribution to Malaysia's new defense arrangements—nicely offsetting an increase of M$75 million this year in Malaya's own military budget—and, after 1965, at least an additional £13 million (M$110 million). With regard to the prickly matter of the common market, Singapore got certain important commitments, including the promise of a 12-year period in which to convert from island-wide free port status to operation of a "Free Trade Zone" to be located, presumably, on Belakang Mati.

Everyone professed to have yielded more than he gained in the London Agreements. Kuala Lumpur's negotiators said they had been rudely pushed around by Singapore. Lee Kuan Yew said he had been "bludgeoned and beaten" by the British. The British thought they had paid rather handsomely to be relieved of their last Southeast Asian colonies. In fact, however, practically everyone was happy about the London Agreements—everyone, that is, except the anti-Malaysia opposition and possibly the Sultan of Brunei, whom nobody was pressuring, at least not just yet, to talk in terms of workable compromise.

Aside from konfrontasi, there still remained quite a few details to be arranged before Malaysia could indulge itself in celebrating what newspaper headlines began referring to as "M-Joy." The Borneo states, as already noted, were busily engaged in installing new state governments. Singapore had to decide what to do about new state elections. The Federation of Malaya's Parliament had still to consider the final terms for the conversion of Malaya into Malaysia. The Parliament did its part expeditiously. On August 14 it heard the Tengku's presentation of the final plan, including his explanation of the two weeks' delay, which signified, he said, not that he had yielded to Indonesian intimidation but rather than he had ensured the peaceful realization of the new nation. The Parliament voted 67 to 11 to endorse the London Agreements. In Singapore, naturally, it was not that easy.

Lee Kuan Yew returned to Singapore with two immediate agenda items—first, to elect the Singapore members of the new Malaysian Parliament; second, to get Singapore Assembly approval of the London Agreements. He was faced, as usual, with rather a delicate set of political problems. Even his worst enemies now admitted that his London performance had been brilliant and that it had enhanced the prestige of the PAP to the extent that in any new popular elections the PAP might recapture a significant amount of the support it had had in 1959 and lost in 1960. At the moment, however, as a result of defections of PAP Assemblymen to the Barisan Sosialis and of other disasters, it held only 24 out of 50 seats in the Assembly. (The 51st seat was vacant; one PAP member had died and no by-election had yet been held.) To carry any measure in the Assembly, the PAP had to rely upon the support of its political enemies, all of them bitterly anti-Lee Kuan Yew. In particular it had to rely upon ex-Chief Minister Lim Yew Hock and the six other Alliance members. Lim Yew Hock was now busily at work building up the Alliance for the next elections, hoping, quite obviously, that he would retain the balance of power and gain new seats as well. Lim Yew Hock, furthermore, enjoys the confidence of the Tengku, who treats him as his favorite Singapore politician, and he commands the vigorous support of Tan Siew Sin, head of the Federation MCA, who was feuding with Lee Kuan Yew and the PAP. Lee Kuan Yew could depend upon Lim Yew Hock not to torpedo Malaysia, but he could also rely upon him to torpedo any further move to enhance PAP prestige.

Lee Kuan Yew introduced two motions into the Singapore Legislative Assembly. The first called for popular elections prior to Malaysia Day of the Singapore members of the Federal Parliament. The vote (on July 25) was 23 to 23, with two PAP and two Alliance members absent. The Alliance demanded that the Singapore Assembly itself elect the members of the Federal Parliament, call for new general elections, and then dissolve itself. Lee Kuan Yew next introduced a motion calling upon the Assembly to "welcome" the London Agreements. The vote (on August 2) was 25 to 17, with seven Alliance members and one Independent abstaining. The Assembly then adjourned sine die, postponing until after Malaysia Day some extremely thorny problems.

Lee Kuan Yew's troubles with the Singapore Legislative Assembly were almost completely overshadowed at the moment, however, by Tengku Abdul Rahman's troubles with Sukarno and konfrontasi. As the Malaysia states—without Brunei—moved toward the Malaysia date, which suddenly receded from August 31 to September 15, the real focus of attention was not Malaysia but Indonesia. Malaysia, left to itself, would have been assured as smooth and propitious a launching as that of Malaya had been on August 31, 1957. Introduction of the Indonesian factor had complicated all predictions and clouded all prospects. For the new Malaysia, whether or not it emerged as a single nation, the international problems might loom much larger than the domestic. The chances for steady, orderly, successful internal development, such as Malaya had enjoyed, now seemed to depend not so much upon the Tengku as upon Sukarno.

CHAPTER
XXIV

THE MAPHILINDO FORMULA

September 15, 1963

The new Federation of Malaysia, now scheduled to be formed on September 16, 1963, is the voluntary merger of four formerly separate political entities—Malaya, Singapore, Sarawak, and North Borneo —each of which is making important concessions of sovereignty in anticipation of mutual advantage. Despite the last-minute withdrawal of the fifth original candidate for membership, the Sultanate of Brunei, the emergence of Malaysia represents a notable victory for a new sort of Southeast Asian supranationalism, as contrasted with the sometimes irresistibly and irresponsibly potent forces of nationalism, irredentism, and ultranationalism.

Nationalism, together with revolution, by which it generally asserts itself, has been the key factor in postwar Southeast Asian political developments. The Malaysia area, however, has been anomalous in that it has achieved national independence without resorting to revolutionary violence. Irredentism, similarly, has been a major factor in creating Southeast Asian tensions—witness Indonesia's campaign for Irian Barat (West New Guinea), China's territorial demands against Burma, the Thai-Cambodian and Cambodian-Vietnamese border disputes, and most recently, within the Malaysia context, the Philippine assertion of claims to North Borneo and disguised Indonesian aspirations to Sarawak, Brunei, and North Borneo as well. The Malaysia states themselves have no "irredenta." Ultranationalism has been the inevitable outgrowth of nationalism, revolution, and irredentism, but Malaya has been the least nationalistic, just as Indonesia has been the most ultranationalistic, of all the Southeast Asian nations. Indonesia's objections to the formation of Malaysia, in fact, have been based in large part upon its political practice that whatever is once formulated by President Sukarno as a national demand must not thereafter be compromised. Malaya has made no national demands.

The achievement of Malaysia constitutes, in many important respects, not only a successful resistance to prevailing Southeast Asian political forces. It also constitutes a graceful coup de grâce to European colonialism in the area. Only minute British "protected" Brunei, Portuguese Timor, and huge but not strictly Southeast Asian Australian New Guinea remain as targets which can automatically attract the anticolonial fervor of the revolutionary. Whether the achievement of the new Malaysia and the virtual elimination of colonialism as "provocation" foreshadow a reduction in some of the destructive manifestations of recent Southeast Asian politics and a significant increase in constructive co-operative effort, the fortunes of the new Federation of Malaysia will help to show.

Malaysia represents a limited and practical type of supranational and regional co-operation which attaches at the outset, however, to two other schemes—one small and hopeful, the other big and dangerous—either or both of which may condition Malaysia's own success. The smaller scheme is ASA (Association of Southeast Asia, inclusive of Malaya, Thailand, and the Philippines); the larger is the newly proposed Maphilindo (a "loose confederation" of Malaysia, the Philippines, and Indonesia). ASA has operated on the theory of starting small and growing big; Maphilindo is proposed on the basis of thinking big and awaiting opportunity. On the basis of experience to date with regional co-operation, it would seem that the better results come from the more modest starts, and also that the big schemes prejudice the little ones. Nevertheless, just as Malaysia is being born and as ASA is beginning modestly to prosper, the new Maphilindo has attracted attention amounting at times to accolade. Maphilindo, it should be noted, is the politically potent sort of proposal which almost everybody, regardless of his private misgivings or his motives, feels impelled to endorse.

In order to place Maphilindo in perspective, it is necessary to flash back to the first important effort to achieve Southeast Asian regional organization and to trace the Philippine, the Indonesian, and the Malayan record from there. In May 1950, the representatives of seven Asian and Southeast Asian countries (the Philippines, Indonesia, India, Ceylon, Thailand, Pakistan, and Australia) assembled in Baguio on the invitation of the Philippines to consider regional co-operation. The Philippines, which misjudged the mood of the other nations, especially Indonesia, India, and Ceylon, attempted to key the conference to anti-Communist philosophy and action. Indonesia, then just newly recognized as independent, rejected the Philippine lead and plan. The Baguio Conference—at which colonial Malaya was not represented—ended in failure, and the Philippines forfeited to Indonesia the initiative in Southeast Asian leadership.

The next important effort, one in which Indonesia exercised the initiative, was directed only incidentally toward Southeast Asian co-operation; it was calculated explicitly to result in creation of a third world bloc, an association of Afro-Asian nations dedicated to neutralism. Indonesia staged the conference in Bandung in April 1955. The result was an electric quickening of Afro-Asian self-consciousness and aspiration toward world influence, and also a general acceptance into the Afro-Asian family of Communist China and a reinvigoration of the world-wide "anticolonial" campaign. At Bandung, in what the chief Philippine delegate later described as a "boxing match," the Philippines endeavored to spar for the anti-Communist world, thus reconfirming its reputation among the other delegations for being atypically Afro-Asian. Malaya, not yet independent in 1955, was represented by unofficial observers, Malayans of Indonesian origin and sympathy who have since then headed the anti-Tengku political parties. The Afro-Asian Conference resulted in virtually no co-operative effort, regional or world-wide, for other than strictly political objectives. It exposed such wide, deep political differences among the Afro-Asian nations themselves that none except Indonesia has been enthusiastic about staging a full-scale sequel.

The Baguio Conference was in many respects a preliminary move of the Southeast Asia Treaty Organization (SEATO) type. The Bandung Conference was in many respects a reaction against SEATO. The next attempt at Southeast Asian regional organization on the part of the Southeast Asians themselves was an attempt to divorce regional co-operative projects—such as SEATO itself was undertaking with limited success—from SEATO's military and political implications, most specifically those of Western and anti-Communist involvement. Malaya's Prime Minister Tengku Abdul Rahman and Philippine President Garcia, after having expressed independently their desire for greater regional co-operation, took the occasion of the Tengku's state visit to Manila in January 1959 to get things started. They announced their intention of setting up a Southeast Asia Friendship and Economic Treaty (SEAFET) organization. Indonesia, they said, would be invited to join. Indonesian government spokesmen immediately and indignantly rejected the notion that Indonesia would in any way participate: Indonesia, they said, was interested only in "binational" or "Afro-Asian" arrangements and in nothing which smacked of anti-Communist motivation or of Western world alliance.

SEAFET languished for over two years while the Philippines and Malaya canvassed other prospects, but only from Thailand did they receive any very clear or favorable response. Representatives of the Philippines, Malaya, and Thailand met, therefore, in Bangkok, and on July 31, 1961, they announced the formation of ASA. Being determined

that ASA should not founder on impractically grandiose schemes, they
deliberately set themselves modest objectives. In the course of the
two years since ASA was launched, the member nations have set up a
regional and three national secretariats to which they have each contributed US$1 million for the implementation of projects. One project
has resulted in the simplification of immigration and travel formalities
—fewer forms, fewer photographs, and other breath-taking breakthroughs
in bureaucratic impediments. Another project has resulted in the integration of communications facilities—joint schedules for national air-
lines, a through train from Kuala Lumpur to Bangkok, radio-telephone
service from Singapore to Manila—and yet another has led to the inevitable exchange of cultural missions, including dance groups and other
"ambassadors of good will." Then, just as ASA really got under way,
the 1963 Malaysia crisis disrupted relations between Kuala Lumpur and
Manila and resulted in postponement—almost in cancellation—of the
Second Annual ASA Conference. ASA survived the strain, however,
even the new strain which was imposed upon it when the Conference
finally opened (April 3, 1963) with the Tengku delivering a forthright
address about healthful and unhealthful regional developments, an address which Indonesian auditors readily construed as anti-Indonesian.

         The Malaysia crisis of early 1963, which threatened to destroy
ASA, in fact resulted in the creation of Maphilindo. Malaysia, ASA,
and Maphilindo, however, are all three in serious trouble, and the very
complicated circumstances demand a recapitulation. In early 1961,
then, the Federation of Malaya invited the three states of British Borneo
along with Singapore to join in forming a new Federation of Malaysia.
Thereupon, the neighboring Republic of the Philippines revived a long
dormant or semidormant claim of its own to North Borneo, and on
June 22, 1962, after the Philippine press and politicians had agitated the
issue, President Macapagal took official action to assert this claim.
Soon, on July 27, 1962, he proposed a compromise arrangement: the
creation of a "Malayan Confederation" inclusive of the Philippines, Malaysia (presumably Malaya and Singapore), and the three states of British Borneo. Malaysians either ignored or deplored the proposal. The
Republic of Indonesia, however, which had been so preoccupied with its
own campaign to gain possession of Irian Barat that it had taken little
notice of Malaysia, noted the Philippine position with interest. It soon
began to develop a public position of its own, basically that British Borneo was an area of vital interest to Indonesia itself. In late 1962, beginning immediately after the outbreak of the December 8 Brunei insurrection, Indonesia denounced Malaysia as a "neocolonialistic plot." Sukarno and Macapagal thus found themselves aligned with each other
against the Tengku, the conflict of Philippine and Indonesian interest in
Borneo—and elsewhere—being obscured by their joint determination to

prevent the Borneo states from joining Malaysia.

During early 1963 the Malaysia dispute kept boiling up, particularly as a result of Indonesian konfrontasi (confrontation) tactics, which included constant threat of military intervention and constant agitation of anti-Malaysia sentiments both without and within the Malaysia area. As the area of dispute extended, Macapagal came forward (March 11, 1963) with an extension of his earlier proposal—this time a "Pan-Malayan Confederation" inclusive also of Indonesia. The Macapagal proposal received little serious consideration at first, even in the Philippines, but as the Malaysia dispute worsened, and as Sukarno's tactics shifted, the "Pan-Malayan Confederation" idea, which virtually nobody except Macapagal regarded as administratively feasible, began to seem politically expedient.

Sukarno gave the signal on May 31, when he staged a dramatic reconciliation with the Tengku, relaxed konfrontasi, and talked brotherhood and co-operation—tactics calculated, it seems clear in retrospect, to put the outside world off guard and to secure for Indonesia the hundreds of millions of American-aid dollars of which it stands desperately in need. Sukarno instructed his foreign minister, Dr. Subandrio, to meet the Philippine and Malayan representatives in a conference at Manila (June 7-11) and there to be conciliatory. The three foreign ministers failed to achieve any agreement on Malaysia, but they produced a diversionary and face-saving formula. This was a vague endorsement of Macapagal's Pan-Malayan proposal. Subandrio rechristened the proposal "Maphilindo," a felicitous coinage such as would appeal to the slogan-fancying Indonesians but signify no commitment unacceptable to the Malaysians. Through Maphilindo, or rather, since Maphilindo was more a semantic than a practical device, through the "Maphilindo Spirit," the three nations exhorted each other to resolve their differences over the Borneo states.

Maphilindo, then, had no blueprint, no timetable, no agenda; and within a month of being launched it was virtually stranded on the shoals of renewed and intensified Indonesian konfrontasi (July 10, 1963). Once again, however, Sukarno performed a volte-face. At a summit conference in Manila (July 31-August 5), the three chiefs of state first engaged in rancorous debate over Malaysia, and then followed the precedent set by their foreign ministers. They obscured serious disagreements by re-endorsing Maphilindo, with the "clarifying" declaration that they "agreed to take initial steps toward the establishment of Maphilindo by holding frequent and regular consultations at all levels, to be known as Mushawarah Maphilindo."

According to President Macapagal, Maphilindo is a double triumph for Philippine diplomacy: an assertion of both Philippine identification with and leadership in the new Southeast Asia. Its creation, he says, is a first step toward realization of his lifelong dream of reuniting the Malay nations—"triplets" long separated by colonial foster parents, now at last about to "rediscover their common origin and shape their common destiny." To many outside observers, Maphilindo looks less like Malay triplets than like a modified and ill-matched Southeast Asian troika—two small anti-Communist nations and one "non-Communist," "anti-Communistphobia" giant hitched together by rainbows.

Politically, the Philippines practices a no-fixes-barred, free-scrimmage democracy; Malaya, a staid parliamentary system with even a king; Indonesia, a "guided democracy" in which the guidance is toward rejection of all known codes and standards. Economically, all three are producers of raw materials and importers of manufactured goods, also of rice and other foodstuffs. There is more basis for economic rivalry than for co-operation, unless it should be co-operation on cartellike arrangements to fix the prices of rubber, copra, sugar, tin, and spices. Their currencies—a hard dollar, a soft peso, and a worthless rupiah—are even less interchangeable in ordinary traffic than are their cultures. In the Philippines, it is the American and, still to a very significant extent, the Spanish cultural influences which prevail and the self-conscious search for "national identity" has only recently begun. In Indonesia, Dutch and other Western influences are officially regarded with outrage, and the nation's own glorious cultural tradition is being deliberately "retooled" in a fiery quest for the "pure national soul and spirit." In Malaya and Malaysia, self-conscious realization of a relatively weak cultural tradition and the unself-conscious acceptance of British standards, including that of tolerance, are resulting in an effort not to isolate and to glorify but to fuse the Malay, the Chinese, the Indian, and other elements, so that a new composite will emerge which will be Malaysian. In their more searching moments of self-analysis, Malaysians aspire these days to understand each other; Filipinos, to bridge the gulf between America and Southeast Asia; Indonesians, to counterbalance both the Communist and the non-Communist worlds by creating and dominating a vast new "emerging" Afro-Asia which includes the major part of the world's population, territories, and resources. President Macapagal's "parable" of Malay "triplets" finding themselves reunited in happy adolescent fellowship is sharply at variance with the Malaysian concept of bottle-feeding querulous infant "quintuplets" right at home (Malays, Chinese, Indians, tribesmen, and others) and the Indonesian concept of the Afro-Asian "David" outwitting triplet but mutually inimical Goliaths (i.e., the United States, the Soviet Union, and Communist China).

Maphilindo faced its first prenatal test in devising and applying a formula whereby Indonesia and the Philippines could accept the formation of Malaysia, their own presumed Maphilindo partner. The Manila summit conference, after prolonged and acrimonious debate, agreed to apply to UN Secretary-General U Thant to determine the views of the people of North Borneo and Sarawak on the question of entry into Malaysia, and they committed themselves in advance to accept his findings. The Tengku had argued that the people of the two states had already clearly expressed their views in free and fair elections; Sukarno and Macapagal had demanded a plebiscite. The British, whom Sukarno and Macapagal accused of "neocolonialistic" manipulation, announced that they would not countenance a UN plebiscite, but that they would afford every facility to UN investigators. U Thant decided that he would send a nine-man team to make a quick "assessment" as to whether the elections had indeed been free and fair and whether Malaysia had indeed been the issue. Macapagal and Sukarno, who had anticipated that U Thant would himself insist upon a long drawn-out referendum and that much could happen in the interval, disguised their dismay over U Thant's plan of quick "assessment"—it was a foregone conclusion that the result would be favorable to Malaysia—by initial enthusiasm for Maphilindo and subsequent recriminations about who was violating its spirit. The Tengku, in view of the time required for even a quick assessment, announced that there would be a "brief postponement" of Malaysia Day in order to allow the Philippines and Indonesia, in accordance with their Manila commitment, to "welcome" the new nation once it had the United Nations seal of approval. The Tengku's decision regarding postponement dismayed a great many Malaysia sponsors, including Singapore's Prime Minister Lee Kuan Yew and North Borneo's new Chief Minister Donald Stephens, who feared that the anti-Malaysia saboteurs would get busy during the unexpected interval. The postponement, furthermore, complicated many technicalities—August 31 having already been stipulated in various official documents as the day on which Great Britain would renounce and Malaysia would assume sovereignty over Singapore, Sarawak, and North Borneo.

The sequel to the Manila Conference was pandemonium. Indonesia, as many observers had expected, contrived to delay, dispute, and disrupt all the subsequent proceedings, challenging every detail of the assessment, while whipping up intense anti-Malaysia propaganda at home and abroad and increasing both the scale and the frequency of its guerrilla nuisance raids across the Sarawak border. The Indonesian government quarreled about the number and the rank of the Indonesian observers who might travel to British Borneo, the movements and the methods of U Thant's assessors, and the decision of the British and the Malaysian governments—in view of Indonesia's own obvious tactics of

delay and diversion, once the original Malaysia Day date of August 31
was well past and September 15 had been set as the day for announcement of U Thant's findings—to fix the new M-Day as September 16. The
Philippine government sided always with Indonesia. The Singapore government complicated matters by declaring de facto independence on
August 31, assuming de facto interim control of defense and foreign affairs, both of which were to be functions of the new Federal government,
and engaging in a heated exchange with Kuala Lumpur regarding the validity of its actions.

As September 15-16 approached, the UN assessors were clearly
about to find in favor of Malaysia. The Indonesian government was openly
building up to an outraged rejection of U Thant's findings and a renewal
of konfrontasi. The Philippine government was confronted with a choice
of dilemmas: whether to adhere to its word and thus affront the powerful Indonesian neighbor with which it had been cementing what it regarded
—naïvely, many outsiders thought—as a genuine anti-Communist alliance,
or to support renewed and possibly violent Indonesian konfrontasi—Sukarno's defiance of what he termed "neocolonialism" being characterized by the practice of what might be described by his unkinder critics
as neoimperialism abroad and neoanarchy at home. To almost everybody except its Filipino partisans, chief among them President Macapagal, Maphilindo, as an instrument of peace and friendship, seemed stillborn.

Maphilindo, conceivably, might even yet lead to the fruitful co-
operation of the 100 million Indonesians, the 30 million Filipinos, and
the 10 million Malaysians occupying the highly strategic and richly en-
dowed mainland axis and island arc of Southeast Asia. First, however,
it will certainly have to go through numerous and difficult transforma-
tions. If only it results in any significant change in Indonesia's record
of active obstruction in the direction of fruitful co-operation, even an
expiring Maphilindo may yet prove to be that long hoped-for turning
point in postwar Southeast Asian history—the point at which conflict
between nationalism and colonialism begins to be transformed into full-
scale co-operation among ex-colonial areas for purposes other than
anticolonial agitation. If it serves merely as a tentative formula for
easing pressures so that the new Malaysia may have a chance to take
hold and Malaysian participation in ASA to become significant, even a
briefly resuscitated Maphilindo can serve a very useful purpose. The
very real and immediate danger, however, is that Maphilindo, if it functions at all, will serve as a vehicle for Indonesian expansionism rather
than for regional co-operation—as a hazard, therefore, and not an advantage to the new Malaysia.

POSTSCRIPT

MALAYSIA IN REGIONAL CONTEXT

The new Federation of Malaysia emerges into a region which
in 1964, ten years after the Southeast Asian nationalist revolutions
against colonialism had already been won, seems even more highly
nationalistic, revolutionary, and anticolonial (now "antineocolonial")
than ever before. The Indonesian and to some degree the Philippine
objection to the formation of Malaysia has been based, for instance,
upon the accusation that the new Federation is not and has not been
truly (i.e., violently) revolutionary. The two neighboring nations maintain, furthermore, that by continuing to tolerate British military, economic, and political influences, Malaysia lends itself to a "neocolonial
conspiracy" for neoimperialist domination of the area, thus constitut-
ing both a provocation to the "truly independent" nations and an invitation to the international Communists to intervene and subvert.

Malaysia, presumably the last of the new Southeast Asian nations
(assuming that Brunei will join the Federation and that Portuguese Timor
will fall to Indonesia) thus enters a world in which the nationalist revolutions against the onetime colonial West, instead of being allowed to
burn out, are being deliberately refueled. It is a world, furthermore,
in which some of the long-established leaders are indulging in purges
of onetime comrades now deemed counterrevolutionary for resisting
newly formulated mystiques which glorify sheer revolutionary activism. Southeast Asia today seems even more troubled and explosive,
therefore, than in the immediate post-World War II period when the
concession of national independence seemed the best formula for re-
ducing tensions and building strength. Independence, obviously, has
not brought the expected or promised benefits, among them stability,
one important reason being that far too much attention has been diverted from national development into nationalistic agitation. Many
of the original "freedom fighters," now self-consciously recasting
themselves in the role, hold that the region exhibits too little rather

than too much nationalistic and revolutionary fervor.

The fact that Malaysia has emerged as the result of internal conciliation rather than of conflict indicates that forces of rationality still persist in Southeast Asia, notwithstanding the appeal of recklessness. The conflict between the adherents of the evolutionary and of the revolutionary processes now seems, nevertheless, to be the critical factor in the region, there being little evidence that violent upheavals subside once the original objective of independence has been attained. Both within and among the new nations, the disagreements regarding the strategy of nation building are extremely great; the contrast in manner and degree of national development is correspondingly sharp.

Huge Indonesia and little Burma have opted for unending revolution and thus, inadvertently, for accelerating deterioration. Thailand (the one long-established independent nation) together with the Philippines and Malaysia has opted for evolutionary development and hence for progress. North Vietnam has elected communism; South Vietnam has become a battleground; Cambodia is a never-never land; Laos is an enigma. With the weight of Indonesia's 100 million people and its vast resources thrown in favor of domestic and regional disruption, and with other states only precariously sustaining themselves, the combined gains of Malaysia, the Philippines, and Thailand (total population 70 million) seem dangerously inadequate even to maintain a balance. Even the most optimistic observers, furthermore, must take cognizance of nearby China and of the distant Soviet Union, whose own interests in Southeast Asia now conflict but whose influences have been exerted in the past deliberately to encourage trouble.

The new Malaysia, therefore, takes its place in a seriously disturbed region which defies any swift or easy development. With some 225 million people living in nine different countries of more or less arbitrary national boundaries and nationalistic demands, Southeast Asia is still further split into scores of linguistic and ethnic groups living at widely different stages of civilization ranging from the aboriginal to the highly cosmopolitan. Over the centuries the indigenous societies and cultures have been profoundly modified by waves of Indian, Chinese, and Arab migrants. Portuguese, English, Dutch, French, Spanish, and American colonial penetration has worked still further transformation—and division. Major elements of the population have adopted Hinduism, Buddhism, Mohammedanism, Confucianism, and Christianity. Other segments still adhere to the animistic religious traditions of earlier centuries. Primitive tribesmen may still outnumber, although they may themselves be transformed into, the high school graduates and the politicians. Regarded by the Western world as potential prizes in the cold war contest, the educated classes and political leaders of Southeast Asia have preferred in general to regard themselves as the harmonizers of widely diverse influences, to which some of them seek of their own volition and as a corrective to the influence of the West to add those of the Communist nations. They have achieved an unassimilated Southeast Asian mélange in which fermentation may result either in an excitingly different new world or in more and bigger explosions.

In the global context, Southeast Asia is the focus today of massive efforts on the part of the United States, the Soviet Union, and Communist China to offset the influence of each other, a fact which various of the area's leaders accept as an invitation to exact aid from everyone, without either conditions or commitments. Quite possibly, the basic objectives of many of the Communists, the anti-Communists, and the Southeast Asian nationalists do, in fact, at this point coincide throughout a great part of the area. In some cases the best that any of them can hope for is not so much clear-cut advantage to themselves as denial of advantage to anyone else, in other words, neutralization. Perfect neutralization, however, is a delusion, and imperfect neutralization is a highly unstable arrangement in which the power conflict becomes exceedingly murky. At times not power but powerlessness becomes an advantage, since the possibility of the collapse of any Southeast Asian nation becomes in itself a compelling argument for somebody to support it. The best illustration is Indonesia, one nation which does deliberately aspire to gain advantage, indeed domination. Out of the apparent Southeast Asian stalemate and by recklessly risking self-destruction, Indonesia gains immense influence which it could not otherwise command.

In Indonesia, as throughout Southeast Asia, the patterns of maneuver between and among the world powers and the Afro-Asian nations grow more, not less, intricate with the passage of years. So far as one of the three great Asian nations is concerned, India has lost in Indonesia as well as elsewhere a great measure of the "moral authority" it exercised only a few years ago—Nehru's own declining energies being one explanation, China's deliberate discrediting of his world policies being another. Japan, which might have aspired to political influence, seems more than willing to settle merely for trade. Communist China, which has inspired both admiration and apprehension by reason of its swift consolidation of power at home and its hold over the Overseas Chinese communities, has obviously become enmeshed in its domestic difficulties and in its quarrels with the Soviet Union. For the time being, it has become for the Indonesian leaders, at least, an ogre less frightening to themselves than to the Russians and to the Americans, and extremely useful, therefore, as a demifriend. As for the Soviet Union, after making a US$1 billion gamble on arms for Indonesia in 1961, in anticipation of gaining an ally, it has apparently conceded that it has lost the major part of its investment. The United States, after gambling almost US$1 billion in aid to Indonesia since 1950, seems to have come to the same conclusion. Indonesia, meanwhile, threatens momentarily to move into a phase of outright anarchy which will make its regional position even more nearly incalculable than before, save that, quite clearly, it has become the most influential nation in Southeast Asia and, along with China, Japan, and India, one of the four most influential nations in all of Asia.

Impending and possibly contagious anarchy in Indonesia, the nation incomparably richer in human and natural resources than any other of the area, now seems an even more formidable threat to Malaysian and regional stability than does its military adventurism, or even the international Communist conspiracy. If the situation in Indonesia is bad and getting worse, so too, unhappily, is the situation in Burma and South Vietnam and the rest of Indochina. Malaysian and regional prospects are threatened both from Indonesia in the south and from Burma and Indochina in the north.

The situation in South Vietnam looked very nearly hopeless before the demise of President Ngo Dinh Diem, and since then prospects have darkened rather than brightened. Vietcong military and political strength is growing throughout the countryside. The Vietnamese urban and rural population is demoralized, the government is disorganized, the military is no more ready than before either to fight the Vietcong itself or to co-operate very effectively with the forces which the United States has committed to combat. In Vietnam the experience of the past decade suggests that improvements are brief and illusory, that deterioration is the norm, and that Communist North Vietnam is much more able and willing than South Vietnam to resort effectively to the devices which seem best calculated to work in the conflict between the two: in propaganda, subversion, and invasion.

The Union of Burma, under General Ne Win and his Revolutionary Council of military men who run a revolutionary government, is now being guided rather aimlessly down a "revolutionary" "Burmese Way to Socialism." This new routing is distinguishable from U Nu's dreamy path mainly in that it involves doctrinaire albeit inconsecutive detours into nationalization and coercion. General Ne Win, it has become apparent, intends to eliminate almost all the remaining residue of parliamentary democracy, private enterprise, and freedom of opinion. He has backed away from Western influences, and in so doing has sidled up close to the Chinese Communist camp. Nevertheless, Burma can easily feed itself, its population is inured to inefficiency, and the state seems, on the whole, more likely to go on moldering and smoldering than to ignite.

Laos and Cambodia seem each more improbable than the other and more susceptible to swift Chinese Communist scooping up, if indeed Communist China is able or ready to start scooping. Laos, a total incoherency which has no logical basis for nationhood, seems to serve Chinese Communist purposes well enough exactly as it is, for it absorbs substantial and futile American efforts directed toward achieving some faint degree of stabilization. The Chinese Communists or their North Vietnamese agents can and do infiltrate Laos at will. The infiltrators can then provision themselves by requisitioning the American rice intended for the consumption of remote tribespeople who are being kept both fit and loyal, presumably, by American helicopter rice drops. In Cambodia, Prince Sihanouk baffles alike the Americans, the French, the Russians, the Chinese, the Japanese, the Poles, the Filipinos, and many others, all of whom proffer aid. From them he gains handsome new installations such as schools, hospitals, roads, and factories. In consequence, he has achieved the appearance if not the actuality of national development, while threatening at any moment to consign himself and his state to the safekeeping of Communist China, which, he says, will eventually prevail throughout the area.

Thailand and the Philippines, in addition to Malaysia, have denied themselves many of the excitements of revolutionary activism and have devoted a reasonably high share of their time, energy, and resources to constructive enterprises. The Philippines has achieved a rough-and-ready sort of constitutional democracy in which corruption is an expected motivation, a free and easy private enterprise in which shady practices are virtually mandatory, and a mobile society in which the educated—even those educated in the madly proliferating diploma mills—can and frequently do manage to rise. The Philippines is a "show window for democracy" mainly in the sense that it demonstrates how basic democratic principles can in fact survive and grow in circumstances which might seem to precede totalitarianism. Thailand demonstrates much the same thesis with regard to limited constitutional monarchy and limited military dictatorship. After a long succession of coups, beginning in 1932, and after prolonged refusal to become serious about national development, Thailand has begun in recent years to enhance its basically happy condition by swift modernization in Bangkok and by the export of progress even to the retarded and restless provinces along the Laos border.

Thailand, the Philippines, and the former Federation of Malaya, the three most promising of the Southeast Asian nations, entered in 1961 into an Association of Southeast Asia (ASA) arrangement for regional co-operation in economic and cultural matters, with intimations of intent to preclude further Communist inroads into the region. The ASA arc of nations, which might effectively have interposed themselves to block Chinese expansion from the north or Indonesian expansion from the south, has been disrupted, however, by the recent controversy over Borneo. Although the Philippines now shows signs of changing tack, it has sided in general with Indonesia against Malaysia, and Thailand has mainly deplored the dissention. The consequent sidetracking of ASA and the attempted launching of Maphilindo (a proposed "loose confederation" of the Philippines, Indonesia, and Malaysia to resolve the Borneo dispute and other problems) signifies, therefore, suspension of a co-operative project which served to unite the three genuinely progressive nations of the area. It signified also the introduction into the ASA region of massive doses of Sukarno's "revolutionary" doctrine that "progressive" nations must militantly combat "neocolonialism" in order to achieve "true national identity" regardless of all costs and consequences.

The new Federation of Malaysia expected to emerge into a world in which it would be allied with regional partners in truly co-operative endeavor. It now finds itself plunged into a bitterly and violently disputatious area in which its very existence is a cause of conflict. One gigantic neighbor, Indonesia, is poised to "smash" it. Other nearby nations seem reluctant to give it even moral support. Colossal China stands ready to support Indonesia in brewing up a regional typhoon, after which the two may fall into dispute over the wreckage. Malaysia's own bright prospects flicker alarmingly as President Sukarno and other national leaders fan the flames of a regional revolution which Tengku Abdul Rahman might reasonably have assumed would burn itself out once Southeast Asian colonialism was at last liquidated with the formation of Malaysia.

INDEX

The AUFS Reports Service, which published in serial form most of the material in *The Formation of Malaysia,* is one of the several program activities of the American Universities Field Staff.

Established as a nonprofit corporation in 1951 by a group of universities and colleges to undertake a new approach to the study of foreign societies, the American Universities Field Staff functions as an academic foreign service. Staff members live in foreign areas with which they are thoroughly familiar to report firsthand on significant developments. Periodically, they return to the United States, where they serve as visiting faculty on campuses of the sponsoring colleges and universities. They lecture to classes, hold seminars, participate in faculty roundtables, advise students, and are available as consultants to teachers and administrators.

The AUFS Reports from abroad were at first distributed only to the academic institutions that sponsor and help to support the Field Staff program. The usefulness of the Reports as authoritative source material on political, economic, and social trends in Asia, Africa, Latin America, and (to a limited extent) Europe brought such favorable comment that the AUFS Reports Service was instituted.

The Reports now go to a steadily growing list of subscribers among colleges outside the AUFS membership, libraries, organizations interested in international affairs, business firms, newspapers, secondary schools, and individuals who have a professional or personal interest in foreign affairs.

For details about the AUFS Reports Service, write to:
AMERICAN UNIVERSITIES FIELD STAFF
366 Madison Avenue   New York, N.Y. 10017